ENEMY
TERRITORY

ENEMY TERRITORY

THE CHRISTIAN STRUGGLE FOR THE MODERN WORLD

ANDREW WALKER

Academie Books Grand Rapids, Michigan
Zondervan Publishing House

Enemy Territory
Copyright © 1987 by Andrew Walker
Published by special arrangement with Hodder & Stoughton, London

ACADEMIE BOOKS is an imprint of Zondervan Publishing House,
1415 Lake Drive, S.E., Grand Rapids, Michigan 49506.

Library of Congress Cataloging in Publication Data

Walker, Andrew, 1945-
    Enemy Territory : the Christian struggle for the modern world /
Andrew Walker.
        p.   cm.
    Bibliography: p.
    Includes index.
    ISBN 0-310-51551-3
    1. Devil.   2. Civilization. Modern–20th century.
3. Christianity–20th century.   4. Apologetics–20th century.
I. Title.
BT981.W35 1988   88-20828
239–dc19
                                                                    CIP

Printed in the United States of America

88 89 90 91 92 93 / DP / 10 9 8 7 6 5 4 3 2 1

FOR SUSAN

Contents

Part three: Enemy engagement –
the struggle for the kingdom

THE C. S. LEWIS CENTRE

The C. S. Lewis Centre for the Study of Religion and Modernity is a Christian research organisation working in partnership with Hodder and Stoughton to publish thought-provoking material concerning the relationship between the Christian faith and the modern world. Following C. S. Lewis's example, it is the Centre's deliberate policy to reach a broad market, speaking to 'everyman' in an intelligent and informed way, and responding to the challenge presented to orthodox belief by the secular culture of our contemporary society.

Preface

Enemy Territory is not intended as a book for academic specialists though it is written with the intelligent lay person in mind. Neither is the book aimed at a specific Christian constituency: it is for all those who would call themselves 'Mere Christians' and who stand by the historic gospel of the Bible and the ancient creeds of the early church.

It would also be a mistake to assume that this is a book exclusively for Europeans because it happens to be written by an Englishman. Not only is it the case that much of the material here is gleaned from American thought and experience, but also it is my conviction that those of us who live in modernity in the advanced industrial nations are bound together by common institutional and ideological realities.

Many of these realities are, I believe, a threat to all our peoples and in particular to the Christian church. It is a matter of urgency that Christians should wake up to the dangers inherent in modernity and begin together to take responsibility for our part in confronting the cultures in which we live. All cultures come under the judgement of the gospel. This is as true for capitalist countries as it is for socialist ones. There is nothing wrong with pitting our free countries in the west against totalitarian ones as long as this does not prevent us from also seeing what the secular values of our post-enlightenment civilization are doing to our own nations.

In order that I do not throw a wave of sociological jargon at you – hitting you hard and leaving you cold – I have tried to see our contemporary struggle for the modern world within a theological context of what I call 'the Great Battle', which is no less than God's war with the Devil.

This may seem a very primitive way of talking, but this book is primarily a work of propaganda for a primitive gospel. Such a gospel insists on a proper Christian dualism that understands Christ and his church to be confronted by a real and terrifying enemy. The early church fathers called him the Evil One.

You cannot really blame non-Christian people today for dismissing the possibility that evil can be personified into some sort of creature opposed to God and his creation. Most people are not reacting against the reality of evil but against silly and unhelpful caricatures of evil. For myself I would rather refer to the Devil as 'it' than 'him', because 'him' denotes someone who is a person, or at least a being who can be said to exhibit the traits of personhood. Strictly speaking, I feel that only God is truly personal, and we as human beings are only persons in so far that we can be said to bear God's image. I am not sure that we can say that about the Evil One: the Devil is all that God is not (see also pp. 33–35). However in order that I do not mislead readers into thinking that I do not believe that the Devil is real or has no intelligence, I shall stick to traditional usage and call it 'him'. I have no objection to personifying evil, but I am rather loath to over-personalise him and award him attributes that I believe he lost with his rebellion against God.

To mention a rebellion is to suggest that a war is on. While this clearly does not relate to the obscenity of human warfare, there is a real war to be fought: it is a spiritual warfare that Christians cannot avoid if they wish faithfully to follow Jesus.[2]

I owe many debts to the following advisers of the C. S. Lewis Centre for their support and encouragement. In particular this book reflects some of the ideas of Bishop Lesslie Newbigin in *The Other Side of 84* (BCC 1983) and his later Princeton lectures. Readers will note a considerable debt to the sociology of Peter Berger and to Os Guinness's *The Gravedigger File* (Hodder & Stoughton 1983) – my chapters entitled 'Captive lives' (chapters five and six) in particular. I am thankful to Professor Colin Gunton for his criticisms, and for showing me a copy of his '*Christus Victor* Revisited . . .' (*Journal of Theological Studies* 36/1, April 1985), which prompted me to think of the Great Battle. I also wish to thank Tom Smail, whose unpublished paper on modernism was invaluable.

As is right and proper, C. S. Lewis (1898–1963) pops up throughout the book; it was his wartime *Broadcast Talks* (Geoffrey Bles 1942) that first stimulated me to write *Enemy Territory*.

It follows that, although I have borrowed from Lewis and other Christian writers, they are in no way responsible for what I have made of their works. Neither does this book represent the views of all the officers and advisers of the C. S. Lewis Centre.

I would also like to thank: the librarians of the Imperial War Museum for their help; my colleagues in the Department of Christian Doctrine at King's College London, where this book was started in tandem with another; and lastly, but not least, special thanks go to my colleagues at the West London Institute, Arthur Giles and Gavin D'Costa, who supported and cossetted me when I needed it most.

Andrew Walker,
The C. S. Lewis Centre
for the study of religion and modernity,
London 1987

Style of References

The citation style used in the text is an adaptation of the Harvard system. References are to authors and dates (the additional digits being to page numbers) and are linked to an alphabetised book list at the end of the volume.

Foreword:

'CHOOSE YOUR SIDE'

This is a propaganda book about war. We usually – and rightly so – associate war with evil, and 'propaganda' is not typically used to describe Christianity (except by our enemies). Propaganda, however, need not be false ideology or distorted truth. 'To propagate' is to spread or to proselytise a cause with zealousness. Many of the fathers of the early church would use 'propagate' when speaking of the success of the gospel in the pagan world. Even in its modern usage the word propaganda suggests claims or opinions that are forcefully transmitted with the aim of effecting change or promoting reform. In the strictest sense, then, to preach the gospel is to engage in propaganda.

Even if this seems reasonable enough, surely it is absurd to talk about propagating the desirability of war? Here I must be careful, so let me be clear about exactly what I am recommending. It is not, God forbid, human war that I am endorsing, but the necessity for Christians to engage in spiritual warfare. To put it as bluntly as I can, 'To be a Christian is to be at war with the Devil'.

Many modern Christians are resistant to this idea, and would prefer to see their witness and vocation in some other terms. There is nothing wrong with this in itself – there are many ways of understanding our life in God – but I believe that what I shall call the Great Battle is a fundamental reality of our Christian faith and not merely a metaphor that we can adopt or reject as we choose. That is why Book One of *Enemy Territory* is sheer propaganda: it is nothing less than a plea to return to the traditional and classic position of the early church concerning Christ and his followers' battle with Satan for the life of the world.

The danger with such an approach, if we are not careful, is that one can fly off into spiritual platitudes and theological niceties that are not grounded in our present historical situation. It is one thing to say that we are at war with the Devil, but where is the battlefield? This needs to be clearly located, otherwise we could be seduced into a phoney war or become embroiled in a mythic battle of our own invention. Spiritual warfare does not mean that we turn our backs on the world of everyday existence, whether it be political, economic or social. We are not some kind of cosmic warriors for Christ, living out some fighting fantasy game with ourselves as heroes. Neither are we battling on some superior spiritual plane, like the heroes of Dennis Wheatley's book *Strange Conflict*.

An over-fascination with our spiritual prowess will not take us into the realm of a Holy Ghost supernaturalism where the power of God's light smites the spirits of darkness, but it may very well lead us into the shadows of self-delusion. There is nothing more pathetic in religious life than witnessing the noisy and frenzied rattling of spiritual sabres that have long ceased to carry a cutting edge. The only spiritual reality we are called to, if we wish to do battle with the Enemy, is down to earth. As Metropolitan Anthony once put it, we need 'a spiritual reality that operates at the level of the kitchen sink'.

It has fallen to our lot, as modern followers of Jesus, to fight the Devil in the heart of the contemporary world. Our *existential situation* is the same today as it has been for Christians throughout church history: we fight our enemies – sin and the Devil – in the geographical districts and historical epochs in which we find ourselves. But our *historical situation* today is radically different from all other historical eras. It is the central contention of *Enemy Territory* that the modern advanced industrial world, what the academics call 'modernity', confronts the Christian church with not merely new dangers, but dangers that are so deadly and damaging that if it were possible the very elect would lose heart and faith.

These new problems, these dangers of modernity, are the most up-to-date military strategies of the Devil against the church. I believe that although our spiritual weapons are as powerful today as they were when they were given us at Pentecost, our strategies have to be re-evaluated in the light of our present confrontation with the Evil One.

The world—though never the material universe—has always been enemy territory. With the coming of modernity, the Devil has come out more into the open (yet few believe in him any more). This is cause for alarm but not despair. I believe that it provides grounds for a proper Christian hope. The Devil has always overplayed his hand, and as he flaunts his authority so Christians will wake up and cease to believe the lies of the modern ideologies whose babblings have almost silenced the still small voice of the heart.

But who will join in the fight? It is no good mouthing pious affirmations that Christ is already the victor and that we can therefore go back to sleep. Or again, it is no good thinking that there is no need to respond to alarmist propaganda because everything will come right in the end – that, as we often say, Christ will reign on his throne whatever happens. Such an attitude is fatalistic, and fatalism has never been a Christian doctrine. It is a truism that God will not and cannot be vanquished, but what is that to us? We are faced today with the challenge of *our* responsibility and part in the Great Battle. If we are Christians, we have to fight. Having chosen God and entered his church, we find that we are surrounded by comrades-in-arms, not members of an exclusive club. If our experience of the church has so far been that of the safety of a sanctuary or the healing security of a hospital, we must understand that this is meant to be no more than a temporary respite from enemy engagement. We must not think that we have arrived in a sanctified sanatorium: we are merely resting in a makeshift medical tent on the battlefield. As soon as we are ready for action – and that means able-bodied, not perfectly fit – we are needed at the front.

In Great Britain during the First World War, you could see the face of Lord Kitchener on recruitment posters that had been pasted on to walls throughout the country. His right arm was thrust aggressively outwards with his index finger stabbing the air, and written in bold print were the words 'Your Country Needs You'. Many young men, fired by patriotism and a romantic sense of warfare, took the king's shilling and marched off to war with a song and a smile. Millions were to die in the mud of Ypres and Flanders as the horrible reality of modern warfare obliterated what romance there was left in war.

In contrast to Kitchener's, God's propaganda really is straight from the shoulder. He appeals to persons of both sexes to 'join up'. There is no emotional gimmickry, sentimentality or romanticism. He tells us simply that he needs us – not of course in the sense that he is incomplete or unfulfilled without us, but because he loves us. And because he loves us he has made us free to choose good or evil, and to take personal responsibility with him for the fate of the world. This, then, is no conscript army; there will be no compulsory 'call-up'. The army is strictly for volunteers only. God calls us to join him in ridding the world of enemy occupation, and yet he leaves us free to join the Enemy against him if we so will. But because we are in a liberation army, if we choose to join God's side there can be no question as to whether we shall fight or not; to fight is the only reason for joining.

To choose to join God's side in the Great Battle is then an option for volunteers but not for mercenaries or soldiers of fortune. No promises are made that we will be rich or even happy. Jesus promises that we will not be overcome and that there will be peace and joy, but nowhere in the New Testament will we find offers of happiness[1] – the Greek concept of 'well-being' – or pleasure. Neither does joining God's forces ensure rapid promotion (on or off the field). The belief that we will be entirely free from injuries, strife, pain and poverty is the invention of 'health and wealth' doctrines that are grounded in neither scripture nor Christian experience. On the contrary, to fight in Christ's army is inevitably to temper our resolve and joy with pain – for we, like our Lord, will grieve and bleed for our brothers and sisters not yet freed from the Enemy.

Choosing between God and the Devil (and I am afraid that

we are not free to choose neither) does not mean choosing the army with the most troops and the biggest guns, but between the right and the wrong side. God does not want us to join him because we want to be on the winning team. He wants us with him because we believe in the right(eous)ness of his cause. We have to accept that, like many of the saints of the past, we may die in full hope, while not receiving all God's promises in this life.

Perhaps all this sounds too idealistic, too serious by half. Can we not watch the Great Battle from the sidelines? Unfortunately this is not an armchair war, and there is no doubt that it will be difficult for many of the present generation to adjust from being spectators at other people's events to being participants in actions of our own. One of the consequences of television has been to turn us into watchers and 'voyeurs' of world events so that our involvement in them is always secondhand. I have even heard a preacher proclaim that we will all be able to watch the second coming on TV!

No doubt many of us are realistic enough to realise that the Great Battle is not a game, a television spectacular or a Hollywood blockbuster. But maybe we feel that we can join God's side only if we will be able to share in his glory and victory. These are part of the promises of God to us, and the hope of eternal life and the final shout of triumph should be a spur to our cowardice and fear of involvement in war.

Sometimes, however, we get so carried away with the final victory that we gloss over the battle itself and what it will mean in our lives. When James and John asked Jesus if they could sit on either side of him in glory, he did not promise them that they would, but he did let them know that they would share in his cup and baptism (Mark 10: 35–40). All of us are called to partake in Christ's cup of suffering. Before we have won the right to resurrection and eternity we have to discover that the Great Battle involves the way of the cross. If we want to be soldiers of Christ we have to be soldiers with him. We so want the resurrection life of Jesus and the power of the Spirit that we imagine that we are exempted from Gethsemane and Golgotha.

If this sounds like uncompromising hardship, it is because

God's propaganda is not written to soft-soap us but to face us
with reality: it is tough on God's side. Some Christians let
their commitment to salvation by faith alone become such a
fixation that they imagine that they do not have to work or
fight. Faith, which is itself God's gift, is no faith at all if it
produces no works. To have faith is to be faithful, and
faithfulness means work and effort, and sweat and tears. God
only asks of us faithfulness – an ascetic faithfulness full of grit
and determination – and it is he who works in us all the
miracles of power and holiness.

If we do decide to choose God and enter the Great Battle
for the modern world on his side, we must recognise that we
are the forces of revolution and liberation and not, as it were,
the establishment troops of law and order. We must not
expect our army to be a 'big outfit' or well equipped, or even
respectable. The glittering armies belong to Satan. When I
keep hearing in certain Christian fellowships that it is time the
church minikin became the church militant, my joy is tinged
with doubt when I hear of such images as 'God's mighty
army', or 'a battleship bristling with warheads and big guns,
ever ready to bombard the enemy'. Is this really the sort of
war we are fighting? Does it accurately portray the nature of
the church's struggle for the modern world?

I believe it is both more biblical and closer to the reality of
our present historical situation to realise that we are the
despised irregular soldiers of Christ – hit-and-run guer-
rillas, resistance fighters – and that at our strongest we are
commando units behind enemy lines.

These images are not meant to be 'radical chic', even if they
are distasteful to moral-majority America or middle-class
Britain. Normally when we use phrases such as these they
evoke pictures of terrorism and anarchy. But the crucial point
is this: until God's invasion of the world – the final campaign
in the Great Battle when the Devil will be defeated – we
remain God's militants in enemy-occupied territory.

At the incarnation Christ raised the standard of human
resistance against the Devil, but as the *eschaton* he will return
as rightful King in full power and majesty. In anticipation of
that return we remain a people's army. We are the advance

forces of liberation, the shock troops who, as it were, have been parachuted behind enemy lines. We must never forget that, in the words of the old hymn, 'this world is not our home': it belongs, until it is liberated, to the Enemy.

The basic purpose of *Enemy Territory* is to alert brothers and sisters in Christ to the nature of our modern world, and to encourage us to throw ourselves into the heart of the Great Battle.

BOOK ONE

THE GREAT BATTLE

I submit that it is impossible to understand the meaning of the Christian faith about man and the world, that it is impossible to be faithful to the significance of the Cross of Jesus, without admitting that Evil has a personalised existence, and therefore, a strategy, a sense of reacting and planning (or rather plotting) against God's work.

(Meyendorff 1978: 318)

Christian, doest thou see them on the holy ground,
How the hosts of darkness compass thee around?
Christian, up and smite them, counting gain but loss:
Smite them, Christ is with thee, soldier of the cross.

Christian, doest thou feel them how they work within,
Striving, tempting, luring, goading unto sin?
Christian, never tremble; never be downcast;
Gird thee for the conflict now by prayer and fast.

Christian, doest thou hear them, how they speak thee fair,
'Quit thy weary vigil, cease from fast and prayer'?
Peace shall follow battle, night shall end in day . . .

'Well I know thy trouble, O My servant true;
Thou art very weary, I was weary too;
But that toil shall make thee one day all Mine own,
And the end of sorrow shall be near My throne.'

(From the Greek of St Andrew of Crete (died c. 740)
translated by J. M. Neale, 1862)

1 THE DIVINE DRAMA LOST

'Christianity is a fighting religion', claimed C. S. Lewis (1942: 39). Did Lewis mean us to take this literally, or is it an example of an author's dramatic licence? At one level this statement is clearly metaphorical and rhetorical. Britain was at war with Germany, and Lewis's famous religious broadcasts were replete with images of sabotage, secret wirelesses and enemy-occupied territory.

But at a deeper level Lewis wanted to make it plain that talking in this way was not *mere* metaphor. That is to say that although he was clearly not endorsing a militaristic brand of Rambo-style Christianity – say, fighting modern crusades against Muslims, or shooting atheists – he was insisting that to be a Christian meant to be a person engaged in the Great Battle. This battle, which is still raging, is no less than the fight between good and evil: the war between God and the Devil.

Today in the 1980s many Christians don't like this fighting talk. Sometimes their reservations are due to sensitive reasons concerning the proper use of language. More often, however, they are a consequence of the trend in much modern Christianity to deny the reality of spiritual warfare. To be specific about it, many of the Christian circles that I enter from time to time do not believe in the Devil. Even in those denominations which claim a Christian orthodoxy, I have often found that the Devil is a formal proposition only. Rather like the concept of Holy Trinity, the Devil hangs around as part of the religious baggage that belongs to tradition or 'our church doctrine' but seems to have no life or substance.

But if the Devil has no reality or active role in the divine drama of salvation then the vision of the Great Battle is lost. Now, of course, it may well be that such a vision exists in your church, and that to insist on the importance of spiritual warfare, some of you might say, is only to preach to the converted. But I believe it to be true that in many corners of Christendom spiritual warfare is no longer a central concern. Furthermore it is not only 'liberal' or modernist churches where this is true. The reasons for this are complex, and are partly related to modern scholarship and partly connected to an over-rationalistic view of redemption in both Catholic and Protestant denominations (both of which I will elucidate towards the end of this chapter).

Despite the complexities behind the loss of the vision of the church at war, the net result has been simple: either the Devil has ceased to exist, or he plays no essential role in the history of salvation. This being so, I would like us to examine some of the implications of a Christianity without the Evil One as opponent. Not only does the Devil's absence from the picture alter how we see the purpose and destiny of the church, it fundamentally changes how we understand God's redemption through Jesus Christ. The New Testament ought to be understood not as a resource for abstract theological thinking, but as a divine drama: the story of the Great Battle. Furthermore, the early church (and in particular during the great patristic era of the first five centuries AD), despite its many internal disagreements on matters of doctrine, saw redemption in thoroughly dramatic terms. But if – for whatever reason – you take the Devil out of the redemption story, the divine drama is lost.

ARGUMENTS AGAINST THE DEVIL AND 'DEVILS'

Some people say that they believe in the Devil but not in demons. I once taught a student who claimed to believe in Satan but thought that demons were used by the biblical writers as a means of explaining the sources of diseases and mental illnesses that were not understood in modern medical terms. Certainly it is true that we cannot expect that writers in Palestine thousands of years ago would have talked about sicknesses in the jargon of medical aetiology. Neither do I think it altogether heretical to wonder whether some diseases attributed to evil spirits may not have been forms of mental illness. I am thinking in particular of the spirit that came upon Saul and drove him mad (1 Sam 16:14–23).

The German theologian Rudolf Bultmann (1884–1976) believed that we need to demythologise the New Testament because demonism was part of the cultural world-view of first-century Palestine that we must reject in order to discover authentic faith (Bultmann 1953:5). I know also that many modern scholars believe demons are part of a primitive *Weltanschauung* (world-view) that smacks of pagan animism where gods and spirits dwelt in rocks, streams, and trees.

There are two points here. Firstly, it is not the case that the evil spirits of the New Testament are remotely similar to animist spirits. The story which most reminds me of animism (if anything does) is that of the angel who stirred up the pool of Bethesda (John 5:1–15). Secondly, and crucially, it is not sophisticated exegesis that leads scholars to disbelieve in devils. It is because evil spirits do not fit – have no logical place or space – into the modern scientific world-view. This view affects more than just clever scholars; I believe that for the same reason many Christians who hold to some belief in the Devil do not believe in evil spirits either. (A favourite way of disposing of demons is the same trick as is used to deal with miracles: assign them to the New Testament era, where they can do no harm or cause any embarrassment.)

It is possible to do away with demons and still cling to a belief in the Devil, but once the Devil is denied then *ipso facto* so are the demon hordes. Once belief in Satan is overthrown then the church has to see its role not in conquering the 'Devil and all his works' but in overcoming ignorance, disease, superstition and injustice. The 'good fight' is then no longer the Great Battle but the fight for human rights, human equalities and human justice. When we squeeze the Devil out through the front door, we unwittingly let in all sorts of secular ideologies that masquerade as Christian ones (which is just another way of saying that he comes in again through the back door). Fighting for justice should indeed be part of the Great Battle – God forbid that our fight has no social and political cutting edge – but it must never become a secular substitute for it.

A few years back I was invited by the Church of England to be an ecumenical guest at a consultation, held at Ely, on the charismatic renewal movement. Just before this a number of leading members of that church had written to *The Times* declaring their disbelief in the Devil. At the consultation a leading psychiatrist, who was from the Society of Friends, insisted that the Devil had no objective reality but was a projection of our fears and insecurities. The Devil was an invention, he claimed, that prevented us from taking responsibility for our own destiny. (Sigmund Freud (1856–1939) said similar things about God the Father!) I met a number of people at the consultation who concurred with that view.

Now I believe it is the case that some Christians do project their own failings on to the Devil.[1] But these people's delusions do not convince me that Satan is a fiction, and psychological arguments against him by psychiatrists have no philosophical bite that carries conviction. Modern psychology has been too taken with human drives and the abolition of guilt to take seriously enough the problem of evil in the world.

DUALISM

The main philosophical argument I come across that has a bearing on the Devil is the old one of dualism. This is the ancient belief that there are two separate and equal forces in the universe. Or, as it appears in Manichaeism (which influenced St Augustine in a number of negative ways), metaphysical dualism posits good and evil in eternal opposition. Although I have heard many a Christian sermon that was implicitly dualist, the orthodox Christian position on this is quite clear. God alone is the sole author of the universe, but, as it were, one of the characters created by God refused to accept the dependency of a created being and insisted on equal powers and rights with the author. There was war in heaven and a rebellion began.

This, of course, brings us right back to the beginning of the divine drama. And there is no doubt that although Christianity rejects metaphysical dualism it has a proper dualism of its own. C. S. Lewis (1942: 45–46) sees that this is the essence of the divine drama:

> . . . real Christianity (as distinct from Christianity-and-water) goes much nearer to Dualism than people think. One of the things that surprised me when I first read the New Testament seriously was that it was always talking about a Dark Power in the universe – a mighty evil spirit who was held to be the Power behind death and disease, and sin. The difference is that Christianity thinks this Dark Power was created by God, and was good when he was created, and went wrong. Christianity agrees with Dualism that this universe is at war. But it doesn't think this is a war between independent powers. It thinks it's a civil war, a rebellion, and that we are living in a part of the universe occupied by the rebel.

For some people this perspective creates its own problems. They are pleased that belief in God does not mean one has to believe that there is another (evil) god, but they do wonder whether on this view God is in control of the universe. Does not the divine drama seem to suggest that the Devil is calling the tune? To look at Christian dualism in this way is actually to advance an argument against God, not the Devil, and some people feel that in discrediting God such a view calls into question not only the Devil but the whole of Christianity.

The early church faced this problem too. In the Old Testament the Devil is usually portrayed as an adversary, not as the supreme evil being. In the story of Job we see the adversary bargaining with God over the righteous man. He seems to be on talking terms with the creator and is able to gain permission to tempt Job in a number of horrible ways. In the New Testament Satan is much more the Evil One that we associate with Christian theology.

Wishing to be faithful to the whole biblical tradition (unlike many moderns), the church fathers insisted that Satan was a rebel but that he was also somehow connected to God's purposes and plans for the world in terms of both judgment and deliverance. In other words, they insisted that Satan's rebellion was itself part of God's overall plan of redemption.

The Anglican Charles Williams (1886–1945) once daringly called the Devil 'God's shadow'. There is – let us admit it – a mystery about the Devil and his role in God's providence.

But the fathers also insisted, and believing Christians have proclaimed it ever since, that although we do not fully understand the relationship between God and the Devil, the inescapable fact about Satan is that he has declared war on God and his creation. The Devil, like all of mankind, was created free. It was not that God let him get out of hand because he was too weak to control him. Like all of us, the Devil is free to serve and love God or reject him. God is love, as St John tells us (1 John 4:8), and as love, by his very nature, cannot command even creatures to love him in return. God's communion and kingdom know of no masters and slaves – only lovers.

The Devil was created both free and good. God as creator has never willed evil. But goodness can choose to change its nature if it has true freedom of will. And the Devil – the angel Lucifer, and the apple of God's eye – wanted to be equal with God. In other words he wished to be God himself, and not a creature. The wish was the mother of the deed and Lucifer rebelled, choosing – in the words of John Milton (1608–1674) – that it was 'better to reign in Hell than serve in Heaven'.

To reject the dualism of Christianity may be a refusal, or an inability, to accept any form of philosophical dualism. Christian dualism, however, is not a philosophical dualism, because the concept of a rebel is not an alternative god: it is a creature trying to be God. It is this sin that Satan taught the human race (Lewis 1942: 48–49).

Another reason why Satan and demons are more usually rejected by modern scholarship is because they are seen as mythological explanations of realities now explainable by science. Or, more simply, there is a belief that the status of the Devil is very uncertain in the New Testament. To this we now turn.

NEW TESTAMENT SCHOLARSHIP AND
THE DEVIL

There is no doubt that the Devil is a complex and changing figure in the sacred scriptures. The Hebrew word for destroyer or devil (*Abaddon*) is not used in the Old Testament to describe Satan, who is seen as the adversary or the accuser. We find in the New Testament that the satanic accuser (*diabolos* in the Greek Septuagint) becomes the full-blown Devil of Christian dualism. In fact the different Greek roots for the Devil in the Septuagint – *diabolos/apollyon* – are of very little importance, for what emerges is the concept of the Devil as the supreme Evil One, the Dark Power. He is not only the tempter and accuser: he is 'god' and 'prince'.

The Devil seems to play multiple roles: he is the angel of the pit (Rev 9:11), the god of this world or this age (2 Cor 4:4), the prince of darkness (Eph 6:12), the prince of this world (John 12:31), and the dragon (Rev 12:7). Not only does he appear in many guises – far more than the few I have mentioned here – but the Devil seems to be chief of the evil spirits. Not only are the gospels and the Acts of the Apostles full of demonising stories, but demons are understood as the opposition forces to the church. They are not simply nuisances or vicious spirits, but are 'principalities', 'powers', 'thrones', 'dominions' (Col 1:16).

Modern scholarship has tended to try and distinguish the different meanings and uses of the words 'Devil' and 'demons'. This has been not so much a question of exegesis but of hermeneutics, searching for the underlying meaning and background to the understanding and belief in the demonic world (see Carr 1981).

In this search many scholars since the nineteenth century have stressed the influence of Jewish intertestamental literature on the New Testament. As he is depicted in many Jewish apocryphal documents the Devil is certainly closer to the New Testament Devil than the Hebrew Satan of the Jewish Bible. There seems to be considerable evidence that the New Testament Evil One is influenced by apocryphal literature, which in turn was influenced by Persian Zoroastrianism.

I have no problems with this evidence, but it never ceases to amaze me what some modern theologians do with it. Because they have shown that the Devil of the New Testament is influenced by sources other than the Old Testament they seem to think that this somehow undercuts the authenticity of the Christian Evil One. But the lure of this historical explanation is to be resisted. To provide an aetiology is not to pronounce on matters of authenticity. In the Great Britain of the early days of the Celtic church, for example, the old Druid ways made their mark on Christian ritual and symbols. The Celtic cross, a cross in a circle, which probably related to the sun and solstice rites, was one symbol with such a pedigree. But once the church sanctioned the Celtic cross it was sanctified; it was exorcised, if you will, of all the previously pagan associations. The etymology of the word Devil and the influence of pagan religion on Christianity, though perhaps interesting in themselves, are of no great *theological* significance. The central theological question is whether the picture of the Devil that emerges from the New Testament is true and necessary for a proper understanding of the Christian story.

Another view of modern scholars is that the New Testament Devil and his demons became augmented by the fathers of the patristic era and were made even more devilish, as it were, than they are in the Bible. Henry Kelly takes this line in *Towards The Death of Satan* (1968: ch. 2), and I think there is some justice in such an approach. There is no doubt that for the fathers the Devil is the Enemy, and on the whole most of them stress this even more than did St Paul himself. However, as Gustaf Aulén (1879–1978) points out (1965: ch. 4), the New Testament provided the basic groundwork for a full-blooded belief in the Evil One and the dark powers. It is true that the fathers tried systematically to translate biblical beliefs into essential Christian doctrines. But if we are going to accuse them of this then we had better also accuse them of inventing the doctrine of the Trinity, for although the New Testament provides evidence for such a cardinal Christian belief it does not set it out in a clear or distinct fashion.

What really grates about Bultmann's demythologising and Kelly's historical spadework is not the scholarship but the network of assumptions. Kelly, for example, can hardly control his incredulity when looking at the mythological world of demons. For him they are not myths that express spiritual reality; instead they are mistaken myths. Similarly with Bultmann. He cannot bring himself to believe in dark powers and evil forces as expressed in biblical language.

This is why I think Walter Wink's recent study on the 'powers' of the New Testament (Wink 1984) is so interesting; he demonstrates that power concepts not only saturate the New Testament but are an essential aspect of its message. Therefore, if modern scholars are 'modernist', they reject the Devil and the fallen angels not because of the lack of evidence or authentic bases for their existence in the New Testament canon. They reject the Devil because they do not believe in him. As heirs of the philosophical Enlightenment and the modern scientific world-view, they cannot grasp the possibility that Evil could be personified or exist as a spirit opposed to God and his creation.

DEMYTHOLOGISING SATAN AND EVIL SPIRITS: A PROPER CHRISTIAN APPROACH

There is a further argument against the existence of the Devil that is, I believe, a very important one. It is not so much an argument against his existence *per se*, but an argument against the way he is so often portrayed. This takes two major forms: either as a monster or as a pathetically funny being. People find it difficult to believe in a personification of evil that looks like something out of a horror movie or a cut-out from a medieval painting. Cloven hooves, pitchforks and horns invoke in most of us laughter or ridicule. On the other hand the modern world, which finds it so difficult to deal with evil, nearly always treats the Devil as a figure of fun if it rejects the monster personification.

In 1986 I wrote an article for the London Arts Festival on C. S. Lewis and *The Lion, the Witch and the Wardrobe*. This was to accompany the first showing in Europe of the musical *Narnia*, which played in All Hallows by the Tower. It was a

very professional and creative production. But one fundamental flaw completely undermined the whole production:
the White Witch (Lucifer) was played strictly for laughs. We
sat and watched not the coldness and menace of evil but a
pantomime dame who was obviously too stupid and incom-
petent ever to pose a threat to goodness. Instead of being
treated to the confrontation between the great lion Aslan and
the forces of hell, we sat and watched a game of cat and
mouse. No wonder people cannot believe in a Devil like that;
it supports the old adage that the Devil likes nothing better
than to be denied.

The image of the Devil as a monster, however, does
occasionally gain some unusual supporters. A number of
people told me that the film *The Exorcist* was positive because
(they thought) it put the fear of the Devil into people. I find
this view curious. No doubt I am perverse, but I found the film
sensationalist, spurious and totally unbelievable. I think that
people enjoyed it (if that is the word) because it was shocking
and frightening, but this is not the 'fear of God' that leads to
conversion or belief.

I am afraid that charismatic circles are sometimes influenced more by the horror genre and the barmier corners of
the Bible-belt than the Bible when it comes to the Devil and
evil spirits. I remember once reading that the evangelist A. A.
Allen had taught that there was a nicotine demon! I have seen
exorcisms that have been totally unbelievable because they
were either trivial or ridiculous. Demons of unbelief, demons
responsible for masturbation, demons responsible for unhappiness and depression, demons that control our cities – all
these and many more seem to have popped up with alarming
regularity in recent years. An excess of demons, like the
proverbial 'reds under the bed', can too easily lead to the
belief that there are no such things. There are many people in
classical Pentecostal churches and the renewal movement
who are worried about an over-emphasis on exorcisms. As
David Tomlinson put it, 'We want to be charismatics not
charismaniacs.' A wrong emphasis on something that is true
trivialises the work of the Evil One. One would think, in some
Christian churches, that the Devil is entirely concerned with

tripping-up the faithful on a day to day basis and has nothing to do with racism, class hatred, war, ecological disaster, and political oppression (see chapter nine). If one pursues an untheological and obsessive interest in demons, committed Christians cease to believe in them, and the Devil applauds.

That is why I find the recent cult book *Pigs in the Parlor* (Hammond and Hammond 1983) totally unacceptable as a Christian document on demons – it is totally unbelievable. Demons are real, I believe, but the moment we try to literalise them – describe their shape and detail their habits – we tend to slip into fantasy. Interestingly I have come across this same problem in a totally different context. I remember teaching a class of social workers who had once received some lectures on Freud. They started to talk about the ego, id and superego as if they were physical realities located in the body. Some of them even seemed to think that the ego was a sort of ecto-plasm that walked – or perhaps swam – about in the head!

C. S. Lewis (1979: 9) surely put his finger on the proper Christian approach to evil spirits in the preface to *The Screwtape Letters*: 'There are two equal and opposite errors into which our race can fall about the devils. One is to disbelieve in their existence. The other is to believe, and to feel an excessive and unhealthy interest in them.'

I once helped a lady to believe in the Devil by playing devil's advocate. She told me that she believed that evil was real, and not merely the absence of good, which, I felt, was a good start. (For example, the power of Stephen King's novel *The Stand* is that evil is a living reality, not the negation of goodness.) Her problem lay in the question of a personal Devil. She could not bring herself to believe in Evil with a capital E, as personified in a spirit-being called Satan or the Devil. So I told her that the most ancient creeds did not mention the Devil. Nowhere do the creeds say 'I believe in the Devil'. Nevertheless it is indisputable that all the early church fathers believed in the Devil as the Evil One,[2] although it was never found necessary to define him in the way we must do so about God.

God reveals himself to us as personal in a very unique way. Personhood is in fact what God reveals to us about himself:

God as a being is in communion (as Father, Son and Holy Ghost). The Holy Trinity is in a sense a communitarian concept, for God dwells in perfect communal relationship. The Greek word for this is *koinonia* and the fact that God reveals his being as persons-in-relation, the Trinity, tells us something about the relational nature of personhood.

Now the Devil, I argued, is not revealed to us by God at all. We know nothing of his being or his nature, except that he is a created spirit that has lost his relationship to the Godhead. Milton tells us in *Paradise Lost* that Satan, even after his fall, still dimly reflects his former glory. But cut off from God his source and out of relationship with the Trinity and the angels, that glory is almost extinct. In a sense, therefore, I told her, the Devil is no longer a person-in-relation that can truly be called personal at all. He is not impersonal like stones or bureaucracies: he is a non-person. The Devil has become all that God is not; he is not beyond personality – he is without it. His purpose in creation is not to destroy God; he knows that he cannot do that. He wants to draw us into the vortex of non-personhood that he has become, and the nothingness or non-being that he is becoming. Satan, in short, aims to take as many of us with him as he can.

In order to believe in the Devil we must rid ourselves of unhelpful images of him (though we do not need to wax philosophical about him as I did for the doubting lady!). We do not have to define him, or even believe that he is a 'person', in order to believe that he is real. John Robinson was telling us all in his 1963 book *Honest to God* that we should get rid of pictures of God as an old man with a beard living in the sky. I have no idea what Satan's personal appearance is like – if a spirit with virtually no personhood left can be said to have an appearance – but the divine drama knows him for what he is. He is, in the words of Lewis, the 'Dark Power in the universe' (Lewis 1942: 45).

We are entitled on the basis of the biblical witness to see the Evil One as the rebel against God, the usurper who became the prince of this world, and the Enemy of the church. What we are not entitled to do is to assume that our own mythological conceptions of him are scriptural. We have all been too influenced by medieval demonology and Milton. (Although I have twice referred to Milton myself, I did so because I was grasping for images to convey something of the reality of the Devil. Milton, for example, sees Satan, Death, and Sin as the trinity of hell. It is an interesting literary image, and one that is well worth developing, but it is not the gospel.)

It may be true that Satan and the demons plot against the church in hellish councils, but we do not really know. It is legitimate to speculate about the Devil as long as we do not assume that our speculations have the solidity of holy writ. Thus, for example, I am not convinced that Satan is a centre of pure malicious but rational evil. On the contrary, I think it more likely that, cut off from the source of rationality, the Godhead itself, the Devil is evil but irrational. One might say 'fey'. I once heard a sermon in which the preacher defended atomic weapons on the ground that Satan would never use them because it would hasten his own destruction! This assumes, of course, that the Evil One is rational and sane. Evil may have intelligence, but the Devil's strategies against the church are not, it seems to me, to be understood as rational military strategies, rather they are more like desperate and increasingly vicious attacks (does he know his time is short?). Perhaps God in his wisdom has told us only a little about the nature and personhood of Satan so that we are not tempted to dwell on him with morbid fascination. We are called to resist him (1 Pet 5:9), not to know or understand him.

THE DIVINE DRAMA, MYTH, AND BIBLICAL SCHOLARSHIP

So far in this chapter my argument has been that by entirely removing the Devil from the Christian world-view, or simply silencing him by demythologising him away à la Bultmann, we undercut the gospel as divine drama. I have looked at some of the reasons why people today cannot (or will not) believe in him. Before looking at how, albeit unwittingly, orthodox Christianity has too often failed to appreciate the dramatic nature of the Great Battle, I want to add a footnote on myth, the gospel, and modern scholarship.

It could be said that scripture's view of the Devil and the evil spirits is mythological. If by this we mean that we explain real spiritual forces in mythic language because there is no other adequate language to explain them, that, it seems to me, is reasonable enough. It is understandable and no bad thing that people should react against crude literalism. When we read, for example, that there was 'war in heaven' (Rev 12:7) we should not assume that there was some sort of cosmic version of *Star Wars*, or that the archangel Michael and Lucifer fought it out with spiritual light-sabres.

The tragic thing is that in reacting against such unhelpful literalism too many of us assume that the war is not real. Some of the stories and images of the gospel are literally true (the incarnation and the resurrection, for example) while other stories are *real* but not necessarily literally true. The great poetic truths of the Psalms and the spiritual truths of the parables would be good examples. Even so-called 'funda-mentalists' usually insist that although it is an axiom of faith that God really created the world, he did not necessarily do so in a literal six days of twenty-four hours each.

C. S. Lewis's approach to the nature of myth is very helpful to us at this point. He believed that the truths of the Christian religion needed to be defended by philosophy and logic. (Christian apologists, for example, appeal to reason in support of revelation, and theology is concerned with truth.) But he also believed that Christian apologetics needed to be explicated in order that their meaning could be made clearer to us. He felt that this could best be done by resorting to myths. Unlike many modernist theologians, however, by myths Lewis did not mean stories that contained spiritual truths without any historical basis whatever. And he certainly did not mean legends and fairy stories (some of which would be mythical in his sense, some of which would not). A myth, for Lewis, was a 'real though unfocused gleam of truth falling on human imagination'. The Narnia chronicles, for example, were written as a mythological expression of the gospel story.

Lewis, who was never a crude literalist, understood the

scriptures as a divine drama containing great truths—some of which were historical and physical—explicated and interpreted by mythology. But the Bible is more than a great storehouse of myths, of unfocussed divine truths; it also reveals God in full-focus. Jesus Christ is sacred myth located in time and incarnated in the material universe. He is the Word made flesh. Myths are no more than refracted images, the logi[3] of the Logos, but with the appearance of Jesus Christ truth (God incarnate) is fully revealed.

I do not mean to suggest that Lewis thought that the Bible was only half true. He stood foursquare on the ancient creeds precisely because he believed in their truth. The Bible for him, however, contained many truths, and he understood far better than many theologians that you must never tamper with the mythology of scripture. If you do—if you insist, for example, in assigning the Devil, the war in heaven, and evil spirits into the realm of legends or outdated world-views—you are playing with the gospel itself.

If we want to tell the gospel story as drama, as opposed to elucidating the truths of revelation in dogmatic theological form, then we have to take the story as it comes, neat. Some of us might go so far as to say that the Genesis accoust of creation is not literal history but myth in Lewis's sense. But to suggest that we should toss out the Garden of Eden story because it is not *necessarily* literal historical fact would be a dangerous precedent. The fall is real enough (remembering my earlier distinction between *real* and *literal*, p. 36), and to take out the story of Adam and Eve is to make a terrible hole in the gospel. It also creates serious difficulties for the theological understanding of Christ as the second Adam. We can be too clever and it is wiser to take the gospel story as revealed throughout the sacred text of scripture.

To reject the mythological character of much of the Bible is to run the serious risk of looking for the truth of scripture as if it were like the kernel in the nut, and ending up with nothing but the shell. Is this not what happens to Bultmann's programme for freeing the authentic message of the gospel for modern man? (See chapter eight.)

The mythological character of the gospel is also essential

for the telling of the drama. The Great Battle cannot be told entirely as a series of truth statements: the Gospel is not philosophy. It is no coincidence that the drama of salvation is kept alive by preaching and story: this is how epic poetry works – and the early church believers in particular were tellers of the story, not New Testament critics. Epic poetry is essentially spoken poetry. It was intended to be heard, not read (Ong 1982); the gospel, likewise, speaks to the heart when the redemption story is presented rhetorically and dramatically.

Of course the Bible is not epic from cover to cover, but there is an epic dimension to the Great Battle. One wonders why it is that Lewis could see the reality of this divine drama dancing throughout the pages of the scriptures even though many notable theologians could not. Lewis could state boldly, as we have seen, that Christianity believes that there is a civil war on, a rebellion, 'and that we are living in a part of the universe occupied by the rebel' (Lewis 1942: 46). He could see the Bible as drama not only because he believed in the Devil but also because he read the Bible as literature. For Lewis the Psalms were poetry, Job sacred fiction, and St. Mark's gospel narrative, and yet he could detect the flow of the divine drama through and in the different mediums of the biblical writers.

He could, in short, recognise the epic quality of the Great Battle. For Lewis it was not enough to have the Bible: you had to learn how to read it. During Lent, in the Orthodox churches, the gospels are read at a single sitting. Despite the different styles and theological stances of the writers, the epic quality of the gospel reveals itself.[4]

Such a practice is enough to give some modern scholars apoplexy. But too many have been weaned on the habit of chopping up the New Testament into bits (sorting out the sources, contemporary themes and ideologies of Aramaic Palestine or the Hellenistic world) so they no longer see the scriptures as a sacred text aflame with divine drama.

The Bible as holy literature, the oracles of the Logos, has become for them an inanimate object of scientific investigation. The divine drama illuminated for us by the Holy Spirit

disintegrates into puzzles, conundrums and endless interpretations. Instead of the great epic being told over and over
by the bards and preachers of the word, we are offered by the
critics snatches of data to be dissected, truncated, and – most
scandalously of all – 'authenticated'. The 'old, old story'
becomes under the critics' needle the ever-unravelling story,
and the drama is lost.

THEOLOGY AND THE LOSS OF THE
DIVINE DRAMA

What, I believe, makes Lewis's view of the Bible so important
today is that it is very similar to the view of the fathers of the
primitive church. For them, the gospel was essentially a story
in dramatic form, to be told not as isolated theological truths
or a series of philosophical axioms supported by mythological
stories and poetic exhortations. The drama to be told was an
epic of cosmic dimensions and significance, played out on the
world stage. This epic I have called, throughout *Enemy
Territory*, the Great Battle.

That the fathers took this view of the Divine Drama is not
obvious, the reason being that if we look at the development
of theology from the first Great Council of Nicaea (AD 325) to
the Council of Chalcedon (AD 451) it is dominated by the
disputes concerning the nature of the Holy Trinity and Chris-
tological issues. And what we today call 'soteriology' (the
doctrine of salvation) did not exist in any systematic way at all
(Kelly 1977: 375).

There are two essential points to be made from this. The
first is that the absence of a systematic theology of redemption
was simply due to the fact that in the early church no great
disputes had yet arisen about it. The problems the fathers
faced were more related to the nature and person of Christ
and his relationship to the triune Godhead than the meaning
of the cross. The second point is crucial to my argument. The
absence of an elaborate and systematic theory of the atonement does not mean that the redemption story was not told.
On the contrary, I believe the evidence is overwhelming that

although there were many different emphases on salvation there was a general agreement as to the nature of atonement and its role in the purposes of God (see chapter two).

And if we look at the patristic understanding of atonement, what hits us with startling freshness is that the Divine Drama is alive and pulsating with the tension and conflict of the Great Battle. Ironically, what we also find, as we shall see in a little while, is that when soteriology was really put on the map in the eleventh century much of the drama was lost.

Perhaps the most famous attack on the Western development of the doctrine of the atonement comes from Gustaf Aulén (1965). He argues – irrefutably, I believe, despite his oversimplification of Latin theology – that the early fathers' understanding of God's war with the Devil was obscured by rejigging the drama of what I have called the Great Battle into a legalistic rational framework. The view of the early church, which Aulén insists must be seen as the classic theory, he calls the 'dramatic'. 'Its central theme is the idea of the Atonement as a Divine conflict and victory; Christ – Christus Victor – fights against and triumphs over the evil powers of the world, the "tyrants" under which mankind is in bondage and suffering, and in Him God reconciles the world to himself' (Aulén 1965: 4).

THE DEVIL AND THE ATONEMENT

It may not be immediately obvious what theories of the atonement have to do with the Great Battle in the modern world. The connection is this. In order to understand how we are to fight the Devil today, we need to realise that our fight is directly related to Christ's own victory over the Evil One. If we push into the background God's warfare with the rebel Lucifer, we are liable to underestimate its importance in our own spiritual lives. Some theories of atonement do precisely this.

The early fathers were Christian dualists and saw, like Lewis, that the Great Battle is the essence of the gospel story. Many of the later Latin fathers (and some of the fathers of the

Reformation) tended to see it only as a backdrop to the *true* meaning of the atonement. The roots of this belong not in the New Testament but in Latin legalism. It was Tertullian (*c.* 160–220) who first introduced into the theology of the third century the concepts of 'merit' and 'satisfaction' from Roman law. In the fifth century Augustine retained many of the bold and dramatic metaphors of his contemporaries, but moved towards a view of atonement in which Christ the mediator between God and man was pre-eminent. In his schema great emphasis was laid on Christ's expiatory death: Jesus the perfect man is accepted as a substitute for sinful mankind.

Of course the Latin fathers not only had St Paul's reference to Christ as the propitiation (with its notions of appeasement) for sins,[5] they also had the whole history and logic of the Old Testament to draw on. But from the tenth century onwards this whole strain of soteriology predominated in the West, and under Anselm of Canterbury became far more systematic and juridical. The love of God, the war with the Devil, and many of the earlier incarnational theories of atonement (which we will see in a moment) fell away to be replaced by a story of God's wrath and its appeasement by Christ's death.

The epic of human redemption was now recast as a domestic tragedy between the Father and the Son, in which the Devil, and incidentally the Holy Spirit, do not seem to be directly involved. The sacrifice on the cross and the 'merit' of Christ's death is the dominant motif. The virtue of Christ's human life, and the control of the world by the Devil, fade into the distance. Now there are some serious theological problems here which we cannot go into in this book (see Aulén 1965, and Walker forthcoming), but we can grasp the essential issues.

In the early church most of the theologians taught the efficacy of Christ's sacrifice, but tended to see it within the context of his whole life, and also against the cosmic background of God's war with the Devil. The later, more sophisticated theories tended to view the question of salvation not so much as God winning back the world from the Evil One and reconciling humanity in himself, but in terms of a legal arrangement entered into by God and man because of the perfect death of the sacrificial Lamb: God the lawgiver lets off sinners, as it were, because of Christ's substitution.

The dramatic and mythological language disappeared and was replaced by a doctrine more fitted to legalism or the language of the ledger: salvation came to be seen as a question of balancing the books, or paying debts to the debtor. (In the nineteenth century the great preacher Edward Irving (1792–1834) once scornfully called such a language a 'stockbroker theology'.)

It is, I think, not untrue to say that too much has been made of an explanation of salvation couched primarily in terms of the law courts – crime and punishment – in which God the lawgiver demands and receives satisfaction. Professor James Torrance, I know, sees this as a weakness in Calvinism, and it cannot be denied that, despite the Reformation, a great deal of this legalism passed over into Protestantism.[6]

The philosophical Enlightenment of the eighteenth century onwards saw a change in mood on the part of many Protestant theologians. They tended to cast doubt on the objective nature of the atonement – at least the Catholic scholastics and Reformers had held on to that – stressing instead the subjective changes wrought in mankind by Christ's sacrifice (such as a growth in God-consciousness or moral transformation).[7] But more interestingly for our purposes, they poured scorn upon the primitive church, seeing the dramatic and mythological story of redemption as crude, unsatisfactory, and even immoral!

Fortunately the Christian church is not dominated by theologians, but by the praying faithful, and the Divine Drama, although suffering numerous attacks and emendations, has lived on in popular spirituality and liturgy. Wherever the New Testament is preached, the divine drama breaks through the restrictions of theological theory and rational presentations of the gospel and continues to win men and women to God's cause.

When the Devil was driven from the centre of the Divine Drama, as he was by the medieval scholastics, he resurfaced elsewhere among the superstitious beliefs of medieval Europe, where he remained despite the Reformation. Indeed the great Puritan era of the seventeenth century saw the heyday of witchcraft.

Aulén makes the telling point that no amount of legalism or rationalism could entirely destroy the Divine Drama, because the mythology of the Great Battle is too dominant in the New Testament to be suppressed. But let us now look at what the early church fathers made of this mythology.

2 RETELLING THE DIVINE DRAMA

There are many ways of telling the Divine Drama. The essential elements are: God, the Devil, the material world, the fall, the incarnation, the cross, the resurrection, and the continuation of the struggle until the *eschaton* – Christ's return. It would be arrogant to suggest that the West no longer tells the story, but I think that it is not untrue to say that the Devil is not as central to that story as he was.

I intend to retell the story (rather than talk about it) from the perspective of the primitive church. The fathers were as close to the New Testament as we are to the Enlightenment of the eighteenth century. Their theology was saturated in the gospel, though they often contended for it in the language of Greek philosophy.[1] In retelling the drama I shall make use of some of my own images and those of some Catholic and Protestant divines, but I shall remain faithful to the spirit of the Greek fathers[2] and their understanding of the Great Battle.

Four notes of explanation will be helpful.

1   It is often said that the Eastern fathers neglected the cross in favour of the incarnation. Too much has been made of this by Western critics. St Irenaeus of Lyons (b. *c*. AD 140) explicitly stated, for example, that it was the blood of Christ that paid for our sins. And both St John Chrysostom (*c*. 347–407) and St Gregory of Nazianzus (*c*. 329–389) in the fourth century talk of Christ nailing our sins with his body to the tree. It remains true, however, that the Greeks see the cross within the context of the incarnation perhaps more so than most Western thinkers. (Karl Barth would be an exception.)

2   The Eastern fathers, and many of the earliest Western

theologians, tended to see the atonement in terms of what is known as the 'physical' theory: God enters into sinful humanity in order to restore it from within. This incarnational theology was partially recaptured by Luther, who accepted the classic position of St Gregory of Nazianzus that Christ in becoming a man became a real human being, the same in nature as ourselves – excepting that the Lord never sinned. (Gregory's slogan was: 'That which he could not assume he could not heal.') Such a view is found in partial form in Calvin, and it surfaces again in the nineteenth century in the thought of both Edward Irving (who was wrongly convicted for heresy for believing it) and the great Anglican churchman, F. D. Maurice (1805–1872).

3   The Eastern fathers, and nearly all the Latin fathers too, held a view of the Devil which eventually fell into disrepute. This view was the belief that the ransom for sin which Paul tells us is Christ's sacrifice (1 Tim 2:6) was paid not to God but to the Devil. All the fathers of the early church saw the Devil as holding rights over this world, but some of them believed that God had to pay him his dues in order to win back the world. That even the Evil One must be treated with justice was the idea. (Do not we see this in Lewis's *The Lion, the Witch, and the Wardrobe*? The White Witch reminds Aslan of the 'deep magic' – the ancient law.)

   This view eventually fell away because, as Tom Smail puts it, the theologians 'could not cash it out' as a fully-blown doctrine of atonement. In the West the juridical view soon dominated, the ransom for sin being seen as paid to God (to appease his wrath). The Devil consequently disappeared from the story. In the East the ransom view also fell into disuse, but the Devil remained as a major opponent to be defeated by Christ on the cross. The Evil One is seen after St Gregory of Nazianzus as having no rights at all – on the contrary he is seen as a robber and a liar who stole the world from God and who holds humanity as captives in bondage to their own sin and his influence and power.

4   Another strand of thought survived in the East from the primitive church, namely the belief that God outwitted Satan

on the cross. (This view outraged the sophisticated German theologians of the liberal school in the late nineteenth century.) It saw Jesus as the victim on the cross who in submitting to Satan became his victor. In the words of St Augustine, 'the cross was the devil's mousetrap'. St Gregory of Nyssa (c. 335–394) uses an even more shocking metaphor: Jesus is the 'bait on the fish-hook'.

I will not make use of the ransom theory in my retelling of the drama, but I shall cling on to the primitive belief, which I believe to be the correct biblical one, that God's atonement in incarnation and cross was the crucial victory in the Great Battle not only over sin but also over the Devil and the powers of darkness. However, let us now turn to the Great Battle itself.

THE DIVINE DRAMA:
God's epic of salvation retold in three parts

Prologue

God is love, and in a moment of ecstasy, of uncalculated desire,[3] created outside his personal communion the spiritual universe. This universe contained no matter but intelligent and free spirits: free to choose and free to love.

In a time before history existed, and while the all-holy Trinity was hymned by cherubim and seraphim, and angelic hosts communed with the divine love, a rebellion began. Lucifer, the morning star of creation, dreamt the impossible dream: to be a creature of God that is equal to God. This fantasy was not fuelled by disinterested speculation but by envy. Others were told the insidious lie, 'We too can be as gods.' A conspiracy was conceived that gave birth to a revolution. And the courts of heaven rang with the sound of warfare.

The rebellion failed and the pretenders to God's throne were cast out of heaven. Cut off from God's communion and divine love, the rebels still clung to their leader Lucifer, their fallen star, who still glowed with forgotten glory and the heat of defeated bitterness.

Part One: The Fall

God continued the inexorable course of his divine love, and again from that immeasurable passion spoke the word of creation and out of nothing called into existence the material universe. It too, like the angels, was created good and without corruption.

In this our world God breathed his spirit into the dust of the earth, and matter became articulate and personalised in the forms of man and woman. Though they were made just a little lower than the angels, they were stamped with God's character, bearing his image and divine likeness. To them was given dominion over the world, and all the created beauty of earth was theirs to hold as regents and stewards of God's kingship.

To remind them that their rule was derived from God himself, and that they were neither creators nor rulers by right, God forbade them only one thing: they were not to partake of the knowledge of good and evil; such a mysterious *gnosis* belonged to God alone. If they disobeyed this one command, God told them, they would die.

The fallen angel Lucifer, having failed to defeat God in the great battle of heaven, saw his chance to enlist new recruits and continue his rebellion in the material universe. Once so full of envy and pride, the great angel became a devil of meanness and spite, and he resolved to spoil the joy of God's new creation.

'Do not be afraid of God,' he told the man and woman. 'Discover good and evil for yourselves: reach out and taste reality.' And repeating the well-tried lie he told them that they too could be gods and would never die.

The man and woman chose to disobey God, and their act of disobedience severed their relationship with their creator: they lost the divine likeness and his image in them was clouded over – though not lost – through this separation. The loss of innocence marred their communion with the divine love, and terror entered their hearts as they were cast off from the sustaining life of God.

The corruption of the material world through human folly led to a process of decay and death, so that the whole cosmos mourned the loss of sustaining communion and groaned and yearned to be set free. And the fall of man resulted in the curse of separation falling upon the whole of the human race and its future history. God's wrath cast a shadow upon the earth, and the fallen angels settled on the darkened world like vultures on a dying prey.

When man and woman were innocent the Evil One's power was not great enough to take the world by force: he could only operate *outside* the human race as a whisperer of lies and delusions. But with the act of disobedience the will and the hearts of the human race were unlocked from the *inside* and the Dark One scuttled in and, like a 'thief and a robber', took the world by stealth.

The Dark Power continued to influence the world by encouraging evil, but he could not control it completely. Despite the fall, the human race still contained the dim image of God within it. Men and women were still free to choose good from evil, though the corruption rooted in their very nature tugged them towards their captor and now ruler of the earth.

Three wills contended for the world.

The Evil One sought totalitarian control by wresting the allegiance of all human beings away from God and fostering the human stubbornness that refuses to submit to any authority. His methods were twofold, either dominance by the fear and brutality of superior force or seduction by the enticement of power, sensual pleasure without constraint, or flattery. The Dark Power had lost for ever his eternal brightness, but his strength and intelligence were derived from God and he could still disguise himself as Lucifer the angel of light.

Against the Evil One and the principalities and powers of darkness God also contended for the world. Human sin and devilish enticement could not obliterate the divine image. God whispered in the secret chambers of the human heart. His Spirit breathed a longing for communion and a nostalgia for the God who was lost. When persons responded to the wooing of the divine love, a breach was made in Satan's empire and hope and joy would enter the world. Men dreamt dreams of salvation and the human imagination created divine myths and received the signs of God's grace.

And to show the world the meaning of faithfulness the Holy One established a prophetic people who would prefigure the restoration of human obedience and divine communion. He spoke through prophets and in acts of history, through poetry and prayers of contrition. Through this people God called for resistance to the great rebel and usurper of the world.

The third will that contended for the world was the human will itself. As human history and experience progressed humankind oscillated between God's light and the depravity of darkness. Every culture, however imperfectly and blindly, either turned towards the light or fell back into the darkness. Each human soul was in tension between the divine dignity of sonship and the degradation of Satanic enslavement.

To choose neither God nor the Devil was an illusion of freedom, for in reality every step of human endeavour, however unwitting, was either a step homewards to God's kingdom or a step closer to hell. The human will could not stand back from the Great Battle raging in its own soul as well as in the world at large: it had to choose to contend either for God or the Devil.

Although individual men and women, and sometimes whole nations, took God's side against the Evil One, the world remained enemy territory. The weakness of the human will betrayed by generations deprived of God's inner communion was no match for the Dark Power. God's authority would sometimes flash across the universe in miracles and signs which illuminated the true nature of Satan's shadowed kingdom. But after the flashes would come an even greater blackness as men and women continued to show that they preferred darkness to light.

Despite their unfaithfulness to him the people chosen by God continued to dream of deliverance, and their songs spoke of an anointed one who would champion his people in the lists and free them from oppression and enemy occupation. And if their poetry was ostensibly about a political and cultural freedom, it also spoke of the bondage of the human race, the yoke of the Evil One, and the hope of salvation.

Part Two: The Restoration

While people were dreaming dreams and singing songs, and the Evil One and his angels strutted their mastery over the world like cocks in a barnyard, the omnipotent God made the decisive move that was to win the Great Battle for the world.

He took everybody by surprise.

While the prophetic people waited for a great military leader, and the Dark Power scoured the skies for signs of a cosmic invasion, God slipped into the world almost unheralded. Only a young Jewish girl, her betrothed husband, a handful of shepherds, and a few wise men had any inkling who had arrived.

At the fall Satan was not able to take the world by force. It was only because the human beings sinned and let him in that he was able, like some robber baron, to plunder God's territory. The divine love on the other hand was strong enough to invade and recapture the world, but God chose a different avenue of attack.

The community of the Trinity is a companionship of love, and the God who is love refused to force free creatures to love him by command. He knew also that the human race freely chose to reject him; it was only right that they should take some responsibility: mankind as well as God must be responsible for reversing the effects of the fall and for moving on to the mature relationship with the creator that had been ordained for them from all eternity. God knew, however, that without divine intervention and the presence of his glory in the depths of human life such a reversal was impossible.

And so in the sanctuary of the triune Godhead, whose secrets we can never know, and whose mystery we must never probe, God the Father prepared him a body, and the Word from the beginning, the Son, humbly said, 'I come' and the Holy Spirit overshadowed a young woman of Israel so that the uncreated one was joined to creature-flesh and became man.

And just as it was that the woman was instrumental in the fall of the human race, so it was that another woman was instrumental in its restoration. All heaven was hushed as the maiden heard the annunciation from God's messenger that she would bear God's child. She assented freely and only with her full co-operation did the Spirit quicken her body, and the God-Man enter the world.

> Who can grasp the wonder or the truth of it!
> 'Whom have we Lord, like You.
> The Great One who became small, the Wakeful who slept.'[4]

The myths and songs of the dreaming world had found their people's champion in the form of a little child. The Omnipotence who smashed the rebellion in heaven freely entered Satan's stronghold, naked and helpless. The restoration of humanity had begun, and God's standard-bearer of the true kingdom had arrived.

The alarm rang out in the temples of hell that something was up in Judea and that there was a baby born in Bethlehem who posed a threat to the rebellious empire. The human king of the region was persuaded to act, and all the first-born sons in the district were slaughtered. But the young God-child escaped with his mother and her husband.

And the child grew in wisdom and strength, but his flesh was no mere phantom or merely the appearance of flesh: he belonged to the human race. As he grew he fought the temptation of sin in his body, and felt the pain of separation in his heart, but he never faltered in his faithfulness to his heavenly Father. Quietly, away from the crowds and demon curiosity, he came to manhood.

He began to teach men and women the kingdom of God and declared that it was already in their midst. Sometimes he spoke straight from the shoulder and sometimes in puzzles and parables. In solidarity with his fallen race, though he himself was without any sin, this man called Joshua in the Hebrew and Jesus in the Greek entered the river Jordan to be baptised for the remission of sins.

The mystery of the communal Trinity was revealed and the Holy Spirit descended upon Jesus, who received him gladly from the Father who spoke of his love for his Son, though the crowds at the baptism did not understand the significance of the event.

The Spirit urged Jesus into the desert, where he resisted the temptations of the Devil, who did not seem to know that he was tempting God himself. And Jesus, endowed with the Spirit, breathed love and fellowship and yet stood sternly for the truth. He commanded the weather and rebuked the demons. The man who had mastered self-control and resisted sin from within now openly declared war on the outward corruption of the fall and the bondage of the Evil One. He healed the sick, raised the dead, exercised authority over the evil spirits and forgave sins. Both the councils of men and devils were perplexed and awed: there had been prophets, healers and magicians before, but none like this man. Who was he?

No doubt some of the angels who had faced God's holiness before had a premonition about this man. Intuitively they knew this was no ordinary son of Adam. But the angels of hell are not party to the councils of heaven. God's invasion plans and strategies of salvation were not known to them. Was this man leading a resistance movement against the Dark Power? How could a man, however unique, win such a struggle? The devils knew that all men sinned, and all men must die.

As the prophetic people flocked around Jesus, and as they saw the transformation in the lives of his disciples and heard the words of life and hope, they longed for a rebellion against the Roman occupation of Judea or a reformation of the Pharisaical law. But Jesus had come to defeat not an occupying human army but the forces of hell. He knew that he had to die to free the captives from the corruption within and the Captor without. All his life he had fought, resisted, and overcome sin. He had obeyed the Father in all things and would not only have to die but had also to become sin for the sake of the captives.

The agony of his death confronted Jesus as he prayed in the garden of Gethsemane. It was not just the natural fear of a cruel crucifixion: suffused with the divine life, the person of Jesus could not die in any ordinary sense. He had to will the rending of his divine nature from his human nature, and die a man alone – the human Jesus cut off from the Father; the Son denied the sustaining power of the Spirit. The naked baby helpless but safe in his mother's arms would now have to become the helpless victim of unrestrained evil.

And as Jesus awaited the betrayal by one of his own disciples to the Sanhedrin authorities, Satan nearly broke him. The time for subtle temptations was over; all of hell, in its unimaginable horror, unleashed its powers on this one person alone in the garden. Perhaps the devils still did not know who this holy man really was, but they could see that he was without sin. If he was to die in perfect innocence, could the effects of the fall be reversed and the time of their dominion be over? They would be routed for the second time in their existence, and their slaves – the people – would be set free and return to fight with God against them!

Lucifer also could not be sure who was before him in the garden. Once, long ago, at the dawn of time, he had persuaded man to disobey in a garden. Perhaps he could do it again.

If he could not persuade the man to desist from dying, then he would claim his pound of flesh and his right to Jesus's soul on the cross; the rebellion of this holy creature would then be over.

As Jesus agonised over his death – a death unique to the Son of God – he sweated drops of blood and he felt his heart failing him. 'Don't let me have to do it,' three times he begged the Father. (Hell cheered him on.) But the Father asked only obedience, even to the end, and Jesus resolved to die.

The forces of hell reflocked around the cross. They had missed him in the garden, but now if he was truly a son of Adam he would die. When Jesus was scourged by the Roman soldiers he bled like a man. His crown of thorns wounded him like any other victim of torture. Hell was confident, and the Evil One moved in to claim his prize.

Jesus the Son of Man and Son of God, who had conquered sin *within* the depths of humanity was taken '*without* a city wall' to die on a Roman gibbet.

The champion of the people was nailed to the wooden beams and lifted up between two murderers. God in the middle contending for the world, a man on his left choosing to side with the Evil One till the last, and on the right a thief who with his last gasp offered his broken solidarity back to God for healing and restoration. Above the head of Christ were the words – ordered by a conscience-stricken Roman governor who refused solidarity with him – '*Jesus, King of the Jews*'. The crowds jeered and mocked, not knowing that he was the king of the universe and the deliverer of the captives.

The human world and hell joined forces to scoff at the dying man. 'I thirst,' he cried. One man alone remembered his forgotten humanity, and the Spirit of God flared within him with the brightness of Eden, and against the crowd, with the dignity of a true son of God, he offered some unrefined wine on a sponge to the dying king.[5]

By now the intoxicating swell of success had unseated the demons, who, fey with the scent of victory, yelled at their victim to leap off his cross and show them his tricks. The mob, more demonised than human, took up the cry: 'If you are the Son of God, get off the cross.'

Amid the banter and foul jibes of the crowd – drunk as all crowds are at a blood-letting – the God-bearer Mary and a few disciples stood numb with horror and dread as they saw their Lord and their champion humiliated, despised and broken.

Jesus called out to the Father in his spirit and with his voice: 'Father forgive them for they know not what they do.' The final words of forgiveness had a threefold action. Firstly, the cry was the cry of solidarity with the corrupted hopelessness and dereliction of all men and women broken by sin and separation. It was the cry to let them be; from one who knew no sin came the plea from the heart of humanity, 'Have mercy on us.' There was no question of an appeal to justice: it was the penitent's cry for forgiveness.

Secondly, the cry of forgiveness was for the covert bondage of unwitting sins, the habits of sinfulness that bound a lost humanity. The cry for forgiveness was also the cry for inward healing and deliverance from the mental and physical effects of sin.

Thirdly the cry to the Father was to set the captives free from the Devil, who ensnares and traps what goodness is left in human beings. The human and material world needed to be cleansed from within, but it also needed to be liberated from the powers without.

'Father forgive them for they know not what they do' was the threefold shout of victory: of forgiveness, of healing, of liberation.

But the words masked the meaning and reality from the crowds of fallen men and angels who were awaiting the final denouement. And when it came, the sun itself could not look upon the death of God. The sky turned black and, as it were, God the Father mourned and turned his back on his only Son.

It was nearing the ninth hour, and Jesus, who had resisted sin throughout his life, now, because of his obedience, became sin itself – not by wilful act but by being made the crucible of the whole sum of human evil. And the Father could not look at him and the Spirit fled away.

'My God why hast thou forsaken me,' echoed the voice of Jesus in the terror of unrelated naked existence. Cut adrift from sustaining love, and dwelling in the deepest bowels of evil, the divine Logos, the person of Jesus, chose this moment of absolute sin and forgottenness to die.

'It is finished,' breathed Jesus, and he expelled his life with his final word.

For the disciples round the cross the words were the pronouncement of doom: the end of hope and meaning, the extinction of faith, defeat. That was the experience of Christ's death in the natural order. But in the supernatural universe the Great Battle was won in the twinkling of an eye.

As the Devil (feeling the final breath of his adversary leaving him) lurched forward to seize his prize, and as the demons howled their triumph like a frenzied pack of wolves falling upon their slaughtered prey, Jesus appeared to them in terrifying power.

The disciples heard 'It is finished' as the scream of defeat, but the devils heard the words as the shout of victory. In a moment the reality of God's judgment crashed through the barrier of their self-delusion. Jesus the Christ was, after all, not only a perfect man but the Ancient of Days.

Instead of hauling another lifeless victim into Hades, the Evil One's power was destroyed, and Jesus entered the gates of hell in triumph. He harrowed hell[6] with the same spiritual vigour with which he had overturned the tables of the money-changers in the temple, and the faithful dead were set free.

The Devil knew that if hell could not hold Jesus, neither could death. He had lost the second war in the Great Battle of the universe and had forfeited his power over humankind for ever.

And on the third day after his death the human body of Jesus, still reposing in the sanctity of the divine presence, was quickened by the Spirit and the person of Jesus of Nazareth was restored to life. But now the human nature of Jesus was not only perfect – as it had been from conception – it was a risen humanity beyond death. Jesus was and is the new Adam: not the unfallen Adam of innocent humanity restored, but the first of a redeemed and resurrected humanity – a greater and more gloriously human humanity than ever the first Adam knew. By his death and resurrection Jesus had smashed the powers of the Devil and in his own person reconstituted the full restoration of communion between God and man.

Part Three: The Completion

Christ's earthly obedience ended in triumph, and the crucial battle against the Evil One was won. But the war was not over. Jesus had shown the way back to God and had demonstrated in his own person that he was the Way, but men and women in order to return to God would need to freely join themselves to the new humanity of Christ.

Having achieved our reconciliation to God Jesus now asks people everywhere to be reborn of the Spirit in order to enter into his new humanity.

By nature we cannot be divine, uncreated life, but we can be adopted into the redeemed humanity of Jesus. In this the threefold action of God is again revealed to us. Jesus the Son was sent into the world by the Father through the Spirit. Jesus departed the world, ascended into heaven, and sent the Holy Spirit from the Father. The Spirit on the day of Pentecost constituted the church that Christ instituted. Henceforth to be a Christian is to be united to the risen Christ through the adoption of the Spirit.

The church is to reflect the mystery of the divine communion: members of the church are to be personally related to each other and, through the Holy Spirit, to Christ the head.

The vision of the church as a body is not an accidental analogy. The body *is* the new humanity: the one person of Christ and his adopted brothers and sisters.

However, because we are adopted by the Spirit and yet naturally sons and daughters of Adam, the old nature still wars with the new. The church is not, in this world, the perfect body of Christ, but is composed of sinful members under grace.

And it is because the new humanity is made up of free men and women that God wishes that all should be saved: his delay in invading the world and bringing an end to history is to allow time for the new humanity to supplant the old. The stay of final judgment upon the universe is an exercise of the divine mercy: God wants a fully redeemed humanity, not a remnant.

Christ entered into humanity to defeat the Dark Power that oppressed us and to set us free from the corruption within. The Jesus who has shown his solidarity with us now calls us to show our solidarity with him. He does not ask us to emulate him: we are not divine, and none of us could die for the world. The Lord's death was a unique and a once-for-all event. However, the final victory over sin was anticipated but not completed on the cross. It was actually achieved but not yet fully realised. And so just as Jesus showed his at-one-ment with us, he now asks us to show our at-one-ment with him, and join him to continue the Great Battle until the final defeat of Evil and the 'restoration of all things'.

Twice the Devil has been decisively defeated by God, but his strategies remain the same. He can never destroy the creator, but he can still spoil and corrupt his creation. Just as he spoilt the old humanity, he now tries to spoil the new one. There is, however, a difference. God never promised the old humanity that it could resist and defeat the Evil One. But the church of Christ has been told that the 'gates of hell shall not prevail' against her. The world was never told by God that it could overcome the evil inherent in it, but Christ tells his disciples to be of good cheer because he has overcome the world.

Jesus departed the world so that he could equip the church with the weapons and armour of the Spirit. When Christians choose to face Satan in the Spirit – in the new nature – they are not only living and adopted members of Christ's new humanity, they are also by definition his soldiers. As companions of the Spirit, a holy company, we are victors as Christ is victor.

Postscript: The Divine Drama Now

Throughout church history, and as we move towards the *eschaton*, we must recognise that the world is not yet kingdom territory. Until Christ's return it remains enemy territory. Sadly, Christians have too often forgotten that the world belongs to Satan and is not our natural home (as sons and daughters of the new humanity). Sometimes Christians have tried to build the new Jerusalem on earth, and church history is littered with the debris of broken dreams, from the wreckage of Byzantium to the forgotten Puritan theocracy of New England.

Christian civilisations have risen and fallen. Today we are supposedly living in the first great secular age of history (though do we not still worship our own pagan idols – of money and success?). Ironically we find that this mixture of heathenism and paganism is rather like living in the primitive church. Perhaps it is less hopeful in some senses, because unlike the early church we are living in a post-Christian age. What is certain is that we need to recapture the vision of the primitive church, for if only we could drag ourselves away from our television sets and unhook our headphones from our portable stereos we would hear the clear call to arms.

The Great Battle is no longer at Golgotha or frozen in church history, it is here now.

We must abandon our leave and return to active service. The Enemy is upon us and we have no time to organise ourselves into battalions and ordered companies. Scattered and divided, we must act like all true liberation armies.

Let us pass the word along and come together to fight in the only way left open to us – the way the church has always been meant to fight – behind enemy lines.

BOOK TWO

THE CHRISTIAN STRUGGLE FOR THE MODERN WORLD

'Christianity is the story of how the rightful king has landed . . . in disguise, and is calling us all to take part in a great campaign of sabotage.'

(Lewis 1942: 46)

Part One

ENEMY-OCCUPIED TERRITORY

3   APPROACHING MODERNITY

In Book One my main concern was to show that the Christian life is one that has to be seen in the context of the Great Battle. This battle, I have argued, is no less than the fight between God and the Devil. I do not believe that the gospel story – of redemption and reconciliation – can be adequately told without the clamour of spiritual warfare or without the primary role of the Evil One.

However, I have also been at pains to show that we need to distinguish the reality of evil from crude and literalistic representations of it. The primitive church employed mythology to augment and explicate the great truths of the gospel. In my retelling of the Divine Drama I have made use of primitive mythological ways of speaking because I do not believe that we have a better language that is available to us when it comes to understanding God's revelation as story – as the great epic of salvation.

I do not think either that we can make sense of the Devil in the language of contemporary philosophy or science; on the other hand neither do I believe that we should try and invent a modern mythology that makes the Devil more credible and accessible. To revamp our old Enemy for contemporary consumption is to run the risk of creating a science fiction that will be seen as fantasy rather than science.

We must be prepared to understand the Evil One as the Dark Power – that which is evil – rather than elaborating (new) mythologies that concentrate on personalised demons and personified devils. I say this because I am anxious that having decided to reject the modernist notion that there is no Devil – and therefore no Christian dualism – we should not be tempted to fall into the opposite error of conceiving our adversary as no more than a fiend. Evil is not literally the 'dreaded Apollyon' of Bunyan's allegory *Pilgrim's Progress*.

If we concentrate *only* on the mythological representations and personifications of evil, we too easily relegate the Devil to our private worlds of personal torments and individual temptations. I do not wish to exclude him from such private and individual arenas, for to do so would be to fly in the face of Christian tradition from the fathers to C. S. Lewis and Cardinal Suenens (1982) in our own time. But I do want us to realise that evil today has to be faced in a far more fundamental and crucial theatre of war: it is in the processes and ideologies of the modern world itself that we find the destructive, impersonal and heartless force of the Dark Power.

We need not wait for evil to swoop out of the cosmos or ascend from the depths of hell: it is here now, not incarnate in human form but embodied in the structures and philosophies of our modern culture.[1] It is this contemporary culture with which we must grapple and fight. This for us is the spiritual warfare to which we are called; it is our small though crucial engagement in the Great Battle between good and evil. I insisted in my foreword that spiritual warfare was down to earth and it is no less than modernity where the battle is now raging. Understanding this modernity is the prerequisite, the necessary intelligence work if you will, of our struggle for the modern world.

DEFINING MODERNITY

'If you want to know what a word means,' said my philosophy tutor, 'never look it up in a dictionary.' I have found this useful advice, particularly if one wants to know what a word means in different cultures and groups.

Modernity is a word that evokes a different response in North America, Continental Europe and Great Britain. While the large *Oxford English Dictionary* defines modernity as 'the quality or condition of being modern', this is not how the word is really used on either side of the Atlantic. The word itself first came into usage in the seventeenth century and was not intended as academic jargon or as a sociologism. It was used simply to stand against all that was feudal or pre-modern.

As a proper noun standing for the state of being modern it has never really caught on as a popular word in everyday speech. Today in Great Britain most people do not use the word. When students come across it they assume it is some sort of technical language. Increasingly in universities and colleges modernity is becoming a major concept whose usage is increasingly following American philosophical and socio-logical meanings. These meanings have given modernity a far more specific content. So, for example, whereas in France or Italy modernity – which enjoys greater popular usage than in Great Britain – tends to mean 'these modern times in which we live', and in Germany modernity means both modern and fashionable, Americans identify modernity as a description of life in advanced industrial societies.

Furthermore, this identification of modernity with life in industrial societies contrasts them with all preindustrial societies (both in a historical sense and in those countries of the Third World that have barely been touched by industrial-ism). But in North America modernity, while retaining this basic meaning, has become a term that is not only descriptive of the central features of modern life in advanced societies but increasingly contains a moral dimension; that is to say, mod-ernity is viewed with concern as a source of conflict, contra-diction and danger. The idea that modernity is problematic has caused sufficient anxiety about the modern world for its use no longer to be restricted to the universities and class-rooms but to spill out into the everyday culture. In America today modernity as a term synonymous with the problems of life in the advanced societies has become almost a cliché.

Modernity understood as the modern world in crisis has now hit us with such force that writers of many different political persuasions are addressing the issue (cf. Kumar 1980 and Greer 1984). In this book I shall be following an understanding of modernity established by the philosopher Alasdair MacIntyre (1981) and the sociologist Peter Berger (1969). Both men are Christians, and in the last few years a number of other Christian writers have followed in their footsteps (Hunter 1983; Guinness 1983; Williamson, Parotta *et al* 1983; Kolakowski 1986).

Modernity for these writers has been used as an all-embracing concept that includes both the ideologies of the modern world – its 'modernisms' – and also the economic, social and cultural realities of modern life.

To understand modernity, then, involves an investigation of modern ideologies and methodologies – in science, theology, philosophy, literature, etc.; it also involves an effort to make sense of these ideologies in the context of advanced industrial societies. It is important, as Christians, to link modernisms with our lifestyles and economic systems, because the crisis of modernity is not just an isolated problem of wrong philosophies or false doctrines, it is also a crisis of wrongdoing and crass social values.

Living in modernity does not mean living in an age that is intrinsically evil because it is modern, but it does mean that we have to understand that we are living in a fallen culture: a culture whose people and institutions and social habits need to be redeemed. It is not our central concern as Christians to get bogged down in the minutiae of academic arguments concerning the merits and demerits of modernity. We would be foolish to believe that nothing good could come out of modernity. But we would be even more foolish if we imagined that modernity is neutral territory: it is enemy territory – as the world, for Christians, has always been.

We shall begin to see in this and the next five chapters that the evils and problems of modernity are of an intensity and subtlety unimaginable a mere two hundred years ago. The Enemy is at work, and our first task as Christians as we confront our adversary in the Great Battle for the modern world is to identify his strategies.

MODERNITY IN THE RIGHT PERSPECTIVE

In order to do this successfully we have to avoid two snares that our Enemy has set modern Christians. The first trap is a sentimental romanticism that turns our attention away from the present battle and leaves us wallowing in nostalgia for the past.

Hankering after the 'good old days' is a way of always viewing history with rose-tinted glasses. Looking backwards with either envy or merely admiration tends to distort history. It has already happened with Victorian England, for example. No longer is it to be seen as an age of poverty, disease and false hopes. Rather it assumes the image of a golden age of progress and stability. Seen thus, there are no 'satanic mills' and violent social upheavals. These are blotted out by the dominant images of Christian England and the establishment and power of the greatest empire the world has ever seen.

If only we could return to the values of the past, many of us dream, how much better life would be! Perhaps if we are American we long for the early seventeenth-century Puritan theocracy of New England. Or perhaps for a return to the first Great Awakening of the eighteenth century, when Jonathan Edwards thundered against the evils of the age. (Such a longing, incidentally, tends to forget certain unpleasant features of the time in question: for black Americans a reassertion of eighteenth-century values would mean a return to slavery.)

No denominations are immune from such romantic longings. No doubt some Catholics yearn for a return to the middle ages before the Renaissance and Reformation shattered the stability of feudal Europe. If only life could return to the 'right believing' of the church fathers, many Orthodox sigh. And is not the ultimate 'nostalgia-trip' beloved of so many Protestants to return to the full power of the New Testament church (the golden age *par excellence* for Christians)? But even this requires a kind of nostalgic astigmatism and amnesia, for the New Testament church is viewed without flaw or corruption, sin or perfidiousness, and we likewise forget the trouble St Paul was having with Corinth, the bitter wrangles over circumcision, and what the Spirit had to say to the churches . . .

And so the Devil is quite happy as long as we dream our lives away, or become antiquarian, seeking to dredge up history in order that we can live out our lives in a museum of our own making. Personally I am strongly committed to a primitive Christianity, but I know that I cannot return to the total world-view of the primitive church. In the first place I do not know exactly what it was like in all its details. Furthermore, there are some features of primitivism, attitudes to women for example, or the anti-Semitism of the church fathers, that I find distasteful and not truly Christian. Crucially, however, the point is this: I cannot pretend that the philosophical Enlightenment has never happened, and that we are not living on the 'post' side of a scientific revolution. Neither can I pretend not to be a modern. In order to be a Christian and to continue the Great Battle against the Evil One, I cannot return to the life and times of the New Testament church as if there had been no history in between. What I need is a New Testament Christianity that speaks to the modern man that I am now; a faith, in short, that is real and challenging to modernity.

But if romanticism[2] suits the Devil because it has a habit of slipping us into unreality – away from the real battle – it has an even more pernicious aspect. At its worst romanticism can be a cloak to disguise naked evil. Nazism appealed to the romanticism of the German people and attempted to re-create the rituals and folklore of its pagan past. From 1933 to 1938 the Third Reich tried systematically to restore the old gods and pagan festivals, homeopathic medicines, and the archaic medieval German language. During the great party rallies at Nuremberg Himmler and the SS hierarchy rode through the streets on horseback, dressed in the full regalia of Teutonic knights.

During this period many travellers to Hitler's Germany found the new enthusiasm for German folklore and the old peasant ways both quaint and charming (but harmless). But all this re-creation of the old ways was also the creation of the *Völkisch*: the racially and culturally pure Aryans who were to be the master race destined to rule the world. Romanticism feeds on the mythology of the past which it tries imaginatively to re-create in the present. Nazism fed on the dark myths of racial purity and xenophobia dressed up in the glories of a supposedly great history and an invented Nordic heritage (Walker 1969).

There have been men such as Samuel Taylor Coleridge (1772–1834) and C. S. Lewis who were so rooted in the Christian gospel that their 'romanticism' was clearly a prophetic warning against modernity. But without such a sure embeddedment romanticism becomes sway to the influence of the Dark Power. Even that great opponent of the industrial system of the nineteenth century Thomas Carlyle (1795–1881) failed to relate his criticisms to the Christian doctrine that he had abandoned as a young man. He became increasingly attached to an almost Greek sense of the hero, but recast in a mould similar to Nietzsche's superman. This form of romanticism becomes not only reactionary, therefore, but conducive to the sort of fascism that took root in Europe in the twentieth century. William Blake (1757–1827), that great romanticist, attacked the new industrial capitalism in the early nineteenth century with great power but not with the radicality of the gospel; he sought to oppose the emergence of modernity with the gnosticism of his mystical Swedenborgianism.

When I was an undergraduate student studying sociology we were all warned of the dangers of romanticism. Early sociologists such as Ferdinand Tönnies (1855–1936) and Émile Durkheim (1858–1917) tended to bemoan the loss of community in the face of modern urbanism; there is a wistful longing for the past in aspects of their analysis of the modern world. In recent years, however, I have realised that although romanticism can distort the past, there is an even greater trap into which we can fall. This trap is the Devil's second snare and is the one he sets if he fails to catch us with the first one. Furthermore, it is my conviction that this artifice is more dangerous than the first and is widespread in the secular culture and the churches. It is a belief that everything in the present is superior to the past.

C. S. Lewis called it 'chronological snobbery' (Lewis 1955: 159). This belief distorts the past because it can see nothing good in it. The old days are always the 'bad old days'. Life before modernity was 'nasty, brutish and short'. In fact such a view tacitly rests on one of the ideologies of modernity: a belief in continual progress (see chapter seven). It is difficult to resist this view because of the great successes of medicine, public health, education, welfare and technology. When I was at school and university in the 1960s, when the myth of progress was still very much alive, my social and political lessons tended to recite the advances of the century as a long list of linear progress: the gradual emergence from primitivism to modern civilisation. Feudalism was basically bad; modern democracies are good. The economics of late feudalism were inefficient; capitalism is efficient as an economic system (and hence superior). Preindustrialism was incapable of generating wealth (and therefore bad); industrialism generates great wealth (and is therefore good). And so on.

Many people living today, in the advanced industrial societies at least, cannot imagine that anything in the past was better than it is in the present. Lewis sees this as a sort of snobbism because it rests on the uncritical acceptance of the notion that our contemporary culture and intellectual ideas are superior to the past simply because they are new. Phrases such as 'out of date' and 'old fashioned' suggest that we are always moving on to better things. Living in modernity facilitates this belief because we live in a world of rapidly changing fashions and technologies. There are always new and better cars, new and better clothes, new and better consumer goods of all kinds, and, it is thought, new and better ideas. To be thoroughly modern, like Millie, is to be 'with it' and 'where it's at'. And where it's at is always the latest though ephemeral social and intellectual fashions of the day.

Looking around us we can see affluence and a long-living and healthy population. But the health and wealth of contemporary society blinds us to the decadence and moral sickness under our noses. If romanticism's distorted view of the past clouds its view of the present, chronological snobbism's myopic image of the contemporary world leads it to look at history 'through a glass darkly'.

If we wish to measure the past in terms of life-expectancy, poverty, ignorance, disease, education, comfort and leisure, then there is no doubt that the modern world in the West has come a long way. There are millions of people in the Third World today who would gladly exchange their lifestyles for a dose of materialistic and scientific modernity. But there are other scales of measurement besides technology, medicine, and even the basic human need for food. These are the scales of spiritual, moral and personal values. Such values cannot be measured by numbers (though Jeremy Bentham (1748–1832), the founder of utilitarianism, thought that they could), but are no less real for all that.

Modernity is a historical process that began in the eighteenth century with the philosophical Enlightenment. It accelerated in the nineteenth century as industrialisation took place, and increased even more rapidly in the twentieth century under the impact of advanced technology and science. Modernity is a radical break, both socially and philosophically, with feudalism. So what did we gain with modernity and what did we lose? Remembering the dangers of our two traps, may I propose that we take an imaginative journey back in time to the year 1700? North America was still such a young country in 1700 that it will be more useful to look at Europe during this time. As the Enlightenment and early capitalism had such a major effect in Great Britain, let us home in on England.

After spending some time there (as if we were actually present) we will gradually come back to the present day, and as we do so we will become more reflective and try and push the present away from us – making it strange – by maintaining a certain distance from our immediate history. Ironically, as we come nearer home we will slip into the past tense.

4 KNOWING THE ENEMY –
The coming of modernity

Going back in time takes some imaginative effort, so please switch off your computers, video games and television sets. (Was there life before television?) Good. There are now less visual stimuli, but it is still far too loud. Could you now unplug your hi-fis, remove your laser playing compact discs, turn off all your tape decks and old-fashioned record players. If there is anyone cheating, I mean those still wired for sound, please remove your headphones and listen. It's much quieter now. But let us go further and imagine a world without 'steam radio' and 'talking pictures'.

There is still too much electrical environment. In Eastern Europe cities are dim and drab compared to most Western towns; there are no neon lights and glaring bulbs to dominate the skyline and illuminate the streets. Imagine first of all that our cities become as dim as these Eastern towns. Having got used to this, be really bold and pull the switch on electricity altogether.

Off go the modern appliances (no more dish-washers, hoovers, microwave ovens and refrigerators). Out go the lights in Times Square and Piccadilly Circus and all the cinemas close down, and the IBM typewriters stop chattering, and the computer screens go blank. Hospitals close, trains stop, radar goes on the blink, satellites spin wordlessly in space, and for everyone dialling long distance or local calls, the pips announce that time is finally up.

Come on you iconoclasts, don't stop now! Let's go the whole hog. Clap your hands and insist that natural gas goes up in a puff of noxious air. As for you 'Greenies' this is your moment: wave your arms and abolish petrol – with all its lead poisoning – and the internal combustion engine along with it.

Well done! Of course you realise that having dispensed with petrol with a quick flourish you have also abolished plastics, polymers and detergents, not to mention over a hundred major products necessary to modern industry. Still, never mind – we will just have to make do with animal furs and leather where we are going. (Sorry about that.)

Let's pause for a while in order to breathe in some pure air. I don't think that we would enjoy the Victorian smog of 1880 London, so let's settle for 1850 England.

Well here we are. Funny kind of place isn't it? There are no rockets, aeroplanes, cars, motorcycles, trams, or even bicycles. Aren't the cities small? But at least there are nice reassuring mechanical sounds and clankings during the day. It's quite nostalgic really – all these steam engines in the factories and those funny little locomotives; nothing but boilers, pistons and rivets.

But the countryside! Absolute deafening silence. Not a tractor in sight. No buzzing saw mills, no electric milking machines humming away. Just horses and ploughs and, for want of a better word, peasants.

Let us take a last look at the towns before we move on. It's difficult to look, I admit, as it is now night-time. Some streets are dimly lit by smoking torches, but the houses have only the shadowy light of candles and oil-lamps. Most people seem to be in bed! Well I suppose there is not much to do. (Is this the real reason why the birth-rate is so high?) Can you imagine that these people have never listened to canned music or swigged a 'Coke', never twiddled with radio frequencies, never seen *Dallas* on TV, never answered the phone, and never played Space Invaders? Those that are still up do at least seem to be talking to each other!

Gosh it's cold here. Have you noticed the chill and damp that pervade everywhere? I mention this not in order to remind you of the central heating that you have left behind, but to warn you not to get ill. Here in Victorian England they have no antibiotics, and medicine is barely out of the Stone Age. Where we are going (1700 England) they have only just got over periodic waves of bubonic plague.

No need to be alarmist, but it's time to be off. Perhaps we

ought to be a little more circumspect. This is not supposed to be a travelogue, and I can see from your faces that you want a little more than a cheery jaunt . . .

. . . Well here we are. (I hope that I have not left anybody behind!) As you can see, not only is there no electricity but there are no steam engines and very little industry. Over in West Sussex you can see the 'Hammer Ponds' where the iron ore is still smelted with charcoal. Believe it or not, it is the centre of the European iron industry.

But I can see that you are bewildered, and I know why. You want to know where all the people have gone. It looks like the Ireland of the 1850s after the great potato famines: there is no one about. The first thing to remember is that the England and Wales of 1700 has a total population of only five and a half million people. Over eighty-five per cent of these are scattered throughout the country in small villages and hamlets.

Outside London, cities are so small that only Birmingham, Bristol, Exeter, Newcastle, York and Norwich have more than ten thousand residents. A real shock for British moderns of the late 1980s is to discover that Norwich, with over thirty thousand citizens, is the largest city outside of London!

London itself is a great metropolis of half a million residents. Even now it is the magnet that draws the rural peasants and small businessmen looking for work and casual labour. All roads lead to London, but thank goodness we can travel by imagination, because there are no hard-surfaced or tarmacked roads. Travel for most people is by foot or horseback. The rich landed gentry and the new but small professional classes may run the risk of travelling in an unsprung carriage on the winding dirt roads (not to mention the risk of highwaymen).

Perhaps an even greater shock for us than the small population, tiny towns and scattered rural communities is the shape of the countryside; the physical geography seems to be different. The river Thames, for example, is much shallower and slow flowing. (So that's why the river is always freezing over in winter!) But the real eyecatcher is the acres and acres of fields unmarked or constricted by hedgerows. Hedges as boundaries have not been invented, and England has yet to be enclosed by the landlords in neat and formal fields. Just as North America once had no barbed wire dividing the range, neither does eighteenth-century England have any boundaries, excepting mountains and rivers (and some fortified towns, agricultural ditches and low stone walls). Perhaps this was the 'green and pleasant land' that Blake was invoking. There is nothing like this countryside in the England of the twentieth century (though rural Ireland is somewhat similar).

But let us keep our attention fixed on 1700. There is a small landed gentry and a growing professional class that make up perhaps eight per cent of the population. They are extremely well educated. Indeed the gentry prefer to leave business to the professionals ('those damn usurers') and concentrate on the arts and natural sciences, religious speculation and, of course, a little hunting. It is the aristocrats in England, as is the case in Continental Europe, who will lead Europe by the nose out of the philosophical world-view of a dying feudal order. As we are time-travellers we can peer into the future and notice that it is the professional class that will have the last laugh; for the 'bourgeoisie' (as Marx called them) took over from the gentry. It was the businessmen, not the lords, who called the tune when the industrial system began.

However, as we know them in the modern world, there are virtually no middle classes in 1700. The vast majority of the population are labouring peasants or artisans in the cottage industries of the villages or the small cities.

Peasants and small town workers are chronically underemployed and the majority of the population is illiterate. The gentry and professional group own more wealth than all the lower classes put together. (Did the romanticists among you imagine that you would have been a member of the gentry if you were alive in this England of 1700?)

Disease and poor diet are endemic. The rich eat too much meat and suffer from chronic constipation, diseases of the bowel, gout, and bladder stones. Looking at the poor, we can see that they eat plenty of roughage, but their diet lacks essential vitamins and protein.

Everywhere there is a total lack of understanding about

hygiene, antisepsis, and the importance of sanitation. Perhaps it is just as well that we are travelling by imagination and not with our physical senses, because many of the towns and cities still carry open sewers in the streets. Medicine is prescientific. Bloodletting is popular among the doctors and apothecaries, but herbal medicine, witchcraft and spells are rampant in the general population. Bubonic plague, as I promised you, is now virtually absent from England, but people in the towns die in their thousands from periodic waves of influenza, dysentery, typhus and smallpox.

Death is literally to be found in the midst of life. Infant mortality is phenomenally high, and many children die before they reach six years of age. Even the aristocracy is not exempt. Life expectancy is so low that the average life span of men just before we got here (in the last quarter of the seventeenth century) was 29.6 years.[1] Admittedly if we stay in the rural districts of England in 1700 we will discover that forty to fifty years is not unrealistic, but old age is rare. For those men and women who live into middle age, pain, disease and poverty are the norm rather than the exception.

My guess is that many of you have had enough of life before modernity. To go back to 1700 is to look at a life that is very little different, for most men and women, from that of 1500 or even 1200. Most peasant cultures remain unchanged in their essential structures for hundreds of years. So by taking a trip back nearly three hundred years we could say that we have covered the pre-modern world thoroughly enough. But, in the words of the film, we cannot yet go 'back to the future'. If we go back now, we will go back with only half-truths. This is one of the Enemy's favourite tricks: nothing is more convincing than a half-truth joined on to a lie.

It has been necessary to look with open eyes so we would not see 1700 as a pastoral idyll or an untroubled world. Let's face it: how many of us would want to live here? Modernity will, however, overcome many of the basic problems of poverty, superstition and disease, extremes of wealth and ignorance.

But let us take one more look before we return to modernity. Family life is very different from today. The emphasis in marriage is not on sexual and romantic compatibility but on the rearing of children and economic stability. Women are bound by their biological functions as child-bearers, and their lack of education no doubt acts to their detriment as full participants in social and political life. But most men are also uneducated and lacking in chances for advancement.

What we do find, however, is that women's work is not so divorced from the work of men as it becomes in later times. The family, not the factory, is the major unit of economic production in 1700. The housewife of modern times has not yet been invented. Women are involved in the cottage industries and farms. Furthermore, women are not as isolated from each other as they are in the world of the 1980s. Sisterhood, in the feminist sense, is a reality here. Mothers, mothers-in-law, aunties, grandmothers, first and second (and third) cousins are all bound together in a community of common suffering and joy. (No less a modern authority than Germaine Greer (1984) has insisted that sisterhood is a greater reality in preindustrial society than liberated modernity.)

Living in community in 1700 may not be living in the kingdom, but there is a world of common commitments, understandings and religious belief. Relationships are personal (sometimes unpleasantly so) because there is no other way to relate; there is no state machinery and there are no bureaucratic organisations or industrial complexes. Men and women may or may not be moral in practice in 1700, but there is no doubt that they have a common sense of morality which is itself bound up with a religious world-view. Peter Berger calls this a 'sacred canopy' (Berger 1969) that informs, makes sense of and interprets the world as the focus of God's concern. Despite cruelty and sinfulness there is a common sense of the moral and spiritual universe which is binding on all persons. In short, people here sin, but at least they know what sin is.

No doubt some of you will find this less than convincing in the face of the superstition and magic that exists everywhere. This is the negative side of rural life, where the gods of old mix with the Christian God in an uneasy alliance. But even this points to a living belief in the supernatural realm. What is more, this is only a whisper away from primitive Christianity, which is kept alive by faithful worship, rituals and community practices. Christianity bites deep into the culture of pre-industrial societies, and in 1700 life may be full of pain and suffering and hardship (which are not good in themselves) but these life-experiences point to the mystery of life in Christ and the reality of his suffering for the world.

If we walk round the towns and villages we will not find the acquisitiveness and competitiveness of modernity. (How many modern Christians value these modern attributes as somehow good! It is precisely because our modern economic system champions these things that we find so little community spirit alive in the advanced industrial societies.) Crime exists, but rape is rare, and murder and theft exist on a minute scale compared to the urban crimes of the twentieth century.

A feature of village life that we cannot help noticing is how people come together to share their common joys and griefs. The sacred canopy of a still Christian England is not just a question of shared beliefs and a common moral perspective: it is an involvement in communal, religious and social rituals which bind people together. People have roots, both spiritually and socially, and these are clearly important to their identity and security. This strange world of 1700 England has a naturalness and simplicity of behaviour not yet tainted by the enticement of big towns and the whims of fashionable society.

Perhaps I had better not go on in this way or things will get too mushy and pastoral after all. But we must beware of cynicism. For too long we Christians have heard the modern world blowing its own trumpet. Yes, it is true that much has been gained, but we need to understand from the perspective of pre-modern rural England some of the things that have been lost.

However, we must return to the present day. We must come back with haste, but as we travel let us also reflect on some of the things we see: looking with the eyes of discernment for the hand of the Enemy on the controls of the engine of progress.

THE ENLIGHTENMENT

Already by 1740 European feudalism is experiencing its death throes. Crucially for Christianity, that great Puritan era of the Reformation is also drawing to a close. The landed gentry of Europe have become a leisured class cut off from the peasantry and increasingly divorced from the authority of scripture.

The humanist Renaissance of the late Middle Ages had already witnessed the gradual emergence of reasoning independent of the church. The Reformation accelerated this process, even though the Bible had become the primary if not the sole authority of the churches. But tragically the Reformation produced a number of unintended consequences that were certainly not in the minds of Calvin and Luther. One consequence was this: once it was accepted that scripture stood alone outside tradition, and could be interpreted correctly by anyone with a pure heart and God-given rationality, it was not too big a step to suggest that the same could also be said of nature.

Although many of the great scientists and philosophers of the late seventeenth and early eighteenth century were Christians, they became increasingly attached to the supremacy of reason. The dawn of the philosophical Enlightenment had almost no effect upon the average European who still tilled his feudal strip and grazed his animals on the common land. But if we move out of the fields and villages and into the great houses of Europe and the salons of fashionable society, we can see a revolution beginning. Among these men where learning and speculation have become a leisured pursuit – where the amateur-cum-Renaissance man is king and the dilettante is the hero – a new world-view is being forged.

Just as the new physics of Einstein will have such a devastating effect upon the philosophy of the twentieth century, so it is the physics of Isaac Newton (1642–1727) that so fires the imagination of the aristocratic intelligentsia. This natural philosophy (science), and the methodology of Francis Bacon (1561–1626) and René Descartes (1596–1650), seems to suggest that the universe is run not by divine decree but by natural laws; laws that can be discovered by the application of the human mind through the senses (by observation) to the physical world. The world – and especially the empirical (the sensate) world – is becoming the prime focus of attention. God and 'eternal verities' are almost out of vision.

It is true that God is not yet totally banished from his creation, but having made it and all that is in it, rather like a watchmaker constructs a timepiece, he is felt to be no longer necessary to explain the inner workings of the mechanism. Perhaps too much emphasis was given in hyper-Calvinism to God the lawgiver? It was not such a great step in reducing him to the laws-giver. Faith in reason and its ability to crack the code of the universe by discovering the scientific laws that sustain it will become the new legalism of the dawning secular age.

And the personal and loving Father, the almighty and awesome Yahweh, bows out to the god of Aristotle: the impersonal first cause in a chain of scientific causation – the 'unmoveable mover'. No wonder that theism is abandoned with such alacrity by so many of these new philosophers. Unitarianism is often the stepping-stone to a rampant deism. When the trinitarian God of biblical faith and credal affirmation becomes the one sovereign God locked into himself, the eternal love of the three persons of the Trinity which is naturally dynamic and outflowing becomes static and inward looking. Deism frees this bound-in monadic god by releasing him as an immanent but impersonal spirit.

Nature becomes her own god and pantheism dances its way through the coffee houses and salons of Europe. What an irony: the great rational philosophical Enlightenment opens the door to paganism! But some of the new philosophers and freethinkers – Voltaire (1694–1778), for example – go the whole hog and, particularly in Catholic France, where anticlericalism spurs it on, atheism takes root. Atheism is virtually unknown in pagan and rural societies, but this new rationalism will usher it into the modern world.

The Enlightenment, then, is far more than a revolution in theories of knowledge (epistemology) or even new methods in science and critical philosophy. We must not move on until we have understood that this philosophical impetus to the modern age is the rise of a new humanism with man at the centre. This is the great 'paradigm shift' – to borrow a phrase from Thomas Kuhn (1970) – of the Enlightenment. God has been replaced by man. And it is men and women in relation to each other, and in relation to nature, that really captures the imagination of these drawing-room philosophers. As Alexander Pope (1688–1744), that great versifier of the Enlightenment, puts it:

> Know then thyself, presume not God to scan,
> The proper study of mankind is man.

And out of this fascination with man two modern versions of him are born. There is the 'individual man', who will become the basis for both modern morality and the principles of democracy. He is not really a man related to other men in natural affinity or community: he is atomised man, human society pared down to a single individual. He is man alone. In the morality of Thomas Hobbes (1588–1679) and John Locke (1632–1704) and the later utilitarians he can only act in his self-interest. He enters into a social contract with other men only in order to preserve his own interest and (in some versions) pleasure. Individual man is not condemned under the fall. He is driven by self-preservation rather than sin. The social contract theories are a metaphysical fiction to explain the origins of society, but they also create the mythology that human beings are essentially innocent. In their different ways both Locke and Jean Jacques Rousseau (1712–1778) saw young children as being free from the taint of original sin.

In the greatest of the Enlightenment philosophers (notably Immanuel Kant, 1724–1804) the individual is seen as possessing ultimate worth and dignity. This is perhaps one of the noblest legacies of the Enlightenment. But out of a concern for restructuring the traditional communities of feudal Europe into mobile free persons with inalienable rights, modern individualism is born. Locke, for example, makes the rights of individuals and their right to private property the basis for his democratic principles of a free society.

Adam Smith (1723–1790) and the Scottish philosophers and economists construct their principles of capitalist economics upon a belief in the rights of individuals to pursue their own wealth and happiness. Laissez-faire is an economic system based on individualism and self-interest. Indeed the whole point of Smith's contention in his 1776 treatise *The Wealth of Nations* is that if individuals pursue their own self-interests then, as it were, an invisible hand will guide all their separate strivings and competition and lead them into the greater good for society as a whole.

But another modern man also comes to life in the eighteenth century: the 'collective man'. Modern democracy in the West is based on the principle of 'one man one vote'. This is the positive side of individualism; no one is to count more than another. This clearly echoes the gospel, despite the distortions of rational philosophy. But the collective man, the man of Georg Wilhelm Friedrich Hegel (1770–1831), and later Karl Marx (1818–1883), but supremely of Rousseau, eschews individualism altogether. Rousseau, who was an incurable romantic, wanted to preserve the community of innocent and primitive social life, but wanted the community to take precedence over the rights of its individual members. Strictly speaking, collective man is no man at all, but an aggregate or abstraction of real flesh-and-blood men and women. These men and women always belong to and are made sense of only as a part of the collective – the race, the nation, the state, the republic, the class, etc.

Modern psychoanalysis has taught us a great deal about the 'splitting' and division that takes place within our own personality. On a philosophical level, the Enlightenment created a whole series of dualisms that have permeated deep into the heart of modernity: the collective is divided from the individual (leaving community a virtual impossibility) and the spiritual world is divided from the material world, leading either to gross materialism or to an other-worldly and gnostic spirituality. (Also, as we shall see in chapter eight, Kant divided the world of metaphysics from the world of the senses and created havoc for theology and philosophy generally.)

In a moment we are about to leave the leisured and leisurely world of the eighteenth-century gentlemen and hurtle through the mechanical and material world of nineteenth-century England, where the revolutionary ideas of the aristocratic philosophers will become embodied in the social, political and economic structures of industrial Europe. But before we go we must understand the full import of what we have seen.

The Enlightenment was the morning star of modernity. Without it, modern democracy and republicanism could not have come into existence and scientific and technological progress would not have been possible (and possibly slavery might not have been abolished). It was a period of remarkable intellectual illumination; a time when a new idealism and optimism transformed man's understanding of himself, his society and the universe. Kant's *Critique of Pure Reason* (1781) was just one of the major works that heralded a new way of doing philosophy: the beginning of that critical rationality that Sir Karl Popper so admired and saw as a turning-point in the history of ideas. Henceforth, tradition, superstition and, later, biblical authority itself would be under continual scrutiny and correction from the empyrean dictates of critical reasoning. There was nothing that would be exempted from rigorous examination. We find after Gottfried Wilhelm Leibnitz's (1646–1716) raising of the question of theodicy in 1710 that even God himself was put in the dock.

Nothing was to be sacrosanct or sacred, excepting reason itself. Men would become gods and taste of the fruit of the (critical) tree of knowledge of good and evil. Eden was not only a historical reality, therefore, but a perpetual temptation for humankind. And lest we be dazzled by the glare of the morning star of modernity, let us not forget that the morning star in biblical imagery is another name for Lucifer: we must not fail, if we are to defeat the Enemy, to detect the dark side of the Enlightenment.

In the early seventeenth century, science was still married to religion. Indeed the great majority of the members of the English Royal Society were Puritans (and mainly nonconformist at that). The divorce of science and religion was a

tragic mistake (Koestler 1959). And for Christians the Enlightenment has meant that the world of phenomena and,
later, the materialistic world have combined to force out the
reality of the spiritual realm. There is nothing intrinsically evil
about a scientific world outlook as long as it is rooted in the
life and authority of God. Cut off from that life it is fair game
for the Enemy (see chapter seven).

But if rationalism and empiricism have a tendency to blot
out God, we must recognise that the Enlightenment's supreme beguilement which has so bewitched modern men and
women is a false understanding of human beings. Not only do
we not get from the Enlightenment an understanding of
human nature that is under the curse of the fall, neither do we
get a true understanding of men and women made in the
image of God.

Most importantly, however, we must recognise that neither
the individualistic man nor the collectivist man of the philosophers is truly Christian. Collectivism would eventually lead
to totalitarianism – fascism and communism are collectivist
ideologies – but it would also surface in the bureaucratic
thinking of Western governments and multinational corporations. Neither should individualism be seen as the Christian
corrective to collectivism. At its worst individualism is rooted
in a hedonism (utilitarianism, modern 'fun moralities') and a
selfishness that the Bible unambiguously calls evil. The consumerism of the twentieth century needs to be understood as
a modern economic mode of hedonistic individualism. Rampant individualism finds so little interest in the collective that
injustice can become the hallmark of some free enterprise
systems. It should be Christians, and not only Marxists, who
assert that capitalism too easily turns a blind eye to its
exploitation of the Third World.

It could be argued that the false views of humanity
perpetrated by the Enlightenment were partly offset by
Methodism and the growth of pietism in the eighteenth
century. Certainly it was the case that the new religious
enthusiasm that was replacing the dying Puritanism assured
the individual of his intrinsic worth, and assured him also that
he was loved and cherished by God. But did pietism, I

wonder, sail too close to the spirit of the Enlightenment? Is there not a certain over-attachment to one's *own* salvation and *individual* worth, with the consequence that missionary endeavour becomes centred on individuals? Pietism, I would suggest, loses something of the communal commitment of the old Puritan covenant and the earlier Catholic spirit.

But there is no further time for speculation and reflection on the Enlightenment, because one of the false views of humanity (the collectivist kind), after ticking away like a time bomb, explodes in a political event of such fury and consequence that the gentle yet élitist world of the Enlightenment philosophers is destroyed for ever.

NINETEENTH-CENTURY INDUSTRIALISM

Philosophy has a habit of creeping out of boudoirs, salons and the libraries of great houses and inspiring (or beguiling) the minds and aspirations of ordinary men and women. When it does, when the populace is stirred with a great idea – for good or evil – then such philosophy is never the same again. The soft glow of the Enlightenment was merely the surface heat of a great fire that exploded in the volcanic fury of the French Revolution. Like a fiery Pandora's box, the lid was thrown wide open, spewing all the good and evil upon the world (and, like the Greek myth, once good and evil are loosed on the world they cannot be called back).

I do not think there has ever been a period in history when there has been such a violent and irreversible change in the political and social order (unless it be the long-term consequences of the Russian Revolution). Up until the French Revolution, as we have seen, life for the ordinary rural peasant had remained virtually unchanged for centuries, in a slowly decaying and dying feudalism. The great changes in intellectual thinking had little effect upon European culture as a whole. The Revolution changed all that. It was this cataclysmic political event that shattered the stability of the old order.

A group of men fired with the heady doctrines of republicanism, anticlericalism and atheism shook French society to its foundations. This was no peasant revolution, but an insurrection led by the intelligentsia of the new middle classes (those professional groups whom the Enlightenment aristocrats despised as base and usurers). The murder of the royal family, the ruthless repression of the enemies of the state and the establishment of Madame Guillotine ushered in not a glorious collectivist state as prescribed by Rousseau, but a 'reign of terror'. Soon the mask of mob rule and anarchy was replaced by the naked face of despotism, and eventually it gave way to Napoleon's personal image of collectivism: an imperial militarism.

The shock waves of this political explosion engulfed the whole of Europe, so that by 1848 only England of the major nations had not experienced a revolution. By the 1790s these shock waves had triggered off another seismic event, sending North America (where the struggle for national independence had already begun in 1774) not only away from the English Crown but on the road to a republican state. By 1818, when the War of Independence was over and the Republican Revolution can be said to have been won, America had rejected both the Crown and religious establishment, and had accepted a creed that granted religious toleration and the 'natural rights of man'.

Indeed New England was a battleground in the eighteenth century between Puritanism and Enlightenment philosophy. The American Constitution reflects this battleground but emerges (formally at least) as more of an Enlightenment document than a Christian one. If one wants to look for the origins of conflict in modern America, one could do worse than line up the eighteenth-century Puritans against the Enlightenment men: say, Jonathan Edwards (1703–1758), Samuel Davies (1723–1761) and Timothy Dwight (1752–1817) versus Benjamin Franklin (1706–1790), Thomas Jefferson (1743–1826), Thomas Paine (1737–1809) and James Madison (1751–1836).

The revolutions of Europe and the New World blew apart the old order for ever; henceforth there could be no going back – no healing of the breach. The modern world had struggled free of the past. Soon after the French Revolution in

England, and starting in the 1830s in New England, waves of religious adventism began to sweep across the nations. The break-up of the old world was seen as a sign of the last times. When the Christian Brethren movement and the Catholic Apostolic Church emerged in Britain in the 1830s and the Millerites in New England waited for the return of Christ in the 1840s, adventism had already taken firm root in evangelicalism (where it has remained ever since).

And if the religious world sought to understand the passing away of the old order and the emergence of the new one, the secular world too, faced with the greatest social change in history, reacted by the invention of sociology and the construction of grand social theories that would explain it all. So while such religious men as William Cuningham (1805–1861), Edward Irving and J. N. Darby (1800–1882) pondered the scriptures to understand and prophesy the future, the secularists, Saint-Simon (1760–1825), Auguste Comte (1798–1857) and Karl Marx, sought to predict forthcoming events through the method of Enlightenment science.

But in a sense the cataclysm of the French Revolution was only the outward political symbol of a much greater cataclasm: the rise of the new system of economics that Thomas Carlyle called 'industrialism'. It is this system, with its marriage of technology and the rationality of market economics, that really embodies – makes incarnate – the philosophies of the Enlightenment.

Modernity began in earnest with this industrialism – like the starting up of a great steam-driven machine, straining and clanking at the mechanical bit and snorting with impatience to be off. Let's follow its progress.

The machine needs feeding, so it gravitates to areas of coal, water and iron. These areas need developing, so entrepreneurs pump in investment: capital accumulated from the slave trade, sugar and cotton. But the machine also needs tending, and its food supplies must not dwindle, so labour is needed. And from the fields and villages of England, where work has slowed to a trickle and where the landlords have enclosed the common lands (after 1802) so that even subsistence living is difficult, from these fields comes a mighty army of labour.

Tears are shed as the traditional homes and communities are left – where the peasants and their families had lived for hundreds of years – and they go to feed the machine. The migration is so great that the countryside looks almost emptied. But the new workers of the modern age must live, and so homes are built around the machine's food supplies; crowded and sprawling, urbanism begins forming part of the machine's superstructure. Yet the workers who tend the machine and keep open its food supplies must also eat. So entrepreneurs, owners of mills and factories, offer them wages. They must keep them low because wages are labour costs that have to be deducted from profit (besides, if the workers do not like the pay there are plenty more around who will take it!). High wages, they feel, will affect the final cost of their product, and if their product is too expensive there is always another entrepreneur who will sell the same product at a cheaper price. This new capitalism is a cut-throat enterprise: to stay in business you must not only compete with but beat your competitors.

And so, founded on its sure infrastructure of heavy industries, free-flowing capital and cheap labour, the machine is off. And what a machine it is. All over Europe the hum and resonance of its powerful engines can be heard. (Ah! This sounds more like the modernity we know.) As the machine gains momentum, so it grows – almost magically – in size. Its interconnecting parts – the mechanised looms, the steam-operated factories, the driven conveyor belts – fit together in an ever-increasing and complicated *system* of cogs and wheels.

The industrial towns grow and the cities swell to take the still coming rural migrants. And if a few romantics mutter against the 'satanic mills', despoliation of the countryside and pollution of the skies from the factory chimneys, the machine shunts them aside as surely as it repulses those Luddites who would shut down its engines if they only knew how.

For though the machine has its critics and it seems clear that not everybody can adjust to its speed and voraciousness, one incontrovertible fact emerges: the machine can generate wealth of such volume as the world has never dreamt. And with wealth (admittedly unequally distributed between the social classes) comes new investment and improved products, money for scientific research and technological innovations.

And as the wealth increases in absolute terms even the poorer classes, those who feed but do not run the machine, begin to improve their social conditions and economic power. Governments begin to slough off some of the wealth in taxes to ameliorate the conditions of the poor and provide public amenities for their citizens. Scientific research begins to pay off with spectacular dividends in the fields of medicine, physics and chemistry. By the 1870s the machine has become so sophisticated that it needs more educated people to run it, to learn new techniques of maintenance and improvement, and to keep up its momentum. Governments initiate education for the masses, and the masses in return are inspired with higher aspirations and demand more leisure time to enjoy their increased earnings. The machine responds by creating new products to enjoy the new leisure, such as the bicycle and the 'magic lantern'.

And everywhere in the newly industrialised world people are on the move. The steam trains revolutionise travel and open up new towns and industrial markets. New social classes appear who run or are run by the machine. People's social and religious habits change and a new materialistic culture emerges where life is influenced by the consumption of earnings on goods and products made by the machine. And the culture glories in the success of the machine and wonders at its might and inventiveness. The machine seems to need neither worship nor fear to make it run; it is built on rational philosophical principles and sustained by money, labour, steam and steel. Despite the fact that religious influence declines throughout the nineteenth century (in the fields of work, welfare, education and government), and social disharmony increases as the gap between the poor and rich widens, the century remains essentially one of optimism.

The machine is a winner. It is as if industrialism and the growing success and power of science confirm all that the Enlightenment stood for: progress, it seems, really is the stuff of the universe. This appeared to be scientifically supported by Charles Darwin's (1809–1882) *On the Origin of Species*

(1859). In the eighteenth century Kant and Hegel preached progress based on philosophical and moral conviction. But the nineteenth century demonstrates it as a scientific fact. If Darwin showed biologically that evolution was nature's way of natural selection and continual improvement, he was backed up on the social level by all the great social theorists who taught one version or another of perpetual progress. Whether it be the positivism of Comte, the social evolutionism of Herbert Spencer (1820–1903) and James Frazer (1854–1941), or the socialism of Marx and the Fabians, the slogan they all chanted was 'Progress, progress, progress'.

The sociologist Émile Durkheim was not quite so sanguine. He recognised that many of the first and second generation of industrial urbanites were morally and socially disorientated – in a state of anomie or normlessness (a sort of perpetual culture shock). Clearly also the rise of urbanism brought a concomitant rise of crime and prostitution. Unless the working classes were caught up in the new sectarian movements of Protestantism (which were themselves a reaction and response to modernity), they were liable to slip into unbelief. It is historically untrue to say that religious decline in Europe began in the twentieth century: the majority of working people in the first one hundred years of industrialism were not regular churchgoers (though the new middle classes were). The process of religious decline that sociologists call 'secularisation' began with modernity and has continued ever since.

As the machine enters the twentieth century we notice that it is more streamlined. The people surrounding it and supporting it – and by now many are living off it – are fitter and are living longer than ever before. They are better educated and more informed – though illiteracy is still widespread among the poor. Daily newspapers are now becoming popular, providing the first phase of what will later become known as the mass media. Family size is shrinking as mothers no longer need large numbers of children to work either down the mines or in the factories (the machine would take anybody to work for it at first) or to ensure that a few would survive; high infant mortality rates are now becoming a thing of the past.

There had been some hints in the latter part of the nineteenth century that the machine was not in perfect working order. As early as the 1860s there had begun a phenomenon that has since become endemic in advanced industrial societies: in a word, recession. Sometimes the machine would boom along, growing and expanding with heroic speed; then strangely it would halt and slump. It would still hiss and make noise, but the energy and power were gone; sometimes it would even shrink and contract within itself. As economic theory had not really moved beyond the 'invisible hand' idea of Adam Smith, not surprisingly no one really knew what was wrong with the machine.

But then, as the new, more streamlined, machine slips into the twentieth century, moving smoothly and with a new confidence – and by now virtually everybody is along for the ride – it crashes catastrophically.

THE GREAT WAR (1914–1918)

Ironically, the Great War would not have been the war that it was if it were not for the machine. With the new science and technology had come new weapons of destruction: armoured tanks, steel submarines and warships, aerial warfare, bombs, machine guns and the huge infantry field-cannons. There were 'Whizz-bangs' and shell-shock, telegraphy and telephones, railways to hasten troops to and from the battlefront, and the new horrors of chemical warfare. (170,700 men were killed by chemical gas – among those severely injured by Allied mustard gas was an insignificant and then unknown German corporal, Adolf Hitler.)

Still feeding off nineteenth-century optimism and belief in the Empire, millions of young British soldiers perished under the combined efforts of the machine and the Continental mud. (Did they wonder who was running the machine? Was anybody at the controls?) It was by now clear that the economic and technological side of modernity was a power of terrible destruction as well as positive social improvement. By the end of the war, according to the United States War Department, 8,634,000 military personnel lay dead. A further

five million civilians were killed (a great number of them in
Russia) because of direct military intervention or through
the indirect and insidious side effects of famine and disease.

The horror of the war led some Christians to look in
desperation for a new understanding of God as the suffering
God. Studdert Kennedy ('Woodbine Willy') wrote, 'The real
truth about the Church is that it is the broken, battered,
bleeding but deathless body of the suffering God revealed in
Christ.'

But for many more intellectuals it was the death knell of
their belief in God. No great and loving God, they reasoned,
could have stood aside and watched the world tearing itself
apart. Meanwhile a young infantry soldier who had fought in
the trenches and had been taken prisoner of war was putting
the finishing touches to a philosophical treatise that was to
bring traditional philosophy crashing down about its ears.
(The young man was an Austrian of half-Jewish descent
called Ludwig Wittgenstein, see chapter seven.) But the
machine, as if unaware of all the spiritual anguish and philosophical commotion, and despite the terrible damage
wrought by its own locomotion, began to move forward
again.

THE INTERWAR YEARS

But this time there was a difference. There was a new
phenomenon: the machine was divided in two. The old
machine continued, but battered and clearly full of technical
faults. However, out of its ruin, yet composed from its constituent parts, a new machine began to thrive and grow with
a power of its own. The outward symbol of this new phase
of the (trans)mutant machine was the Russian Revolution.

It is essential for all of us Christians to understand what was
happening here. Modernity is not merely or even supremely
capitalism. The industrial machine that we have followed so
far has been the philosophies of the Enlightenment embodied
and incarnated in the economic mode of capitalism. It is
capitalism that generates the power of modernity, but the
philosophies of the Enlightenment provide its guiding lights

(or, if you prefer, the 'ghost in the machine' – the software in the computer's brain).

But capitalism is only the individualistic man of Enlightenment creation in economic form. We must also consider the collectivist man who first burst upon the world with the French Revolution. These two men are a Janus: the two faces of the same materialistic coin. Modernity, then, is incurably materialistic but it can look towards either collectivism or individualism. The Russian Revolution, under Lenin (1870–1924) and Trotsky (1879–1940) in direct descendance from Rousseau, Hegel, Marx and Engels, decided to alter the course of modernity towards collectivism.

But because such men were materialists and therefore underestimated the power of spiritual and moral values (despite the Soviet invention of the doctrine of 'dialectical materialism'[2]), they failed to see that they were only perpetuating the problem of modernity in another form. Indeed there is no doubt that in overthrowing capitalism, and seeing it as the source of all modern evils, the Soviets saw themselves as the true heirs of the Enlightenment. They also embraced science, materialist philosophy and doctrines of (socialist) progress. But they went one stage further: Soviet socialism adopted a stance of militant atheism.

With this militant atheism came a ruthless drive against Christianity and an attempt to overthrow traditional ethics as the vestiges of an outmoded and regressive bourgeois morality. The dominance of the collective (the state) over the individual led to the repression of individuals and a denial of the very basic human rights which the Western Enlightenment had bestowed upon democracy. Despite the grand titles of 'freedom', 'democracy' and 'socialism', Soviet-style communism inaugurated a 'reign of terror' far more widespread and horrific than the French Revolution. To this day no one has accurately computed how many millions of people were killed under the rule of Lenin and Stalin. In many ways Dostoevsky (1821–1881) had predicted the spiritual bankruptcy of the new collectivism in his novel *The Devils* (1872) (a novel, incidentally, still banned in the Soviet Union).

Meanwhile in the West, it was not obvious whether the

machine of individualist man would survive. Would the great engine of progress run out of steam? Despite all the wonderful new scientific inventions and the beginning of the electric age (and hence new fuels for the machine), the great power of the nineteenth century simply was not there. People throughout Europe and America began to complain against their new god who seemed to have let them down. The world economic market seemed to be saturated with demands for goods which the machine could not supply. Investment was drying up, businesses were collapsing, men were laid off work and wages were cut. Unrest and revolution were in the air, and strikes, sit-ins and lock-outs were leading to political instability and an increasing possibility that the old machine would be destroyed.

On the other hand, although the machine was in need of a re-fit, the Enlightenment principles that guided and supported it were being increasingly reinforced by changes in philosophy and science. Perhaps the problem with the machine, thought many of the intellectuals, was that it needed a new design and improved principles to guide it. In the field of philosophy logical support was claimed for the absolute superiority of scientific and mathematical thinking over religion and even traditional philosophy. The rise of this logical positivism reinforced the Enlightenment belief in science and rationality (at the very moment that the world was in desperate need of a moral code and a spiritual light to help it through the great crisis – the Depression – of the old machine's apparent demise). This led to the collapse in many universities of not only traditional moral theories but also many of the great idealistic philosophies (such as Kant's, for example) that had come out of the Enlightenment itself. Only science and mathematics, declared the positivists, could be depended upon for reliable knowledge and to provide the true basis for progress (see chapter seven).

Science itself had undergone a radical shift since the Great War. The great Newtonian synthesis of cosmology and physics, which had been the basis of the scientific revolution, was found to be faulty. The great mechanical cosmos understood in terms of cause and effect, and symbolised technologically in the mechanistic world of the age of steam, was reinterpreted in a far more sophisticated and brilliant new scientific synthesis, the theory of relativity (first propounded by Albert Einstein in 1905). This great change in scientific thinking meant little to the masses, but they were able to see the great benefits of modern scientific practice despite the faltering of the economic system. The discovery of penicillin by Alexander Fleming in 1928 was only one of the obvious wonders of science, but everywhere people could feel the impact of scientific research: travel on land, air and sea; new electrical and domestic appliances; moving and talking pictures; radio and the telephone. Modernity was increasingly becoming an industrial system dominated by a scientific world-view.

But science will work for any man. Having no values of its own, it can work equally well for collectivist man or individualist man. Science, in short, does not care which machine it works for. And so the Western machine, although it was responsible for the growth of science, could claim no exclusive ownership of it: it belongs to and supports the materialistic world of modernity, not a particular political or economic system.

Throughout these crucial years of twentieth-century growth, the many colonial countries that had provided so many natural and human resources for the Western machine began to demand an independence of their own, fired by the very principles of democracy that had sprung out of the Enlightenment and inspired the French and American revolutions. And while Africa and Asia were in ferment, modernity faced its own Waterloo on the fields of the advanced industrial nations.

During the late 1920s and early 1930s when John Maynard Keynes (1883–1946) was working out a new economic system where government intervention would stabilise the negative effects of free enterprise – low investment, acute unemployment – individualist man and collectivist man were fighting it out for supremacy. The great fear of the Western democracies was Bolshevism. And with good cause. There had been aborted revolutions in Germany after the Great War, and an international socialism (though factional) was spreading throughout Europe. But collectivism can come in many forms. When Benito Mussolini (1883–1945) invented fascism in the 1920s (literally national socialism), it was not quite clear whether this was going to be a force to use against Sovietism or a collectivist evil in its own right.

In the event, fascism in either its nationalistic form (Italy and Spain) or its chauvinistic and racist form (Germany) was to prove a totalitarian system of terrifying evil. Hitler's Germany in particular was an embodiment of the dark side of the Enlightenment: a regime of science, efficiency and power without morality. But national socialism (Nazism) also fed off the dark side of the counter-reformation to the Enlightenment: a romanticism that was anti-intellectual and irrational. Not without justification did René Guenon understand the hideous strength of Nazism as an unholy marriage of magic and tanks.

THE SECOND WORLD WAR

I believe that the Second World War was a war that had to be won not in order to save Western modernity, or to ensure that individualist man would conquer collectivist man, but simply because Hitler posed the greatest threat to the moral order of the world that history had ever seen. Fascism was the sly trump card of the Evil One. While Westerners were impressed that the trains ran on time in Italy, and that unemployment had been solved in Germany, Hitler was preparing for war.

In 1945, when the war against the Third Reich was finally won, and the Allies had also defeated the Japanese Empire, the total loss of life, including the civilian victims of bombing and famine, was fifty-five million people (a figure equivalent to the whole population of Great Britain in the late 1960s).

Furthermore, the Second World War had resulted in the most terrifying weapon of destruction being not only developed but also deployed against the enemy. When the atomic bomb developed at Los Alamos, New Mexico, was dropped on two Japanese cities in August 1945, the

Apocalypse of St John moved out of the realm of mythology and prophecy into scientific reality. This is not the age of Aquarius, as the 1960s song so misleadingly supposed: it is the age of imminent judgment. The Bomb gives the lie to the false Enlightenment doctrine of perpetual progress. It is a reminder that the social utopias of the philosophers are a delusion. The atomic age has forcefully reopened that old forgotten Christian question: 'What if the world should end tonight?' (Lewis 1975: 82).

COMING HOME: THE POSTWAR YEARS

And yet the end of the Second World War was such a celebration of the defeat of the fascist enemy that there was a failure to grasp the fact that the universal Enemy had merely been rehearsing for Armageddon. The war, far from finishing off the machine of modernity, had given it new life. In the capitalist West new markets opened up, and the industries that had become so busy and productive in the war effort were ready to go again in a postwar boom. The ingenuity of the scientists and technologists, prompted by the necessity of wartime, had created postwar spin-offs: there was the development of the jet engine and radar, rockets and computers, plastics and new synthetic materials.

The Russian Bear, the uneasy ally of the Western powers against fascism, made its own bid for power. It soon developed the atomic bomb. Shortly afterwards both America and Russia developed a fusion bomb. This hydrogen device was more powerful and 'dirtier' (it had greater radioactive fallout). Politically the 1950s saw a Cold War between the superpowers – each battling for supremacy in the world economic markets; each striving to gain the upper hand in military might and ideological influence over the developing countries.

At least the battle for supremacy was somewhat channelled symbolically into the race for the moon. It was surely preferable for the superpowers to fight it out in the space race than blow the world to bits (Wolfe 1979). When, however, the Americans won the competition with the 'giant step for

mankind' in 1969, the peaceful application of space explo-
ration took second place to the development of spy satellites
and military innovations. (The very fact that the proposed
'Star Wars' defensive strategy of the United States involves
computerised laser technology should alert us to the fact that
such a defence has ominous offensive possibilities.)

And all the while the shadow of the Bomb grew longer as
the most powerful nations on earth stockpiled enough mega-
tonnes to blow up the world fifty times over. If this was not
enough, India, Pakistan, South Africa and Israel joined
Great Britain and France in the growing queue of independent nuclear nations who have entered the atomic lists for the
final tilt.

But in the West what really characterises the mid-1950s to
the present day, and marks off the contemporary world from
the earlier stages of modernity, is the bewildering speed with
which the social, technological and ideological changes have
taken place. Modernity went into overdrive.

I once saw a science fiction movie about time-travellers in
the future; towards the end of the film the whole story is
speeded up and re-run in about two minutes. Modernity has
been a bit like that in the last thirty years, except that as the
story progresses, faster and faster – with many Enlightenment
doctrines reappearing in new form – new lines keep being
added to the narrative so that no one knows how the story will
end.

The speeding up of modernity began with the start of
modern consumerism. Of course capitalism is essentially
about selling goods, so there is nothing new about consumerism *per se*. But in the 1950s, with the switch from heavy
industries to light engineering and service industries, a new
age of personal affluence got under way. This affluence was
made possible not only by higher wages (in real terms) but
because new mass markets in non-essential goods were also
opened up for the population at large. It was one thing in the
1830s and the 1930s to provide luxuries for a minority, but it
was quite a different thing to provide non-essential products
at a competitive price for the whole population.

Of course consumerism works by convincing people that

they actually 'need' non-essential products as an aid to the quality of life. As J. K. Galbraith (1979) has pointed out the adman actually creates markets and implants 'needs' in people; he is not merely responding to consumer demand. But in the 1950s the first wave of modern consumerism transformed people's lifestyles so that they came to expect it to be right and natural that they should have consumer durables (and increasingly non-durable goods). Advertising came into its own with the mass media, and soon 'steam radio' turned into portable transistors and the old 78s phonographs became radiograms and record players. Television augmented and soon overtook the cinema as the masses' most popular form of entertainment. And with television the world of advertising came right into the home. What could be better than a captive (and captured) audience!

It may very well be, and I mean this seriously, that the adman invented the teenager. In all pre-industrial societies children pass from childhood to adulthood by a 'rite of passage'; there is virtually no in-between stage. Even in nineteenth-century Europe the passing from young person to 'grown-up' was accomplished with the minimum amount of fuss and transition. But in the 1950s, with the first wave of postwar affluence, young people in transition began to have money and the adman found them a place in the consumer society. This was the period which saw a revolution in popular music and the beginning of rock'n'roll. With it came not only new though ephemeral music, but new clothes, magazines, books and films.

At the same time were born new heroes and demigods; the Hollywood dream factory, which had already indelibly stamped the character of both North America and Great Britain by the 1940s, began to spin its web of enticement over the whole of popular culture. Everyone wanted to be a 'star', either in films, music or television (and perhaps even in religion).

But the new teenagers also created new social phenomena and philosophies: 'the generation gap' appeared, 'angry young men' ranted and raved and 'beatniks' smoked reefers and read about Zen. The 'Teddy Boys' probably heralded that other new aspect of teenage consumerism – the beginning of modern youth subcultures. Over the years 'Mods and Rockers', 'Hell's Angels', 'Skinheads', 'Rude Boys', 'Romantics', 'Neo-Romantics' and 'Punks' were only a few of the pieces in an ever-changing cultural jig-saw.

Lest it be thought that I have singled out young persons as a special problem, let me hasten to add that I think that the behaviour of youth cultures has to be seen as a mirror image of the adult society. Since the 1950s parents have been accumulating more (and always better) consumer goods, domestic appliances, automobiles and luxuries. Adults follow fashion in clothes and social habits as assiduously as their children.

Indeed, I think that the onslaught of modern consumerism is not so much a slavish addiction to fashion as a capitulation to hedonism. Hedonism, for Christians, has its roots not in the Enlightenment but in the fall. Nevertheless, hedonistic doctrines are a natural for individualistic man. And of course after the Second World War and the comparative austerity of the 1940s, having fun seemed natural enough, and justifying having fun is what hedonistic philosophy is for.

Hedonism, however, is not simply a doctrine that says pleasure is good for you. John Stuart Mill had claimed (Rogers 1964: 238) that pleasure could be of a carnal nature or of a 'higher' kind. During the 1960s, and what became known as the 'permissive society', it was perhaps sexuality that became the dominant form of hedonism. 'If it feels good do it' was the carnal end; 'sexual enjoyment as personal fulfilment' was the higher end. Sexual intercourse aided by the technological breakthrough of synthetic hormones (the pill) became normative among unmarried couples. Casual sex (promiscuity) increased rapidly. Probably even more than action there was a great deal of talk about the techniques of sex, its joys, its malfunctions and inhibitions and how to overcome them. This same period saw the end of traditional censorship in films, plays and books. The 'right' of orgasm for women (as well as for men) seemed to have been added to the list of the 'natural rights of man' which the fathers of the Enlightenment seemed to have overlooked!

Sex is like the cat that is let out of the bag: once out it is difficult to put back. The phenomenal rise in venereal diseases and the performance of abortions 'for social reasons' were two of the unintended consequences of sexual hedonism which nevertheless seemed to have little effect on sexual behaviour. Instead we still see an increasing clamour for 'abortion on demand' and improved facilities for sexually transmitted diseases.

But the most subtle – and most high – kind of hedonism that dominated cultural life in the 1960s was known as 'self-awareness'. People were 'into' themselves ('psychological solipsism' as one wag called it). There was psychoanalysis for the status-conscious and assertiveness training for those with low self-esteem. You could join consciousness-raising groups if you were deprived or oppressed. If repression was your problem you could engage in Co-Counselling, sensitivity training and T-grouping. For those who wanted peace of mind or enhanced consciousness there were several off-the-peg forms of Eastern mysticism.

Looked at positively, we might say that all these things were actually a realisation that the stresses and strains of modernity could not be coped with by further doses of materialism. The great spread of drug-taking among the young during this time can also be seen either as 'doing it for kicks' or looking for a road out of materialistic culture. (For some it was simply a road to oblivion.) I mention this because while the 'swinging sixties' was at its height the emergence of the so-called 'counterculture' was more than just youthful rebellion: it was a genuine 'revolt of the soul'. Os Guinness has captured this middle-class revulsion against materialism and affluent decadence in his best-selling book *The Dust of Death* (1973). He saw the counterculture as a desperate cry for help from the captured sons and daughters of the Evil One; a cry, he feels, which went virtually unheeded by many Christians who saw only the law-breaking or iconoclasm and failed to see the spiritual hunger.

The 1960s was a decade of great excitement, creativity and energy. It was, until 1968 at least, a time of great optimism. Taboos were being broken,[3] cheap holidays abroad were all the rage, for, as everybody was taught at school, 'travelling broadens the mind'. New religious ideas and moral codes were made accessible by widescale immigration, cultural exchanges and mass communication. The mid-1960s were the watershed of postwar society, and the creativity and anarchism of the period left nothing untouched. The full effects of the theological liberalism which had been at work since the nineteenth century came into their own in the English-speaking world after the publication of *Honest to God* (Robinson 1963). The fly-by-night theologies of the 'death of God' and 'magic mushrooms' were only the anarchic end of a serious attack by modern scholarship upon the presuppositions of biblical faith and credal affirmation (see chapter eight).

Of course all this change, verve and audacity was enough to give traditional Christians apoplexy, but too many people were having a good time to worry about the consequences of all these changes. And then, like a blast from Gabriel's horn, 1968 declared that the party was well and truly over. That year saw the invasion of Czechoslovakia and the worldwide student protests. In North America hippies and flower children were turning into anti-Vietnam war demonstrators. The Vietnam war had undermined the moral confidence of America, and a mood of recrimination and uncertainty was settling in.

For many people living through that time, 1968 was the unforgivable pin that pricked the bubble: and with the deflation of the great illusion that the 1960s was a perpetual party came the realisation of the cost. In economic terms the truth of the matter was that Western capitalism had underinvested, overspent (as one does at a party) and failed to keep the machine in running order. The 1970s became a decade of high inflation and spiralling unemployment. The world entered a long-term period of recession and chronic unemployment, both of which at the time of writing seem to have become endemic to our advanced societies.

Furthermore, the 1960s was a decade of ecological mismanagement. Too much attention had been given to the short-term goals of profitability and not enough to the long-term effects on the environment of industrial waste, chemical spillage and oil and petrol pollution. In the heart of the great metropolitan areas of America the inner cities became as desolate and hopeless as shanty towns. Urban violence and civil unrest were mushrooming like small bombs threatening to blow up the machine from within.

Violent crime, and in particular rape and the molestation of children, climbed vertically (to the present day), and the violence of domestic crime was matched by the scourge of international terrorism and the regional and local wars of Africa, the Middle East, Asia and South America.

Although the 'swingingness' of the 1960s had been absent in the 1970s and 1980s, drug-taking had increased among young and old alike ('coke' if you were middle-class, glue-sniffing if you were poor), and so too had alcoholism. Many of these features of the modern world were only the surface manifestations of the much greater structural changes begun in early industrialism and accelerated since the Second World War. For example, there have always been high rates of divorce after wars, but in the 1960s divorce was made easier and simpler by legal changes. These changes themselves reflected the changing role of women and the consumer approach to marriage: 'If your partner does not satisfy get another'; 'Shop around until you find what you want'; 'Children are of course important, but not so important as sexual compatibility and personal fulfilment'. And by the mid-1980s in California one in two marriages ended in divorce, and one in three in other high-density populations in North America and parts of Europe.

I will have more to say about family life in the next chapter, here I note merely that in the last twenty years we have seen the large-scale establishment of the single-parent family, the so-called serial-monogamy syndrome (divorced people keep getting remarried) and an endless chain of step-children and step/half brothers and sisters.

And who would have thought that as we face the 1990s the social and moral habits of the 1960s should be visited upon us in the guise of AIDS, which threatens to sweep across the world with all the terror and destruction of the black plague in the Middle Ages?

Admittedly, for optimistic technocrats at least, the 1970s

saw the beginning of a new technological revolution which, it
was hoped, would refuel the flagging machine, create new
jobs and improve the quality of life. At least this revolution
was genuine because the comparatively cheap micro-chip
computers made possible and affordable a computerised
society. But it remains to be seen whether this will exacerbate
chronic unemployment or solve it. And despite all its promise
it is not yet clear whether it will pull capitalism out of its
recession or whether it will only serve the interests of affluent
minorities. The fact that such technology has already had a
major impact upon the leisure industry should not fill us with
wild joy. Videos and computer games, hi-fidelity television
and quadrophonic sound are the sort of toys developed for
people with nothing better to do. Or if you are of a nightmare
disposition, the whole thing resembles the clinical and page-
less world of Ray Bradbury's *Fahrenheit 451*, a world in which
there is sexual fetishism, but no books, and people are wired
for sound and watch TVs implanted into the walls of their
homes. As Paul Simon says in his song 'The Boy in the
Bubble':

> These are the days of miracles and wonder
> And
> Don't cry baby, don't cry, don't cry.

But as the individualist man's machine ticked over at idling
speed, in desperate need of a new surge of power and aware
that the world's supply of oil had nearly run out, the collectivist machine was doing no better. Russia, for example, failed
to keep up with the scientific and technological innovations of
the West. Its economy was in a state of inertia. Neither
superpower could rationally risk a war to get them out of their
malaise – there could be no winners this time round. It is
difficult to apply the medieval doctrine of the just war or the
Puritan conviction of 'God on our side' to atomic apocalypse.

Curiously, in the United States there was an optimism and a
new sense of confidence after Ronald Reagan became president (a confidence later deflated by the Iranian arms fiasco).
It is difficult for a European to find the rational basis for this
optimism. Conservatism (both secular and Christian) was on

the rise and there was a feeling of greatness and destiny: a sense that Americans could again hold up their heads and 'walk tall'. No such confidence existed in Europe, where the new post-liberal conservatism in politics had little positive effect.

BACK TO THE PRESENT

In this chapter we have, through our time travelling, been outside of our own world for some time now, so perhaps we are now looking at modernity with the eyes of a stranger coming home. Bishop Lesslie Newbigin (1983) describes the effect of coming back to England after years in the mission field as one of shock: a realisation that there was little hope. Even India, with all its poverty, he found more hopeful.

Our politicians still speak of help coming just around the corner, but in the inner cities of England and America, among the chronically unemployed, among the young faced with the long-term prospects of AIDS or the imminent threat of annihilation, there is little talk of hope. Belief in utopian progress is increasingly seen as a delusion. As Christians we must surely wonder if the time for Enlightenment man is not up. I have said elsewhere that

> Enlightenment man has undoubtedly been a man of power, but he has also been a barbarian. Now he is stumbling. The Church should not be helping him up, but helping him over: false optimism does not need a helping hand; it needs firstly the truth, and secondly love to salve the lost illusions and move on to a fuller humanity (Walker 1986: 214).

The problem with modernity, Enlightenment man's home, is that it masks the reality of his hopelessness from him. By concentrating on some of the crises and conflicts of modernity through my interpretive and impressionistic historical journey, I hope that I have begun to bring to your attention some of the fundamental problems of the modern world. In the next chapter I want to show some of the more insidious ways in which modernity stops us from seeing contemporaneity as the territory of the Enemy.

5 CAPTIVE LIVES –
The insidiousness of modernity (Part one)

Having arrived back in our contemporary world after our historical journey, I hope that we will be better able to view modernity with a certain detachment. The problem with contemporaneity is that it is right under our noses. Because we are immersed in the culture of the modern world as actor-participants, it takes an effort of will to stand back and look clearly with Christian discernment.

In our impressionistic historical view of the coming of modernity we saw it in terms of crises and radical social and economic change. But to live in modernity is to experience it as home. This is where we live, and for those of us not dwelling in the inner city or immobilised with fear by the threat of atomic war, modernity is really quite comfortable. We do not experience our existence as under constant threat from the Devil. Our life is characterised on the one hand by a certain cosiness of Christian fellowship and on the other hand by a pleasant familiarity with the secular world: we work in it, spend our hard earned income on it, and take some of our pleasures from it. Certainly the modern world has its problems, but so it will always be until the parousia, we could say. Why make such a fuss about modernity? The Devil no more threatens Christians today, we might think, than he did a thousand years ago.

If that is how we still feel, then we must recognise that we can only think this way because the Enemy is not threatening us. And one of the main reasons why this is so is because we are not threatening him. Most of us remain unaware that our Christian faith – however real to us – has already been divorced from the mainstream of modern life. As the great machine of modernity spins remorselessly round, it has spun us away from the centre of social existence – community life, government, commerce, industry, education, welfare, leisure – to the peripheral margins of societal life. Life on the margins characterises the Christian church in advanced industrial societies, and more often than not we do not even notice it. The Evil One may not have come between us and God on a personal level, but as an army he has scattered us all over the place, dumped us unceremoniously in our little religious ghettoes and subcultures, and left us to our own devices.

And so in this chapter I want to look analytically at some of the ways Christianity has unwittingly capitulated to the forces of modernity. We talk about the evils of secularism, but do not seem to recognise that we are ourselves secularised. We all want to do a mighty work for God, but do not realise that we are living on privatised religious estates on the outskirts of the city of the world.

If we want to rescue the captives from the clutches of the Enemy, we must first wake up and realise that we are ourselves leading captive lives. We are not in darkest prison like our brothers and sisters in the flesh, but we are under house arrest. Our adversary lets us out from time to time, to visit other houses, but we rarely enter with power and authority into the heart of the city.

When I was a boy I belonged to a small Christian sect that was my whole world. I thought it was a big world, for we were always going to conventions and special meetings where, so it seemed then, there were thousands of others like myself. When I went to Bible college at the age of eighteen, hardly anybody had ever heard of my religious home. When I later became an agnostic and went to university, nobody had ever heard of my Bible college. And so it is in Christian life generally. We imagine that we are in the thick of it – especially if there are miracles, new liturgical enthusiasm and popular songs – but in reality we are in the thin of it. Hardly anybody in the big wide world has heard of us, let alone been influenced by our lives.

Those Christians who belong to the sort of council of churches where passionate debates take place about atomic war, South Africa, police brutality, racism and urban decay may think that they at least are closer to the real action. But this is a delusion if we think that passing resolutions about the evils of society actually influences world governments and changes the direction of modernity. I am not saying that churches should not state their views about social evils, but it is quite another thing to imagine that clear statements are denting the Evil One's power.[1] (But as we know, a great many Christians caught up in talking about social activism of various kinds do not believe in the Devil.)

Of course it is one thing to state baldly that modern Christians are often ineffectual in their witness and live in a privatised world, cut off from the mainstream of social life, but it is quite another thing to make out a case that it is so.

The central question I want to use as a peg on which to hang various theories is, 'Why are so few Christians aware of the direct threat of modernity to the Christian church?' I will attempt to show that answers to this question have to do with the almost hidden insidious nature of modern life. The social philosopher Alfred Schutz (1889–1959) was concerned to demonstrate how we never notice the way in which everyday life works (Schutz 1943). Because we are engaged in practical actions of great complexity, which we nevertheless 'pull off' day after day, we have little time to stand back and analyse how we do all the things that we do. According to Schutz, we take for granted that the world works in a reasonably rational and orderly way, unless and until something goes wrong. In reality the social world is constantly shifting and changing, yet we experience life as orderly and sane, not as random or chaotic. Despite all the things that happen to us, such as religious conversion, dreams, accidents, bereavement, psychological shock – all those things that pull us out of everyday reality – we tend to slip back to a belief that there is a bedrock of common sense and sensibility at the heart of things.

I remember my father used to say that even those experiences that take us out of ourselves – the 'mountain-top' experiences – can never keep us from having to come down to the valley of ordinary existence. But on the plain, the everyday, where we must live most of the time, we do forget – or never notice – that reality around us is constantly changing. That is why social processes are so much more difficult to understand and combat than ideologies.

Now I believe that the secular ideologies of the modern world do pose a real and direct threat to the Christian church. They are a frontal assault of the Devil not only upon believers but on human beings everywhere. But what worries me more is *the process* of secularisation. I believe this to be more pernicious than secularism *per se*. Many Christians can recognise secularism and have boldly stood up against it. But secularisation creeps up on us announced. While we fight the Devil on the theological front, he sneaks up on us from behind. We must remember that he is waging a dirty war. This is not an equal fight between two evenly matched sides battling it out according to some carefully laid down ground rules of fair play.

Consequently, if we want to engage in enemy combat in order to further the coming of God's kingdom we need to beware of two damaging manoeuvres.

We should avoid an exclusive obsession with 'secular humanism' that sees the problem of modernity only in terms of false ideology. The New Religious Right in North America eschew humanism when it threatens the fundamental truths of God's revelation of himself in the sacred scriptures (at least as they understand them). But they embrace the worldliness and materialism of advanced industrialism and even declare it good! The 'electronic church' pulsates with the secular energy of modernity. This worldliness, as Os Guinness has recognised, is precisely, for Christians, what the process of secularisation is all about (Guinness 1983: chs 3, 7).

Conversely, many 'liberals' in the churches in both America and Europe denounce (but rarely renounce) capitalism, or at least materialism, but praise the superiority of critical rationalism over Christian dogmas and tradition.

The Devil does not mind which of these attacks upon him we make, because taken on their own either one will leave us helpless and impotent in the Enemy's territory.

SECULARISATION

I must come clean and admit that the concept of secularisation has become extremely confusing in sociological usage. The clearest and most sophisticated expositions of secularisation that I know can be found in Martin (1978) and Dobbelaere (1981). Basically secularisation is a composite concept that involves a number of different ideas. Many people erroneously think that secularisation means that religion or religiosity itself has disappeared from advanced industrial societies. This is not so. On the contrary, all the evidence suggests that not even modernity can stifle spiritual hunger. In a country like Great Britain, for example, even though less than fifteen per cent of the population regularly go to church over seventy per cent still claim to believe in a God of some kind. Increasingly sociologists are insisting that although traditional religion (and certainly Christian orthodoxy) is in decline, latent or 'implicit' religion abounds everywhere (Bailey 1976).

Of course this is of small comfort for Christianity. The fact that superstition, occultism, and vague forms of religious paganism persist into modernity is nothing to shout about. On the individual level secularisation has meant, on the whole, a decline in Christian commitment. Throughout Europe there has been a steady drop in religious attendance since the nineteenth century. As I pointed out in the last chapter, working-class attachment to institutional religion never picked up from the moment that peasants moved off the land and became urbanised. Continental working classes are more violently atheistic and anticlerical than their British counterparts. The United States is unique in the advanced countries of the West in maintaining a level of church attendance of closer to fifty per cent than the European norm of some fifteen per cent or less.

This itself gives the lie to the notion that America is a secular republic. Under the influence of its Enlightenment men the American constitution may formally be secularist, but the history of America demonstrates that it is the most religious continent in the Western world. Indeed as Neuhaus has recognised (1986) it is precisely because religion has been forced out of the central corridors of power in America that the New Religious Right has managed to stride in with such urgency and rage.

But this leads us into the area of secularisation that has been the most damaging to the Christian church. The technical term for this is 'laicisation'. There is no English equivalent to the French basis of this concept, but broadly it denotes the fact that institutional church religion has been pushed by modernity out of the centre of social and cultural life and into its own peripheral and private sphere. (This is the point I was making – without the jargon – on pages 106–107.) The traditional sacred cosmos or canopy of preindustrial society that dominated rural life before modernity (remember England of 1700) was dissolved by the amoral technical and specialised institutions that developed with industrialism. The commercial, scientific and industrial world of capitalism (or socialism) does not need religion in order to go about its business. This was precisely why Edward Irving prophetically saw that the great evil of industrialism (to use his friend Carlyle's term) was that it was godless.

Furthermore, the new technical and rational society not only dissolved the sacred order; it disintegrated the communal order. Henceforth the local, stable community where relationships were both personal and persistent became no more than a rarity in the modern world. An excellent example of such a community today would be the Amish groups of Pennsylvania. A student of mine who saw the Hollywood film *Witness*, which featured the Amish community, wondered whether we should think of their way of life not as a residue of the past but the way of the future!

Although 'laicisation' is a process that has become universal in the Western world, it is in North America where it is at its most advanced. In Europe Christians everywhere know that they are in trouble because their churches are empty and attendance continues to decline. Despite the recent successes of house churches and charismatic movements, the overall picture is unchanged. In the United States, however, it is precisely because churches are so full, and wealthy, that it is not easy to see that in fact secularisation in the form of 'laicisation' has gripped the church by the throat.

The philosophical Enlightenment, as we have seen, promoted rationality on a philosophical level. The immediate effects of that philosophical rationalism were felt only by the intelligentsia. But with the coming of modernity proper, that is with industrialisation, what made the philosophies so potent was that they became embodied as a functional rationality. It was the economic rationality of the market and the scientific rationality of research and technology that facilitated the process of laicisation. And it is at this point that we can see the way in which secularisation feeds and nurtures the philosophies of secularism. Functional as opposed to philosophical rationality is experienced by men and women in work, by government and through bureaucracy. There is nothing philosophical about this in itself, but it begins to create the habit of mind that begins to take for granted the *natural* superiority of science and rational thinking. In short, modernity itself creates the scientific/rational *Weltanschauung* (world-view) of modern men and women. This world-view is one in which the material and the phenomenal dominate consciousness at the expense of the spiritual (the numinous) and the supernatural.

Within the crucible of the modern mind, the modern world-view, secularist philosophies are naturally at home and breed with alarming fecundity. I do not mean to suggest for a moment any kind of determinist philosophy here: functional rationality does not cause philosophical rationality, but it does help it along.

A simpler way of looking at laicisation might be to say that institutional Christianity has lost some of its functions: most education passes from church to state; so too do medicine, welfare and human counselling. Neither psychology, psychiatry, social work, health education, social security, nor nursing relies significantly on religious insight or Christian doctrine. They too have passed over into the world of law, business, government and technology, where rational but secular goals and methods dominate.

A more important Christian observation is to note that

laicisation has meant that as institutional Christianity has been forced out of the control box of the modernity machine it has lost its authority. Christianity in the contemporary world in which we live has become a matter of private belief and personal preference in a society that tolerates any old religious beliefs (and new ones) so long as they do not interfere with the running of the machine.

A friend of mine told me that although he is a committed Christian, when he leaves home and goes to work he has to play by the rules of commerce. The aggressiveness and competitiveness of capitalism has little time for his Christian sensibilities. When pushed, he explained that in his line of work 'cutting corners', 'fudging', 'giving out disinformation' and 'cheating just a little' are part of the rules (unstated, but there) of the job. The fact that so many Christians feel the tension between their private family and church life and their public performance at work exemplifies how far removed Christianity has become from modern institutional life.

Anthropologists and sociologists agree that religion as a sacred world-view is virtually impossible in advanced industrial societies. Like it or not, it is a fact that religion is more dominant and persistent in rural societies than industrial ones. It is in the West that religion has declined not only in terms of churchgoing but authority. The great growth in Christianity at the present time is in the Third World and those parts of Eastern Europe that are still under atheistic leadership. It is one thing to attack the Soviet system or Third World countries not yet under the sway of Western democracies (and business), but it is in these countries that the gospel is spreading like wildfire.

To recapitulate, the essential feature of the most important aspect of secularisation, laicisation, is that Christian authority and institutional control have been virtually removed from modern life. The modern world has become dominated by the rational and technical society where specialisation in work is no longer related to traditional skills or crafts (based in the home) but to the economic and functional necessity of the marketplace. This has led to a 'knock-on effect' where the technical world has invaded the church. We have seen the growth of extra church bureaucracies such as the World Council of Churches, and the bureaucratisation of churches themselves. Recently I was shown around the offices of a community church that prides itself on its radical Christian commitment. My abiding memory of the tour was the computers, word processors, IBM typewriter, and management 'know how'. (This is not meant to be a criticism, for I doubt whether we can work effectively without such things; it is merely to point out that modernity enters the church far more easily than the church enters modernity.)

DEATH AND DYING: A SECULARISATION CASE STUDY

There is one monopoly left to the church in modernity, and that not by choice but default: she still controls funerals. Or to be exact, Christianity does not but religions of all kinds do. Death is the unforgivable sin of modernity, and the modern world will have nothing to do with her. She interrupts the pleasures of cultural hedonism, gives the lie that progress is for all and for ever, and introduces suffering into personal relationships. The secular and technical world manages the mechanics of death very well – disposes of corpses efficiently – but will have nothing to do with rites and prayers and personal goodbyes. How could it? And so throwing up its hands in horror and resignation it turns to the priests and pastors of religion – of a more primitive world order – and tells them to get on with it.

But the priests and pastors are caught in a trap. Everywhere in the modern world death is taboo. Victorians loved to wallow in the sentimentality of death because it was so prevalent and self-evident in their society that they had to come to terms with it as best they could. Today we can talk about sex without modesty or fear, but bring up the subject of death and you will be treated with the same social horror as if you had brought up the subject of masturbation at a Victorian ladies' tea party. Not only do we not talk about death, but we do everything we can to hide it from view and pretend that mortality is just a myth.

On a wild and windy day, with gusts of rain driving into the side of the crematorium, an Anglican priest waited for the next funeral to commence. He was one of many ministers on the 'death rota', as he called it. Looking the picture of misery and helplessness, he snatched a few words with me as I waited to go in. 'What are we expected to do,' he said. 'Nine times out of ten we do not know the deceased or the grieving family. Most of the "congregation" [he said it in such a way that it merited being put in inverted commas] do not know how to behave, when to stand or kneel, how to express their grief. I have to pronounce words of Christian hope when I do not know if there is any hope.'

Even more tragically for the vicar is the fact that for many unchurched families he is simply a cog in the death machine; an impersonal professional who has to mumble a few words before the curtains swish and the coffin descends to the fires below. The first concrete experience of the church that many people have in their whole lives is at a funeral. For nominal Christians it is perhaps only the third time they have been at a religious service; the other two being their baptism and marriage.

We see here how widespread and deadly is the net of secularisation that has been cast. Let us see how this has taken place. Firstly, we need to recall that a feature of modernity is that infant mortality rates have dropped, people live longer, and medicine and improved diet have ensured that we have healthy populations. Consequently death is no longer in the midst of life as it was for our ancestors and still is in many Third World countries. Secondly, when people do have the temerity to die they increasingly do so away from home.

In both the United States and Great Britain more people die in hospitals and homes for the elderly than in their own houses. Even if people do die at home, before you can say 'Jack Robinson' the men from the funeral directors are round to take the deceased to the chapel of rest. Dying these days involves a variety of bureaucratic and local government procedures. The undertakers have moved in as the middle-men, the 'third party', who handle all the unpleasantness and worrying details of death. This has resulted in not only strangers and professionals moving into the arena of dying and death, but it has also led to commercialisation and big business. Jessica Mitford's book on *The American Way of Death* (1963) is now nearly thirty years old but little has changed except that death is now even bigger business.

Not so long ago a wife would have 'laid out' her own husband at home. The wife would have been 'laid out' by family or friends. The body, as the material expression of the divine life, would have been treated with respect and care. The deceased loved one would have been left for all to come and see, and grieve over, and most importantly to say goodbye to. There would have been no question whether the children would come; they came as a matter of course and 'right behaviour'. It is, may I suggest, much easier to say goodbye to a face than to a wooden box.

And when a death occurred in a family or a community, mourning would be a ritualistic affair. Curtains would be closed, arm bands worn, and hats removed as the hearse passed by. (What a wonder it is today in atheist Moscow to watch the people as a funeral passes by. Streets are blocked and atheism has to give way as people kneel in the streets and cross themselves with the sign of the Holy Trinity.) Rituals have always been more colourful in 'Catholic' countries than Protestant ones, but many Protestant rites survived until the end of the First World War.

Rites of passage, as anthropologists call them, are not only universal features of all rural life, they also survive in truncated forms into modernity. These rites mark the cycle of life – birth, puberty, marriage, death. Not only are they dramatic representations of personal and social events, they are also outward expressions of inner emotional feelings. But modernity abhors them, and they are repressed. Puberty rites have virtually disappeared; even the ritualistic marking of birth and marriage is less than it was. Death rites remain, but rites that are no longer recognisable as rites or common practices.

We could say quite simply that this is an example of the

decline of religious belief. It would be more accurate to say that it shows the decline of community and public practices. As laicisation has forced religion from community to private practice, we should not be surprised that so few people know how to mourn together and share common griefs. We shall see in the next section that partly as a result of secularisation religion has become privatised and inward looking. Personal grief very often no longer has a communal expression.

The terrible thing about the modern attitude to death is that we pass it on to our children. We do not want them to be upset, so we keep them away from funerals, or from saying goodbye, face to face, to their relatives and friends. We do not even like adults to grieve. Sometimes we repress the natural grieving processes by giving the mourners tranquillisers. We cannot bear emotion in public, and we look at grief as pathological or a sign of emotional instability. If a woman has lived with a man for over fifty years, why should she be expected to get over his death in a week?

Insensitivity while dealing with the bereaved is an endemic problem in our modern world. Where once husbands and wives would 'go into mourning' for prescribed periods ranging from months to years, we like to see people pick themselves up and get on with it. A girl on a health education course I once taught told me of someone she knew whose husband had died after six months of marriage. Nothing had happened to sour their relationship or to lead her to have negative feelings about him. On the day after his funeral, her best friends called at her door with the news, 'Surprise! We have got you a blind date . . .'

I remember only too well a student whose little girl died at six months of age. His best friend did not go to the funeral because he had already decided to go on a day trip to France! After the funeral was over and the bereaved student returned to college, instead of going up to him and holding him – or even just politely commiserating with him – most students ignored him. I realised then how our own personal embarrassment and refusal to face up to our own mortality prevents us from behaving to others in a natural and human way.

And now we must come to the 'hard saying'. When it comes

to death, counselling the dying, or helping the bereaved, we Christians have become secularised. It may be true that we still believe in the resurrection, but we seem to forget that we must first experience death. People do not 'pass away', 'pass on', 'fall asleep' or even get 'promoted to glory': they die. I recall another student who was an Anglican clergyman. He developed cancer, and despite radium treatment – after which all his hair fell out – he was declared terminally ill. But no one would tell him. His doctors would not do so, his wife could not bring herself to do so, and the vicar in charge of the parish did not know how to do so. It was eventually agreed that I could be allowed to bring up the subject.

When I did so, tears of pain and relief broke out. 'I know that I am dying,' he said, 'and I am so angry with God for letting it happen, and with my family for refusing to let me work through it.' I saw him as often as I could and at first we concentrated on his anger. It seemed to me that it was not only natural but positive: it demonstrated that he still had a relationship with God.

But while this was happening another student, who was a friend of both the dying man and myself, became convinced that God was going to heal the clergyman of his cancer. It is very difficult psychologically to prepare somebody for death when you are also trying to heal them. I asked him to desist not from his prayers but from his actions because I felt sure that God wanted to prepare the Anglican priest for his death. More so, however, I knew somehow that my friend was bolstering up his own natural fear of loss and dread of death. He did not turn up to the funeral when his friend died, and for me this was sadder than the loss of the vicar who had found peace and hope before he died.

I believe in healing, but 'there is a time to die'. When we are privileged to know this in advance (and I think that it is wrong in nearly all cases not to tell a dying patient) it is a time for preparation and repentance, and ultimately of acceptance.

The establishment of hospices is a genuine example of moving out of the margins and into the city of the world (Du Boulay 1984). By that I mean it is a way of bringing dignity, caring and love right into the heart of the impersonal secular world of modernity. We must understand that hospitals are not designed for death, and yet they have become institutions of death. Many doctors and nurses are not trained in counselling the bereaved. Death is always a failure in hospital, and the business and routine of life in the medical and surgical wards do not lend themselves to a personal death (Sudnow 1967).

Christians usually think that they have nothing to learn from other religions, but that is because we confuse beliefs and practices. We could learn much from Jewish behaviour (Gorer 1965) and indeed the religions of most pre-industrial countries. Bureaucratic and institutional practices in public life, and idiosyncratic and private beliefs in private life have combined to push out the communitarian and personal dimensions of dying, death itself, and bereavement.

I think that in the Protestant West in general there is perhaps a little bit too much of an emphasis on beliefs and saying the right thing – giving the right word. But when you are involved with the dying, as I have had to learn to be, so often it is more a question of practising the presence of God. You are holding the hand of an old man who is ninety. He is senile, and there is no indication from reading his case notes whether he has any religious conviction at all. His breathing is laboured in that heavy way which so often heralds the end, and as you grip his hand to let him know that he is not alone, you try to love him as the Lord himself would do. This, I am convinced, is one of the strange yet powerful ways we Christians overcome the Evil One.

I do not think that we can turn back the tide of secularisation altogether in the area of dying, but we can call a halt to it by giving some serious thought to practices within our society and churches.

Hospices are clearly an improvement on hospital wards. Our doctors and nurses need far more counselling in this area, as do our social workers and priests. Furthermore, perhaps we should at least ask whether cremation is not really for the convenience of public health, efficiency, and land conservation rather than for people. Purely on a psychological level, it may be that a culture such as ours that has grown up out of a

Judaic-Christian background finds cremation difficult to accept. Theologically, if we are going to accept cremation at all (given our belief in bodily resurrection) should we not at least commit the ashes to a grave and not scatter them to the winds? (We are not, with deep respect to them, Hindus.)

I know that in talking frankly about death I have touched many a raw nerve here, and possibly even stirred up guilt and feelings of unease. Many of the people on my courses on dying, for example, had never really come to terms with the inevitability of death in their own lives, and many a time we had to stop to allow distressed and upset people to leave the room.

I do not want to embarrass anyone or to moralise, but I feel that this is an area in which modern Christians have been caught in the net of secularisation without realising it. Too often, even if we are committed Christians, we are afraid of death and like secular society prefer to imagine that it will not happen to us or our loved ones. And when it does, as it always does, we are caught unawares and unprepared. This is enemy work, and it acts upon us subliminally and insidiously. Perhaps we could start by forgetting our Christian duties and remembering our humanity: the naturalness of grief and the pain of loss. It is precisely because our Lord suffered these things that we recognise him as not only God but human, like us.

Let me end this section with a personal story of encouragement. Recently my father-in-law died, and I was anxious for our children to go and see him and say goodbye. This is the sort of thing, so an undertaker told me, that only the Irish do in Britain these days! Usually when you suggest this action to your family, whether they be Christian or heathen, you will be regaled with horror stories of long-term psychological damage. If that fails to dissuade you, you will be told that it is not very nice: it is frightening and ghoulish. (Well, death is not supposed to be nice.) However, though I cannot speak for others, my three boys found it perfectly normal and natural. (Please be sensible and ensure that the body is laid out decently.[2])

When we came away from the chapel I asked the boys if

they were pleased that they had all gone to say goodbye to their grandpa. They all said that they were very glad. 'But dad,' said Joshua, who is seven, 'I noticed that Grandpa did not have on his ordinary clothes. He was dressed in the robes of a king.'

PRIVATISATION

Already in this chapter I have referred to the idea that Christian commitment has become a matter of private belief. Like secularisation, this 'privatisation', as it is called by sociologists, affects Christians because it affects everybody living in modernity. We live in a fallen culture and cannot be completely exempted from it. If we want to know what is happening to the church we need to understand what is happening in the secular world at large. I have already hinted that perhaps we are not aware how much religion has become detached from public and modern secular life. I think we need to say more about this, because while it is related to secularisation and is partly a direct result of laicisation, there is more to it than that. The fact that Christians find themselves caught up with a religion that is no longer related to work or community life, but instead to leisure, tells us something about the whole process of privatisation. Os Guinness has talked about the modern world in terms of a divide. On the one hand there is the macro-world of big business, government complexes and military machines which we experience as impersonal and anonymous in character. On the other hand there is the micro-world which we find more personal and meaningful, the world 'of the family and private associations, the world of personal tastes, sports, hobbies and leisure pursuits. Very significantly, it is on this side of the divide that the Church has made her home' (Guinness 1983: 76).

It was not a conscious choice to retreat from public life into a private world. This happened more as a result of the need for specialised care and education for citizens to be managed by the state. Churches alone could not handle the enormous demands created by an industrial society in the spheres of welfare and social security. The old system of parish relief for paupers in England, for example, was quite inadequate for a geographically mobile population. Such demographic changes wrought by industrialism meant the decline of rural parishes and the creation of a new urbanised and industrial poor.

More straightforwardly, however, capitalism and technology have no need of religion. In pre-industrial Europe there was still a division between church, work and home, but these divisions were not absolute. Industry was primarily 'cottage industry' where the family was the unit of production. Village life was community life where the church, home, and work, were the living and connected cells of a functioning organism. I have experienced this kind of world in the mountain villages of Crete. There it is difficult to separate the secular world from the sacred. The primarily agricultural work blends in with the liturgical calendar of the church. The regularity of the seasons matches the regularity of the great Christian festivals of Christmas, Easter and Pentecost.

I remember in particular going with the local bishop to an early morning Eucharist. The whole village was there. After the liturgy everyone came to receive the *agape* (delicious warm and scented bread) from the hand of the bishop. And then we continued the 'love feast' by moving into the homes of the villagers, eating sumptuous food, drinking wine and singing songs. There was no sense that we had passed from the holy world of church to secular life: there was a wholeness and a holiness about the whole experience which is difficult to describe.

As modernity has progressed in the last one hundred and fifty years, it is not only the world of work that has become secularised, but also government. Increasingly governments in the Western world have become reliant on their advisers, scientific specialists, experts in systems analysis, and supremely on economists. The great rational market economy (which ironically keeps breaking down) now dominates governments' policies. Perhaps the most significant aspect of the technical and rational mastery of the modern world has been bureaucracy. Government in North America is not really run by the President or the Senate but by the Washington bureaucracy. In England the daily business of politics is not controlled by the Prime Minister or Westminster: it is Whitehall that calls the tune.

Bureaucracy, which was so brilliantly analysed so long ago by Max Weber (1922), is based on legal-style directives and rational – though slow – procedures. Nowhere in modernity has bureaucracy more stifled the cause of human freedom and destroyed a sense of personal identity than in the great central bureaucracies of Eastern Europe. Bureaucracy is the natural tool for collectivist man in modernity. But we in the West cannot be too sanguine, because bureaucracy is a major cause of impersonalism in our societies and the most negative aspect of the collective in our essentially individualistic culture.

Relationships at work, in the technical and scientific sphere, and supremely through bureaucracies, are functional relationships. Our dealings with our fellow citizens in this public domain are based on what Martin Buber has called the 'technical relation'. The 'I-Thou' of personal and communal relationships does not really apply. Of course we all like to get on with people at work, but our relationships are based on our skills, our expertise or our functional roles, not on friendship.

It is precisely because so many of us experience the world of work, government, the military, multinational corporations, etc. as impersonal that we seek personal fulfilment in the private sphere of leisure and the family. This is particularly so for workers whose lives are related to work not as a vocation or as a career, but as a job for earning money to spend in private. Working on a conveyor belt or as a human cog in a vast industrial machine does little for a sense of personal fulfilment. Indeed it creates a sense of alienation from work and the public world (Blauner 1964).

THE FAMILY AND PRIVATISATION

Privatisation, however, is not simply a case of alienation from the impersonal technical world of modernity. It has partly been caused by changes in the family itself. In the typical pre-industrial village the community, even if it was not tribal, was based on mutual rights, duties and obligations. This was reinforced by family and kinship. The pre-industrial family was not mum, dad and the kids. Grandmother, grandfather, uncles, aunties, grandchildren, first, second and third cousins were not simply related by conjugal and marital ties: they existed in a network of meaningful relationships. In short, family and community were inextricably linked.

But it has been a universal feature of modernity that the larger family unit, the so-called 'extended' family, has given way to a much smaller unit, the 'nuclear' family. This has nothing to do with Enlightenment philosophies; again it is a question of process. Industrialism demands mobility of labour. People have to go where there is work. Traditional communities decline. At first new communities grew up around the heavy industries of coal, steel and shipping. But in recent years the decline of these industries has meant an end to many traditional working-class communities where the extended family still survived. The nuclear family is not only smaller, as it is based essentially on the marriage bond and children, but it encourages privatisation. 'An Englishman's home is his castle,' goes the old adage. This is meant to convey a sense of security and privacy: the drawbridge is pulled up and the portcullis is dropped. The meaning persists in the contemporary world, but the castle, these days, is usually a semi in suburbia with mum, dad and two children.

As the family has shrunk it has also lost some of its traditional functions to the public world. Families are no longer units of economic production; they have become solely units of consumption. The education of children has passed to specialised institutions, usually run by the state. But the shrinkage and change in family structure and the alteration of some of its functions has coincided with a rise in the importance of the family as a focus of personal fulfilment. Indeed as the public domain has become more impersonal and technical so the family has increased in importance.

There are many positive aspects of this move, not least the fact that modern families are child-centred. It could be argued also that the nuclear family has facilitated the improvement of women's status within the home. The modern wife is considered more of an equal partner and helpmate than a chattel or a housekeeper. As women increasingly spend some of their married lives in careers, it follows also that they have more economic power.

In many ways, however, the focus on the family as the source of personal fulfilment is crazy. The modern nuclear family is a vulnerable and fragile institution. Witness the rates of marital breakdown in the Western world! In the first place men have expected too much of the 'new' woman. They have expected her to be super-wife, good in bed, a wonderful mother, an efficient housekeeper, a co-counsellor, and an earner of income. The changing role of women has often in practice meant that women go out to work and still do a full-time job in the home.

Not surprisingly, many women have begun to reject the expectations of men and have looked for their own 'role models' among themselves. Feminism has meant in practice that as women change they demand that men change too. Men confused by some of the changes in women's own expectations of marriage have found it hard to adjust to a wife who now expects her husband to be a thoughtful and technically competent lover, a housefather and a co-counsellor. The 'battle of the sexes' has penetrated into the heart of modern family life, leading not only to change but to role confusion. It has certainly not led to a greater family stability.

The great strain for married couples in modernity is the absurdly high expectation of the marriage bond. Of course it is admirable that expectations are high and that women should be given greater autonomy (and hope for more in the sexual area than their Victorian forebears). But both men and women in modernity have been too influenced by the romanticism of popular literature and supremely by the dreams of Hollywood. Marriage is about respect, commitment and graft, not just the 'buzz' of romantic and sexual excitement. Sexual fulfilment is at such a premium in modernity that if marriage cannot provide it, it can always be found elsewhere.

But if marriage turns out to be less than satisfactory in the arena of personal fulfilment, this is not only for the marriage partners. The battle of the sexes is augmented in the home by the generation war. It is in the family that the seeds of teenage rebellion first germinate. 'Honour thy father and thy mother' is not a slogan of the youth culture. But can we altogether blame the children when from the moment they are born they are the focus of adoration? In the 'baby boom' of the 1960s a whole generation of children were reared on Dr Spock and a belief in the right of self-expression.

This approach to children not only makes them precocious (more so in America than Europe) but 'precious'. A belief in the importance of 'self' and 'my ego-fulfilment' becomes a childish occupation that continues into adulthood, militates against the collective (the community generally) and feeds aggressive consumerism, individualism and hedonistic culture. Again we can see how processes and changes in social life facilitate secularist philosophies. I was amused at Dr Spock's comment about his book and his attitude to child-rearing towards the end of his life. When asked if people should still buy his book, he replied that they should, but only in hardback 'so they can hit the little ******* over the head'! It is significant that the great teenage rebellions of the 1960s and much of the counterculture came from those very middle-class families that had practised and encouraged self-fulfilment and personal autonomy.

A desperately sad aspect of the modern family is the way in which so much lavish attention is spent on the (small number of) children who after a life of smothering contact with their parents grow up and become almost strangers. All of us, I am sure, have tales to tell of the anguish and alienation that exists between parents and children. When they grow up, our children leave our private world to move into a private world of their own. There are so many to choose from, so many philosophies and cultures to move into.

All this contrasts vividly with those many families that have not taken on board self-fulfilment for their children, but have left them to their own devices: the 'latch-key' children, those out in the streets, members of territorial gangs. Sometimes children brought up in safe middle-class homes discover that safety is illusory as their parents split up, and the single-parent family becomes a dominant feature of modernity. They too get caught up in the underworld of youth subcultures, where the peer groups become more important (and possibly more caring) than the family.

WHERE HAVE ALL OUR OLD PEOPLE GONE?

But if the private world of family life is a world fraught with tension and danger for parents and children, it is far more frightening for the elderly: they may very well find themselves excluded from it.

We have a number of ways of dealing with the elderly in Western societies. If they have money, they can go into private homes or villages where only the elderly can live. These 'happy homes' are meant to give old people a sense of dignity and worth, but in reality they live in a privatised world cut off from both family and the wider community. If the elderly do not have money, then the answer is to put them in government homes. The move of the elderly from the family to institutions is partly a result of the change from extended family to nuclear family. The smaller family units cannot cope with grandparents either in terms of money or space.

Tragically, as our old people disappear from our midst so that increasingly we do not notice them, the old adage 'out of sight out of mind' comes into its own. It is a feature of modernity that our elder citizens are considered to be a nuisance to be dealt with as quietly and unobtrusively as possible. Social worth in our society is related to the workplace: you are valued by what you do for a job, not what or who you are as a person. Wisdom and experience are of secondary importance in our world; it is expertise that is valued.

What makes this alarming is that we are all living longer and retiring earlier. At the moment, when we should be integrating our elderly into community life and reintegrating them into our families, we are sending them off into social exile. For those old people who want to continue living outside institutional life, it means in many cases living alone or away from their children and grandchildren, or perhaps giving up their own homes to live in 'sheltered accommodation' overseen by a warden and social workers.

But the worst aspect of this whole affair is that so many people do not care about the quality of life for old people. I can talk about this from direct experience. For two years I worked as a residential officer in old people's homes in addition to my academic work. As senior officer on duty I came to know only too well the loneliness of old age. My wife, who works as a field social worker, also knows the problems of the elderly. She faces the same syndrome day after day. It is this: the phone rings and someone tells her that they are worried about an old person in their family – 'What are you going to do about it?' they demand. Sometimes they are only too eager to be 'shot of them'. Sometimes there is an appearance of caring, but really they just want the 'problem' off their hands.

Even when children care desperately for their elderly parents and have to put them in a home because of lack of personal resources, they are not always able to keep up regular contact because of moving to find employment. Many of the residents in homes for the elderly have no family, and many that do never see them from one year to the next. There is nothing more heartbreaking than trying to cheer up an old man or woman on Christmas day, surrounded by decorations and a cheerful staff, when their daughter or son does not visit or even call on the telephone.

And every residential social worker knows that I am not exaggerating when I say that after a death has occurred – often alone or with one of us holding the dying resident's hand – the family will descend like vultures, demanding a complete inventory of all their belongings, ransacking their personal clothes for valuables, and insisting on receiving all that is left of the petty cash. I wish that I could say that it is my experience that Christians are above this sort of thing, but it is not.

And try as hard as they do, residential staff can never turn a residential establishment into a home. Great strides have been made in recent years to offer greater choice and to personalise private rooms, but resources are never enough to provide the optimum living conditions for a comfortable and happy old age. Many homes, in Great Britain at least (and perhaps this is more true of the private sector), still offer no privacy for the elderly who do not have their own rooms, who have no locks on the lavatories and who have to suffer the indignity of being bathed and examined by a non-qualified member of staff of the opposite sex. The first task I was given was to bathe an elderly spinster. I infuriated the officer in charge by asking the lady if she minded. The old lady looked at me in wonder and said, 'Nobody has ever asked me that before, but if you really would not be too cross I would rather you did not.'

In the worst homes the confused-elderly are wheeled in front of the television and left there all day. Institutionalism sets in after a few months, and active people slow down and soon learn not to complain. People who cause trouble are constantly under medication (more for the staff's sake than the residents', so it seemed to me). I have met wonderful doctors who really cared for their old patients, but sometimes the doctors were dismissive and rude, believing that there was little point in wasting valuable resources on the elderly as they were going to die soon anyway. I remember one day I was serving lunch and the doctor strode in during the meal, walked up to his patient who was eating his lunch, pulled his head up and demanded, 'What is it this time?' He then frog-marched him out of the dining hall to the medical room. When I confronted him outside the refectory and insisted that the resident be allowed to finish his meal, he exploded in a torrent of foul language and vowed he would never return.

I could tell you many tales of great joy and hope, but I could also give you far worse than the few examples I have mentioned here. Have they shocked you? I hope so, because residential homes are places where people become cut off from family life and the outside world. Most people do not wish to see what goes on behind the locked doors. Eskimos put their old people out to die on the ice. Some African tribes leave their elderly to die by the rivers and waterholes so that the wild animals will eat them. We lock our old people away.

Occasionally we hear of staff abuse and there is outrage, but more often than not we simply do not think of what it means to be old or shut away. Do not ask the elderly about personal fulfilment in the modern privatised family: they feel betrayed.

Perhaps you would like to help; please do not feel maudlin or offer a vicarious prayer. Why not act and go round to your local old people's home – it will be within walking distance – and take your children with you. Ring the bell and say that you would like to adopt an old person. Do not only go and see them, but take them out or bring them home. This is kingdom work. Nothing less.

THE CHURCH AND PRIVATISATION

Privatisation, then, is not only a question of secularisation. It is something that has deeply influenced all social life. We have seen how the impersonalism of public life and changes in the structure and functions of the family have led to an emphasis on self-fulfilment as something that belongs in the private sphere. I have been anxious to show that the nuclear family may lead not to satisfaction but to frustration and disappointment.

But while the family may still be the supreme focus of privatisation, it is not the only one. The private domain is that world where families, individuals and associations of private affiliation live alongside each other. I say alongside because in no sense does the private world consist of a common culture and identity. Families live separately and autonomously. A feature of suburbia is that many people do not even know their own neighbours; certainly not those across the way. Furthermore, the private world consists of hundreds of different subcultures and associations.

It is doubtful if we can talk about modern nations having a culture in the sense that we can say that there is a monolithic entity called American culture or British culture. We can definitely say, however, that both America and Britain have a vague overall culture that is expressed in its national institutions and 'way of life'. But underneath the umbrella of the popular (and vague) culture there are hundreds of 'little cultures'. Perhaps not so much a way of life, but what Wittgenstein called a 'form of life': small and privatised world-views binding on the group and consisting of accepted social practices, group norms and common languages (by the latter I do not mean natural languages like French or English, but a nomenclature or group argot).

If there is a common culture at all it is usually expressed as part of the public world of government and state. Something like the 'civil religion' of American life, or the compromising good-sense of the British, is held up as embodying the culture at large. But the private world, where people look for both their pleasure and their fulfilment, is a competing world of separate group allegiances, some of which happen to be religious.

The reason I am suggesting that the church of Christ lives in this subcultural world is because I want to insist that God's spiritual family, as well as the human family, has also been radically altered by modernity. I do not mean spiritually altered, but socially transformed. The fact that Christianity is just one option among many shows us that the private world is a competing realm of separate and pluralistic realities. I shall say more of this a little later on, but for now I want to concentrate on aspects of privatisation.

Again we can see how this process of modernity aids philosophical secularism. For what could be better for the life of individualistic man than privatisation? The private sphere becomes the natural home of modern man. In the public world perhaps the older Puritan work ethic still dominates, though more so in the United States than Great Britain. But in the private world(s) hedonism takes root. Capitalism and the sterner Puritan ethic are delighted with hedonism as a private way of life because hedonism encourages consumerism, and consumerism becomes the economic mode of hedonism for modern man. Pleasure, in short, belongs to private leisure and individual patterns of economic consumption.

Even this affects church life, as I shall show, but we must recognise that it is not only rank hedonism that flourishes under private banners. As we have already seen (p. 101), self-fulfilment is the 'higher' form of hedonism. If we do not turn up for work, we are likely to get the sack, but in our private worlds we can dream our lives away at home, church or play. We can do this because the private universe that we inhabit for much of the time is characterised by a philosophy of personal freedom and private choice. '"Do what you want" shall be the whole of the law' was a favourite catch phrase of the occultist Aleister Crowley, but in fact it is the 'law' of the private kingdom – with the added rider, 'as long as it does not interfere with other people's personal preferences'. The 'consenting adults' mentality dominates private life, for there are no community taboos or collectivist laws to inhibit private expression (though, of course, there is the penal code).

To be free in private is to be able to watch pornography or to preach the gospel. Private pietism fits in very nicely with privatisation, but then so too does Transcendental Meditation or the playing of *Trivial Pursuits*.

You have to look hard in Christendom to find a Christian culture which has not become privatised. There are strong cultural residues in Catholic and Orthodox countries that are still primarily rural. It is no small thing to be able to leave your belongings unguarded and your doors unlocked, as you still can in the country areas of Greece (Davies 1982: 85). But it is Islam, not Christianity, that has realised the danger of privatisation and the negative and draining effect it can have on public life.

We Westerners find it hard to understand or admire the growth and success of Islamic fundamentalism, but the traditional Muslims have realised far better than the 'progressives' that if you want to resist consumerism and individualism then you have to capture the public ground and control the country from the centre. We Christians have already lost that battle, and I personally believe that we should not attempt to fight it again. This is my fundamental objection to the American new rightists. It is not because they are rightists (they could just as well be leftists) but because they want to capture the centre not for the gospel but for a 'Holy America'. The church throughout its history has been too preoccupied with building Christian civilisation at the expense of 'realising' the kingdom. I do think, however, that we should hit the Enemy in the public world, and even set up outposts and command centres there, as long as we do not forget that the kingdom cannot be built as a nation state or a political empire.

There is more bad news to come, but let us pause for a moment to take heart. While it may be true that we Christians are living in our separate and little private worlds, this is not to say that nothing significant is happening. On the contrary, a great deal is happening. This is because our adversary cannot have everything his own way. Privatisation is in fact a dual-edged sword. On the one hand we can see it as a master stroke of the Devil: Christians and humans everywhere have been forced into private enclaves cut off from the public world and each other. Private worlds, whether they be families or voluntary societies, turn out to be delusory sources of personal freedom: disillusionment and hopelessness follow behind the many human philosophies and religious ideas that modern men and women discard as carelessly as consumer toys.

On the other hand privatisation can also rebound on the Enemy, for there is no doubt that personal fulfilment is possible in the private sphere. There is real love and joy to be found in families and human life; no person is totally under the control of the Evil One until sin once and for all obliterates the *imago dei*. And we in the church may not yet be an army 'mighty and terrible with banners', but we can muster resistance by coming together in little bands of hope ready to strike in deep raids behind enemy lines. If the private world is where we find ourselves, then it is here that we must first come together.

I would like to suggest, with respect to the historic churches, that we should take a lesson from the sects. Usually we think of sects in totally negative terms; they divide Christendom and introduce strange beliefs and practices, we often think. But we have to understand that sects are a response to modernity that works. For example, my own Confession, Eastern Orthodoxy, has not found it easy to translate its great liturgical and spiritual treasures from rural and primitive existence to the urban and sophisticated life of modernity. Those emigrés who have settled in Western society have found that their *diaspora* churches cannot be like the great populist and establishment churches of Russia and Greece; they have to survive as nonconformist 'sects'.

I do not mean by this that they have had to invent new beliefs, but they do have to adopt the voluntary camaraderie of the sects. That is what we need to learn from sects. We look so closely and with such moralistic scrutiny at the religious content of sects, and the habit of mind that imagines that it alone has the full and unique expression of the faith, that we fail to notice what they have to offer.

Nowhere is this more true for Christianity than in the inner cities. How is Lutheranism doing in Berlin, or Episcopalianism in Detroit, or Anglicanism in London? They all face the same problem: their strength traditionally lay in parish life, traditional communities, and what the sociologists call 'cultural embeddedness'. The inner cities no longer respond, because the communities have dissolved or become permanently disfigured. You cannot predicate a parish life upon shifting populations and broken communities. Anglicanism, for example, may be surviving in the countryside of Hertfordshire, and indeed is truly embedded there, but she is adrift in the East End of London (Ahern and Davie 1987).

What sects do, and are doing with remarkable success in inner cities, is to create 'community' by private association or voluntary agreement. This may very well have to be the hallmark of the future church in modernity, just as it was in the early days of Christian existence. After all, lest we forget, the church, sociologically speaking, started as a sect of Judaism. The question modern sectarian formations have to ask themselves is also the same question as the early church asked: 'Are we to be exclusive or inclusive?' Too often modern sects have been too exclusivist and purist. But it need not always be so: sectarian formations without sectarian spirits are a genuine recipe for a future.

But on a more general level we need to realise that the church is not down and out because she is on the privatised and peripheral margins of society. She is, however, hemmed in by the Adversary. So God is calling us and gathering us where we are. I believe that he is also calling us to break out of the margins and take the battle to the Enemy. We worry about sectarian exclusiveness without realising that we have become used to living under siege. It is not only the sects that are guilty of fortress mentalities: we have come to believe that God is to be found only in our prayer groups, fellowships and denominational congregations.

In Egypt the Coptic church is forbidden by law to proselytise. Her members can convert to Islam, but it is a one-way street. A positive consequence of this is that the church has preserved her spiritual heritage and also maintained her community base. The negative consequence, however, is that Christians there have developed a ghetto mentality that can no longer think in terms of mission, but only survival.

We are a long way from Egypt, but in many ways the secular world is as merciless as Islam. It does not care how many revivals the church experiences in the private world as long as it stays where it is. The Devil is not powerful enough to prevent genuine spiritual and personal fulfilment in the church. She remains for him, even in modernity, enemy territory. His desire is to keep us inside our barracks (or, more appositely, behind the battlements of our homes). An army on the move is what he really fears.

6 CAPTIVE LIVES –
The insidiousness of modernity (Part two)

PLURALISM AND CONSUMER RELIGION

But we have not yet finished with insidious processes that sneak up on us and entangle us in their silent webs. Secularisation has meant for Christians, with the exception of North America, a steady decline in religious attendance. In the form of laicisation, Christian institutions and authority have been removed from the centre of public and social life. Living on the margins of society, Christians have made their home in the private world of the family and religious associations – their churches; this private world is really the world of leisure and personal and private quests for self-fulfilment.

If all this was not enough, Christians have had to discover that living in the private domain means living in a society of bewildering confusion and choice. For the process of privatisation has coincided with a proliferation of conflicting and contradictory philosophies, both religious and irreligious. Christianity, in short, now finds herself as merely one option in a spectrum of almost limitless options. In 1700 in England a peasant could not wake up in the morning and decide to convert to Buddhism, or change his religious allegiance to Islam. Such opportunities were not open to him and knowledge about them (for him at least) did not exist.

But today world travel, mass communications, immigration and emigration, and improved education have meant that the modern world has been turned into a global village where the full range of human *Weltanschauungen* are on sale In terms of social class and ethnic groups, modern advanced societies can be said to be pluralist: there is not a homogeneous entity such as the tribe but a heterogeneous mass of competing groups. But our societies can be said to be pluralist also on the level of world-views; consequently the private sphere of personal fulfilment resembles a giant supermarket with products on sale to suit everyone's personal tastes and pocket.

Religion may no longer control the marketplace, but she finds herself on sale as a consumer product. 'You pays your money and takes your choice' surely fits into the secular 'spirit of the age'. Where John Bunyan would have talked of the pilgrim's quest, we tend to think of the consumer looking for a good buy at the sales. Christianity is now on 'special offer' in multiform shapes and sizes. Competing in the open market with other religions, and with atheistic philosophies, there is a broad choice of 'real' and 'best' Christianities for anyone who wants to buy. I have suggested elsewhere (Walker 1986) that no doubt someone will soon publish *The Consumer Guide To God* so that people can pop in and out of churches with the same ease and comfort as they visit their favourite restaurants.

To be fair to modernity, the seeds of Christian pluralism were already sown before the rise of capitalism or world travel. The Reformation unfortunately also led to reformation *ad nauseam*, and the modern denomination was born. In the United States, which has no established church, denominationalism has always been the hallmark of its religious growth. Capitalism and denominations have grown hand in hand. Modernity has accelerated denominationalism – and sectarian formations – and hastened the commercialisation of Christianity. We all complain at the commercialisation of holy shrines such as Bethlehem and Lourdes, but do not always realise that we have succumbed to commercialism in a far more fundamental way: we have become consumerised.

The reason why cable and satellite television can be a success is because they cater to private worlds. Within the wider culture, there are literally thousands of 'little' or 'sub'-cultures with their own interests and consumer power. It does not even matter if some of these groups are rebellious or anti-capitalist, they can find a pitch in the marketplace. They might even become big business. Punk started as an anti-establishment pop culture determined to stand against the 'star' system in modern music. It soon became sucked into the mainstream commercial world. In England the magazine *Time Out* started as an alternative guide to London. It pioneered new forms of advertising (especially for 'gays'), and produced creative photographic formats and original journalistic techniques. Soon *Time Out* became a success and spawned a whole series of copycat magazines and even influenced religious journalism.

Christians have also discovered that subcultures equal commercial markets. Every time a new religious movement comes to the fore we find new magazines, newsletters, audio and visual tapes. These magazines increasingly look like secular 'rags'. *The Plain Truth* looks like *Time* magazine; Christian youth magazines in England and America are glossy and in full colour. They resemble *Playboy* without the nudes, and follow the formats of secular musical journals and the press of alternative lifestyles. New converts and old believers are asked not only to praise the Lord but to pass the contribution.

The techniques of Madison Avenue are employed to market new religions and personalities. Long before the rise of the New Religious Right, the Bible Belt had learnt successfully to adopt the methods of travelling salesmen and 'medicine men': not only exaggerated claims but also hypes, cajoling and flattery.

But if this seems to be merely the unacceptable face of religious capitalism, we must realise that Christianity finds it almost impossible to resist competition. *Laissez-faire*, in short, has come to dominate Christian behaviour as well as the secular economic order (cf. Templeton 1981: ch. 9). Christians buy television and radio time, adopt the glossy methods of the admen and the graphic artists, because they want to successfully compete with other secular or non-Christian products in the commercial yet private world. 'Why should the Devil have all the best tunes?' – the adage of Wesley, and later General Booth – is translated into 'Why should the Devil have all the best methods of communication?'

We can all be such purists that if we are not careful the gospel will never be preached for fear of offending good taste and traditional sensibilities. But the nub of the problem lies elsewhere. So often we find that the 'Revival Hours' and television specials are selling not only Christ but charismatic personalities and their organisations. When, for example, Oral Roberts told millions of Americans in January 1987 that God was going to 'call him home' unless viewers sent him pledges of one hundred dollars to meet the 4.6 million dollars he needed (a figure which was subsequently increased almost twofold) for his medical and missionary expansion, viewers by definition were asked to support him personally as this was *the* method for supporting God. I have yet to hear of a famous and successful 'televangelist' who has asked viewers to send in money to some other Christian organisation or to funds for Ethiopia or the World Health Organisation.

What is wrong with religious pluralism, and loved by the Evil One, is the spectacle of Christian groups and churches jostling for position in the marketplace. It is unfair to suggest that it is only television evangelists or charismatic leaders who do this. We see Orthodox repressing Protestants, Protestants nudging out Catholics, and Catholics holding off Protestants. Christendom in modernity does not encourage partnership, but rivalry. We all claim to believe in Truth who is the Lord Jesus himself, but we all believe that our special understanding of that Truth qualifies us to disqualify other Christian groups.

I am old-fashioned enough to believe that there really are true doctrines which can be distinguished from the false: apostasy and syncretism have always been problems for the Christian church. Very often, however, it is not doctrine that divides us, but pride and self-interest. Eastern Orthodoxy is united on doctrine but divided by ethnic traditions. She is still formally out of communion with the so-called Monophysite churches of Egypt and parts of the Middle East, but the real differences are so minimal that their separation is nothing less than a scandal. Quarrelsomeness characterises the Orthodox at their worst. Evangelicalism is a world where the fundamentals of Christianity as understood by the fathers of the

Reformation are held in basic agreement. Yet what corner of
Christendom is more factional than evangelicalsim? Anglicans and Methodists agree on virtually all points of doctrine,
but cannot seem to forgive or forget their historic differences
and rejoin together. Pentecostals agree on the essentials of
their faith, but whenever charismatic religion appears we see
not only schism from traditional Christianity but division
among Pentecostalists themselves. Catholicism is growing in
the modern world, but where is the evidence that it intends to
do so in partnership with other denominations?

Division can be a question of conscience and preserving
orthodoxy from heterodoxy. Truth itself divides. But so often
our separateness is a mixture of ignorance, apathy, indifference to other Christian confessions, and self-interest.
Christian rivalry means organisation against organisation,
ecclesiastical   structure   against   extra-denominational
structure, leadership against leadership. Such rivalry is a
competition for scarce resources both in terms of money
and personnel. The kingdom is being proclaimed, but
from a thousand different empires. New visions so often
lead to new structures and sects. The direct result of this is
proliferation and further grist to the mill of pluralism.

I remember going with Os Guinness in 1964 to Speakers'
Corner at Hyde Park. A man from the Protestant Truth
Society was telling us how the Catholic Church was still selling
indulgences up and down the land of England. Another man
from the Catholic Truth Society, who was also speaking on
'Truth', was within earshot. I was violently anti-Catholic at
the time (being under the influence of Dr David Martyn
Lloyd-Jones!) but I was so incensed by the Protestant truth-
bearer that I remember piping-up (I was a very young Christian then), 'Can we have less of this and more of the gospel?' I
was not angry because the scene was unseemly, but because I
thought it was sinful to attack other confessions in that way.
I think that I feel even more strongly about that today. At its
best, our competition with each other keeps us divided and
ineffective in our war against evil. At their worst, our divisions are a refusal to repent of our sins. I have not got much
time for the sort of milk-and-water ecumenism that would

invite us all to come together on the basis of the lowest common denominator. But while I think it unrealistic that we can expect major institutional change to take place in the near future, we must come together in order to stand against the common attacks of the Enemy through modernity. This is not a question of realistic expectations, but a question of moral imperative (see chapter nine).

Pluralism not only means that we compete with false religions and yet remain divided among ourselves, but it also means that our own proliferation and competition in adding more options for the spiritual consumer leads to the likelihood that we are devaluing spiritual commitment. Recently I was invited to preach at a small church in southern England. The minister there was thrilled, as he put it, at the 'real growth we have had'. It turned out that the new converts were nomads who so far in their spiritual wanderings had sampled spiritualism, new religious movements, house churches, and Anglican charismatic renewal. That is the trouble with pluralism: it encourages us to think of spiritual commitment with the faithlessness of consumer whimsicality.

If we are going to win converts, we want good Muslims, faithful Jews and caring atheists who come to us because they see the fulfilment of their hopes in the person of Christ. Christianity is not a 'hard-sell' designed to collect the gullible and the spiritually confused and to keep them in our little world through gimmickry, secularist know-how and frothy excitability. Private but 'turned on' Christians become merely religious variants of the secular hedonistic culture if we are not careful. To be a Christian is to feed on Jesus, not to buy him. That is the essential difference between the Christian concept of commitment and belonging and the vagaries of religious consumerism. Consumerists soon pass on and join either our Enemy (often unwittingly) or return to the open prison of the modern world.

MASS MEDIA AND THE QUALITY OF CULTURE[1]

Up to now in these two chapters on the insidiousness of modernity, I have concentrated on what might be called 'sociological processes', but I want to end this section with a technological process which I believe has transformed the nature of advanced industrial societies, and for the worse. I am talking here about the pervasiveness of the mass media, and in particular television.

But readers must forgive me if I do not launch into a stinging attack upon the triteness of 'light entertainment' programmes, the sheer banality and crassness of TV quiz shows, or even the violence and overt sexuality of adult shows. I do think these things are important, but they are not the crux of the matter. As unfashionable as the thesis now is, I think that Marshall McLuhan was prophetically correct in the 1960s (1967) when he saw that it was not the content of television that posed a danger to civilisation, but the medium itself.

His argument was that the way in which television works as a method of communication affects the way in which we understand and interpret the world. Because McLuhan was considered a romanticist, and because also his theory was prophecy rather than hard fact, it has fallen into disrepute. In particular McLuhan claimed that books would be displaced, and that literature generally would deteriorate. On the surface, at least, this does not appear to have happened. But twenty years have passed since McLuhan's theories, and I think that there is strong evidence that he was right. This is of grave concern to Christians, who spend as much time watching television as everyone else. My central thesis is that television distorts and trivialises reality, and has rendered the citizens of the advanced industrial world into passive spectators who seek only to be diverted and amused.

But first some facts.[2] There are over 576,000,000 television sets in the world. In North America there are 844 commercial stations (as of January 1984) serving eighty-three million families. Nearly all that number of families have colour television and forty-five million have more than one set. In Great Britain by January 1985, eighty-five per cent of the population would watch television on a typical day. (By 1987 the *Guardian* media expert claimed on London radio that it had risen to ninety per cent.)

In the United States in 1983, 19,681,000 televisions were sold. By 1984 in addition to public and commercial aerial television services there were 5,800 cable TV systems serving a population of 34.1 million subscribers (that is: 40.7 per cent of television homes). In 1983 the total advertising expenditure on television was more than seventy-three million dollars (compared to just over sixteen million dollars spent on newspaper advertising).

In Britain in January 1985 the viewing public were watching on average four and a half hours' television a day, or thirty-two and a half hours a week. This is still small beer compared to America, where the average viewing time is 7.38 hours a day or fifty-three hours and twenty-six minutes a week.

Robert Bower (1985), tracing the changes in television audiences since the 1960s, notes that more women watch television than men (though this is mainly because women spend more time in the home), more blacks than whites, and more blue-collar workers than white-collar workers. The majority of Americans see television in a positive light, although those with higher education are increasingly critical and there is a disquiet at violence and sex on television. Between 1960 and 1980, however, the proportion of the population that thought television gave them the best and most complete news coverage had tripled and major surveys in 1970 and 1980 considered the increase in news coverage to be the most important change in television (Bower 1985: 133). Despite the critical views of the better-educated members of the public, there does not seem to be a strong correlation between antipathy to television and actual numbers of hours watched. In short, even when they do not love it people watch it.

The BBC research into trends in viewing demonstrates a major switch from radio and newspapers to television between the years 1960 and 1980. When asked in a recent survey what was the most entertaining medium in Britain – television, magazines, newspapers, or radio – seventy per cent said television. In a similar result to that of the American studies, the majority thought that television gave the most complete news coverage. Television came off as by far the most beneficial, up-to-date, useful and entertaining of the modern media. Conversely, little interest or appreciation was shown towards newspapers. It may be that at the present time the British are more appreciative of their television than Americans. This could of course be due to the fact that British television is much better than American television (most American intellectuals seem to think so). America, however, has been a television culture longer than Britain, and perhaps the novelty effect of the new technology has worn off a little sooner.

In real terms we are now into our second and third generation of television culture. It is precisely because we are immersed in it that we find it very difficult to stand back from it and see what it is doing to our world. The most brilliant analysis in recent years, which has again taken up McLuhan's thesis, but adapted and adopted it to the present time, has been Neil Postman's *Amusing Ourselves To Death* (1987).

Postman argues that we have been too obsessed with visions of totalitarianism and fears of Orwell's 1984. These fears are justified, he argues, in the context of socialist societies where they are already grounded in reality. Certainly it is the case that collective man, with his predilection for totalitarianism, is always likely to end up under the control and in fear of 'Big Brother'. Postman sees Western societies more in terms of what I have called individualistic man: societies committed to hedonism, consumerism, and personal freedom. He thinks that Huxley's *Brave New World* is more apposite to our situation because in Huxley's futuristic novel citizens are controlled by pleasure.

Postman cannot see freedom-loving Americans marching manacled and regimented into oblivion, but wonders whether they may not dance and dream their lives away. In the 1950s during the Cold War, any hint of anti-American sentiment was seen as treason. Today we hear (and more importantly 'see') the New Religious Right standing up against godlessness and communism, but, says Postman, 'Who is prepared to take arms against a sea of amusements?' (1987: 161).

Let us follow some of Postman's arguments and see how they fit into our broader concerns. Firstly, he is at pains to point out that new technology often brings with it far more than sheer hardware: it alters our understanding of the world. He cites Mumford's work *Technics and Civilization* (1934), in which the author insists that the invention of the clock in the fourteenth century changed our attitude to the universe. A piece of power machinery produced a 'product' of seconds and minutes. This product, claimed Mumford, dissociated time from human and natural events and nourished the belief that it was an independent world which could be understood in mathematically measurable sequences. Time is now understood as what the clock says, and what the clock says is measurably true. I shall have more to say about numbers and reality in our next chapter on science and morals, but for now it is sufficient to understand how the clock came to dominate our world. It really came into its own when the commercial and consumer world of capitalism arrived. Rationality in the marketplace could be divided into segments by a timepiece. As Postman puts it, 'the clock made us into time-keepers, and then time-savers, and now time-servers' (1987: 11). The image of Lewis Carroll's White Rabbit bewailing the fact that 'I am late, I am late' haunts modernity, and we think of time as precious time, so precious that in our business we never have time for prayer, for quiet or reflection. Of course in the private world of the home we always have time to watch television.

Postman, however, is not really arguing against technology but against certain forms of communication. The trouble with television, as he sees it, is the medium itself. He argues that you cannot use Indian smoke signals to do philosophy, because 'Its form excludes the content'. He thinks that, 'You cannot do political philosophy on television. Its form works against the content' (1987: 7).

Oral culture is at the heart of all human history: people who live together talk together. Oral cultures, like the Aramaic Palestine of Jesus, or tribal Africa, are cultures which put the stress on personal communication and conveying meaning and truth through narrative and parable. When cultures become literary cultures something happens to language which changes it and people also.

In the first place language in oral cultures is always language for somebody, or a group of persons in particular; you can only communicate by speaking directly to a listener or an audience. But with the invention of writing speech can be 'frozen' for all to see. It can be taken out of its original context and made to stand on its own. A writer addresses an imaginary audience, and once thoughts are written down in a certain order and shape they encourage the 'grammarian, the logician, the rhetorician, the historian, the scientist – all those who must hold language before them so that they can see what it means, where it errs, and where it is leading' (Postman 1987: 12).

The invention of writing, then, led to greater precision, opened up the possibility of a wider discourse than the immediate group, and assisted reasoning itself. But writing remained a specialist and laborious job. A book in the Middle Ages would take many months to copy by hand. The Holy Scriptures were so precious that it is not altogether surprising that they remained as a focus of liturgical meditation and monkish study. Nobody deliberately kept copies of the Bible from the masses. The word of God was in short supply – until the invention of printing.

This printing, or typography, allowed for the dissemination of information, study, science or whatever, to reach the literate population; it also aided a rise in literacy. The Reformation would not have had the effect that it did if it was not for the invention of the printed word. Postman thinks that typography actually encouraged individualism at the expense of community. It aided the Reformation, but it also aided the growth of modern science and undermined religious sensibility. Without a doubt the invention of writing and the establishment of a literary culture through printing destroyed the epic form of poetry which was intended to be oral, lyrical, and of musical resonance. Rhetoric and the printed word are always in uneasy tension.

Nevertheless, argues Postman, although typography may have had negative effects on medieval culture, its benefits far outstripped its less positive features.

That ours has been a literary culture, argues Postman, may

have sometimes militated against oral culture, but in time it came to reinforce personal communication and also influence it in a fundamental way. Whether it is in giving a speech, preaching a sermon, or delivering a lecture, we find that our presentation is directly affected by the use of books.

We can see a useful illustration of this idea in Bradbury's *Fahrenheit 451*, which as we have already seen is about a world that represses the written word for the visual image. Books allow reflection, self-knowledge, personal illumination; people are converted through reading books. In Bradbury's novel there is a wonderful synergy between the book and the person, when at the end of the story we meet the book people who have learnt a book or chapters of the Bible off by heart: they have become the book. This is not a return to pure oral culture, because the written books are still literary even though they are committed to memory.

Postman likes to call the age of typography the 'Age of Exposition'. It is an age, he asserts, that has served us well for over four hundred years. If it helped create the age of Enlightenment, it also sustained the great eighteenth-century revivals of Methodism and the Evangelical Awakenings of the late eighteenth century and early nineteenth century. He argues that Jonathan Edwards, George Whitefield, and Charles Finney were men of learning and culture. They appealed to the heart, but believed in the importance of good theology and 'right believing'.

Postman (1987: 13) thinks that we are now undergoing 'a vast and trembling shift from the magic of writing to the magic of electronics'. A shift, he believes, that is as great as that from oral to literary culture. He calls this new age – somewhat out of desperation – 'The Age of Showbusiness'.

Obviously Postman is attached to literary culture, but it is not because he is bookish: it is because he believes that television cannot deal with serious, moral, and religious issues in the same way that books can. In the past, in a world without electricity, there was little time for reading. Reading was a serious business. Mothers read to their children, and the Bible was part of family life. Perhaps we should add to that much abused phrase 'the family that prays together stays together' the rider 'and that reads together too'. To read was to 'better yourself', to learn and to wonder. Casual reading did not really come into existence before the 'penny-dreadfuls' of late Victorian England.

The mass media did not start with television but with newspapers, but news spread slowly in nineteenth-century Europe and America. The crucial breakthrough, according to Postman, was the telegraph. When Samuel Morse invented the telegraph in the 1840s it meant that news could be sent directly from state to state, and in time from America to Europe. This, Postman asserts, altered communal communication. Usually in the pre-electronic world, knowing something meant knowing something that was useful to me, or something that belonged to my family, group, community. We know from our own experience, do we not, that news which is personal – that is for us – has a different character to mere information? But, Postman adds, 'The telegraph made information into a commodity, a "thing" that could be bought and sold irrespective of its uses or meaning' (1987: 67).

The very fact that the telegraph could pass information out of one context and insert it into another meant that fragmented and disconnected knowledge would pass along the wires whether anyone wanted it or not. The telegraph was not interested in merely passing 'real' news, but would sell gossip, trivia, novelty, scandal or whatever. Soon newspapers started to stock telegraphed information. Papers became internationalised and began to peddle in information for information's sake.

Of course, to return to our own concerns, it is not surprising that individualistic man was happy with a diversion from working for the machine. Newspapers began to appeal to the 'lowest common denominators'. It is true that gossip had existed in the eighteenth century and the age of satire, but that was for a small minority. Today in America and England it is assumed that we all want to know the 'kiss and tell' stories of the 'stars' – and we do. Everybody wants to know what is happening at Buckingham Palace and whether Prince William has got a cold, or Prince Charles has lost a little more hair, and whether it is really true that Princess Diana loves to spend all her time 'dancing the night away'. We may or may not think that President Reagan is the greatest president of the United States, but we all want to know if he dyes his hair, wears make-up all day and night, and is going to have any more parts of his body removed.

It is difficult sometimes to distinguish real news from news about those who are in the news, and even news about those who read the news on television. Postman (1987: 69) asks us to ask ourselves, how often do we hear news on television, radio, or the newspapers, which causes us to change our plans for the day, provides insight into our daily and personal problems, or causes us to take some action that we would otherwise not have taken?

The telegraph introduced a language which was not the language of community or literary culture. It introduced us to a discourse of headlines, impersonal information, fragmented stories, and sensational and novel news. 'News took the form of slogans, to be noted with excitement, to be forgotten with dispatch' (Postman 1987: 71).

Postman thinks that as dramatic as Morse's invention was, and despite its assault upon literary culture, 'the Age of Exposition' might have survived if it was not for the invention of photography. At almost the same moment as Morse was telegraphing, Louis Daguerre was reproducing nature by capturing her in pictorial form. The photograph produced its own revolution – a revolution in graphics – where images replaced words. The photograph aids the dictum 'seeing is believing', but in fact pictures can do many things besides reproduce reality. A photograph of a whip may be just a whip, but it might also evoke sadism or brutality. Images are evocative by definition, and help to create moods and illusions.

Add music to stir the feelings, and you have the ingredients for magic and enchantment. The early cinema did just that, but television, thinks Postman, is the advanced synthesis of the seduction of telegraphy and moving pictures – a seduction that does not happen occasionally on a 'big screen', but every day in your own home. The British journalist Tom Davies has argued that media is obsessed with the novel, the perverted and the bizarre (1982: 315) at the expense of permanence and reflection. And now we are coming to the crux of it all, and it is time to build on Postman's analysis and see where the problem really lies.

Given that information is a commodity – and this is becoming even more true with microtechnology – but given also that so much of this information is garbled, fragmented, unimportant, trivial, what is the best thing to do with it all? The answer is to turn it into entertainment, a peek-a-boo world 'where now this event, now that, pops into view for a moment, then vanishes again' (Postman 1987: 78–79).

No doubt many of us worry about the 'junk' programmes on television and would like to see more serious programmes, but the trouble with television is that it handles 'junk' very well. It is what it does best. The problem is that it cannot resist turning serious programmes into entertainment. To produce 'good' television means for a producer to provide programmes that are immediate, arresting, gripping, informative. He wants high ratings first, critical applause second, and thirdly professional pride in a job well done. He does not expect to provide worthy television; and worthy television, as we all know, is boring![3] Neither does he intend that his programmes should last in our memories, because as we all know television programmes are instantly forgettable: there are so many other channels to switch to, so many dramatic images to catch the eye, to make us forget that 'good' programme we saw only a minute ago.

There is no doubt that television can entertain us, but it is a debatable point as to whether it can do anything else. When television purports to inform, teach, instruct or uplift, it does so within an entertainment framework.

Consider the news. In both the United States and Great Britain emphasis is on dramatic presentation with attractive presenters and colourful music. When in Britain women newsreaders were introduced, this was such a novelty that they became news themselves. For months men up and down the land of England wondered what Angela Rippon's legs might look like. And the BBC, as if knowing that Britain's first lady newscaster was more sensational than the news itself, eventually obliged the public by releasing Ms Rippon in a song and dance act on *The Morecambe and Wise Show*. If that was not enough, Ms Rippon's rival on the Independent Broadcasting Network also became a celebrity. Both ladies featured in the news. They grabbed the headlines of the tabloid newspapers on many occasions. Ms Ford's row with her television boss, over whom she threw a glass of wine, was even re-created in a daily newspaper by an artist's dramatic reconstruction.

The men newscasters have not been left out. They have written biographies and opened supermarkets. Reginald Bosanquet, the newsreader for ITV's *News at Ten*, was constantly headline news. It was assumed that people wanted to know about his hairpiece, his drinking habits, his girl friends, his political views. (I wonder how many people gave it a second thought when he died?)

What could be more bizarre than turning newsreaders into 'stars' and personalities because they read the news! Only television could do that. The news itself rarely deals with news items for more than forty-five seconds. Most people forget the news items within a short time, and in America it has been shown that within an hour of major news programmes twenty-one per cent of people interviewed could not remember a single news story.

Indeed the whole problem with television as a teaching medium is that it is difficult to retain information presented in terms of vivid images and personalities. What television does best, of course, is to create personalities. The British often think that American television is inferior because it is so overtly taken up with 'show biz'. But this is a peculiar view when you recall that British television weathermen are now chosen for their oddity, interesting regional accents, or show-manship. (No doubt this is a cover for the fact they can never get the weather forecast right!) It certainly cannot be said that Independent Broadcasting is more guilty of entertainment wrappings than the BBC. For years the British public have been offered their 'serious' television by eccentrics with strange voices and unusual mannerisms. The British have always loved eccentrics and never more so than when they are seen on TV.

What has been really superb television over the years in the astronomical field? Well of course the answer is *The Sky At Night*, with the amateur astronomer Patrick Moore. With his rapid-fire old English accent, ruffled and never-fitting clothes, and Coco-the-clown hairstyle, he has become an English institution.

And what could be better for science than the English dancing dervish, Dr Magnus Pyke – his arms twirling and whirling like windmills sending meaningless semaphore messages in accompaniment to his breathless reports? I was once on the high street at Chiswick when he was being filmed in front of a Greek store. Before the camera whirred Dr Pyke warmed up with a few swathing strokes, like the blade of a helicopter about to lift off. Who could forget him? But who can remember what he said?

And botany and nature studies will never be the same again after Dr David Bellamy. With his big, burly, rough good looks, the worst blocked nasal passages in history, and an ebullient enthusiasm for all growing things, he has endeared himself to the viewing public. He is a good communicator, a genuine scientist, but above all he is a personality and an entertainer.

None of the above remarks is intended as cheap *ad hominem*, I want only to point out how difficult it is for television not to provide entertainment. The lines between light entertainment and serious television are so blurred as to be invisible. Why is this? It has little to do with producers, script writers or directors: it is the way the medium works. A visual medium presenting a flow of images and ideas finds it is difficult to treat matters with seriousness and reflection. Makers of films and documentaries want to capture an idea, a position, a view as an *idée fixe*. It simply does not work on television if people are allowed to 'think aloud' or ask for a minute or two while they reflect on the issue. People get bored with bumbling or indecisiveness, and film-makers dread an interviewee who cannot make his point in the required time segment.

In my own work on religious broadcasting I have learnt that it is impossible to convey the nuances and complications of an argument that you can develop in a seminar or a lecture, or even an everyday conversation. Most of the filmed documentaries that I have done are divided into forty-five seconds for each reply. So often the replies are not what the director wants, so they have to be redone or edited. Religious people often think that television producers of religious broadcasting are unscrupulous or out to convey false impressions of Christian positions. This is not my experience. It is the medium itself that defeats them, even if they are trying hard to be objective and fair.

Of course religion can be sheer entertainment also. When *The Sea of Faith* was produced for the BBC it was submerged in a sea of images that were breathtaking, but the 'value' of the programme was in its controversy and novelty, not in the seriousness of its content. So much of American religious television is overtly 'show business' that it raises the serious question of whether people think that the content of religion is in fact the entertainment of television shows.

And all the time, particularly in America, serious news items, as well as opera, drama and religion, are interrupted by advertising; each item a 'little show' of its own. Adverts were once a means of conveying facts about products. They have long since ceased to be slogans aimed at what they think people need; it is market research that determines how an advert is prepared, not the excellence of the product itself. And the populace must be amused and entertained and treated with the most lavish and gorgeous colour and flowing images that technology can create.

And after being bombarded with the 'little shows', with their jingles and catch phrases, we return to *Revival Hour*, where we were contemplating whether to give our hearts to Jesus. But if we have forgotten what we were going to do, there are so many other good things to see: with a touch of a button we can watch a soft-porn movie or listen to the president.

But politics itself has become a world of images and personalities. It is so easy to give the wrong impression if you do not look right or do not *appear* to be sincere. Mrs Thatcher has changed her hairstyles and voice in the last ten years. She no longer seems to be so strident. But Michael Foot was never able to appear as a man in charge of the Labour Party. His wild hair and casual clothes had 'Hampstead socialist' written all over them. But more crucially Michael Foot demonstrated a cardinal rule of television: if you want to impress you must be clear, precise, forthright, witty, and preferably funny. (President Reagan has proved that the 'one liners' have it when it comes to political television: 'There you go again' was one of his most successful ploys when he wanted to put an opponent down.) Foot appeared to the British public as a man without direction in charge of a party with no clear policies. And yet this was the man whom most members of Parliament, on both sides of the House, have recognised as probably the greatest orator in the House of Commons in the last twenty-five years! Would Lincoln, with his angular features, strange beard and wonderfully crafted speeches, make President in a televised world? Rhetoric is most at home in the age of exposition. (The Rev. Jesse Jackson's powerful run for the White House in 1988 was at least a reminder that television cannot totally obliterate charismatic appeal.)

It is possible to learn to sparkle in the camp meetings and revivalist tents and become an adept at television, but few have achieved credibility in both arenas. Oral Roberts is probably the best example in America. But Pat Robertson, who is one of the best television performers in North America (and a presidential hopeful), is a thoroughbred 'televangelist' but with little track record in mass meetings. Pat Robertson, like the American president and Harold Wilson the former Labour prime minister of Britain, learnt the art of chatting to the family audience; they knew how to come right into your front room and talk to you face to face.

The informality and chattiness of television make us feel at home with the 'stars' and the personalities. They certainly seem to be at home with each other. Dr Billy Graham swaps one-liners with George Burns, Kris Kristofferson talks to Kermit the frog, Neil Kinnock appears in a pop video, Hollywood personalities mix with the president and appear on Jerry Falwell's *Old Time Revival Hour*, Mrs Thatcher has intimate chats with BBC's Jimmy Young, who is as convincing with the prime minister as he is in his interviews with ladies who use Ariel washing powder (no irony intended).

This cosy, warm and intimate world invites you to participate in it merely by watching and listening. You can feel part of the world events during news time, become caught up in the gossip of the day (which like the news has an ephemeral quality that refuses to stay in our consciousness), imagine that you are present at a court-room drama, and be given a front seat at your favourite spectator sport. If you wish to be really taken out of yourself there is always an exotic location to visit, a 'soap' where you vicariously experience how (you imagine) the rich behave. And in Britain nothing is more alluring than brass-tacks existence with the regulars of *EastEnders* and *Coronation Street*.

So real is the plastic culture that television creates, that when we drag ourselves away from the 'tube' and look in our newspapers we find that they are full of stories about the personalities of television. And television tells us what the newspapers are saying about itself, and where you can get the latest videos and what films to see and what show to pop out and see before you come back and watch 'old faithful', who is always there just waiting to be switched on or switched over but hardly ever to be switched off.

Television says there are no real class divisions any more, because we all share in the same culture. It must be true, for when we go out to work or to school, or to see our boyfriends or our girlfriends, we have so many things in common. 'Did you see so and so last night?' is a good opening gambit for conversation, and we discuss the 'news of the day' as television presents it, and talk of this personality and that programme (some of them are so challenging aren't they?). And if we are Christians we talk about how wonderful *Shadowlands* was. But that does not really matter, for we only thought it wonderful for two days, because something else caught our eye and took our attention.

And in our private worlds, cut off from each other not only by our separate houses but within our own front rooms – for we cannot talk to each other when the television window insists that we watch its amusements – we can sit back and let the prancing and faithless images of a pluralist world walk right into our homes and hearts without a thought of resistance. And if we are truly moral we switch over from the pornography and the violence and we watch the news, the chat-shows, the scientific documentaries and, of course, the religious programmes. It never occurs to us to switch off: we switch over because we expect to be entertained and amused.

And one wonders if Marshall McLuhan was so wrong about literature, for when we reach out for that book before we drop off to sleep it is probably for pulp literature that deals with the absurd, the horrific, the unusual. Or we reach for our *Reader's Digest*, the natural way to read in our post-literary world, for it is made up of fragments, 'howlers', abridged sayings and 'one-liner' jokes. Perhaps we have already bought our *Reader's Digest Bible* so we can read edited highlights of God's holy word.

It is right that we should pay attention to the content of television programmes, because this is an area of ethics and Christian alertness. In Great Britain Mrs Mary Whitehouse has been one of the most despised and abused women of the last twenty years because she has insisted that there are right and decent standards that should apply to television as well as everyone else. Today, in the light of the sexual and violent saturation of the passive viewing community, her stance seems not so much puritanical as simply commonsensical. I am sure that G. K. Chesterton and C. S. Lewis would have applauded her.

But it may very well be that the deeper problem of television lies in its grip upon the thinking and moral processes of our societies. What we need is not better television but less television.

Television is cosy and alluring at the same time. It appeals to the voyeur in us, and beguiles us into thinking that we are participating in the great historical and cultural events of our times when in fact we are powerless in the public world where the military, bureaucratic and scientific estates rule modernity.

But we install television sets in our bedrooms and kitchens so that we do not miss anything, even though for so many of us 'news' and 'soaps', 'religion' and 'pornography' flicker across our screens like the disconnected unreality of stroboscopic light. But thank God for the 'stars' and personalities: they hold the whole fantasy together and give meaning and substance to this moving magic-lantern show. And when the advertisements appear they merely punctuate this grammar of showbusiness so that the whole of television is like a never-ending soap opera: art, it insists, is real life.

We have no difficulty justifying a life immersed in this circus culture; after all, we have a ring-side seat. And there are so many good things about television that we can legitimate it in so many ways. 'Look how it attracts our best brains from colleges and universities.' Of course we might think it a sad state of affairs when our intellectual élite would rather record and comment on the news than make it. So much creativity and talent spent on amusing us in three thousand different ways!

'But, of course, television is educational.' But is it? Like our microtechnology, which is itself linked to the monitor and television screen, we are bombarded with information and quiz shows, but mainly on the level of 'trivial pursuits'. Are not the British *Mastermind* and *University Challenge* quiz games trivia for those with photographic memories? For the rest of us, we are entertained by the brilliance of those who know absolutely everything about nothing of consequence. Can television teach the skills of a literary culture; does it really aid reading, reasoning, problem-solving, debate and moral understanding?

'It is wonderful, though, for the old people. So many of them are alone.' Indeed they are, and never more so when they are forced to watch television because there is no one to talk to. Go into the homes for the elderly and see what television does to old people. Many of them will not be able to talk to you because most of their day is spent being talked at by the 'tube': they never have to talk back and could not even if they wanted to do so. Television keeps them out of the way and keeps them mute.

And what do parents really feel about television for their children? 'Television is so educational for the children, and it keeps them happy.' Often this really means 'Television is wonderful because it gets them out of our way' or 'Television keeps the peace' – when will we learn that peace and quiet are not the same thing? – 'and gives us more time to ourselves.' 'We do not need Dr Spock any more, or educational toys, and we certainly do not need books: we have open access to the world.'

A FINAL NOTE ON PROCESSES

I have tried in these two chapters to look at some processes which I believe are insidious and the work of the Enemy. We have looked at *secularisation*, and in particular the concept of laicisation, and we have seen how this process has pushed the church out of the mainstream of public life into the tributaries and backwaters of modern society.

The whole of modern culture, not just the church, has become privatised and individualised. Self-fulfilment is sought at home and in our leisure hours. This *privatisation* has no culture of its own but is the abode of a myriad subcultures and competing world-views. It is a private world of separate realities, a *pluralism* of views and peoples.

And if all this was not enough, the technology of *mass media*, and especially television, keeps us locked in our homes – and away from each other – where we passively absorb the fantasy world of media-amusement. And we are living *captive lives* though we think we are free.

Part Two

ENEMY PROPAGANDA

7 SCIENTIFIC SORCERY –
Science, scientism, and the collapse of moral philosophy

In the previous section I have attempted to show some of the ways in which the processes of modernity insinuate their secular habits into our consciousness. Subliminally and insidiously we become conditioned into these habits – these modes of thinking and acting – without noticing the effects they have on our lives.

As Christians we need to recognise that modernity has meant a fundamental change in the infrastructure of Western culture, forcing out the world of community and face-to-face relationships and replacing them with what Martin Buber (1959) has called 'technical relations'.

The modern world, whether it be capitalism or socialism, is dominated by the technical and impersonal power of science, bureaucracy and industry. Rationality and scientific mastery have now taken precedence over personal and spiritual values, which have been relegated to the private and competing worlds of consumer choice.

Modernity, however, has not only brought with it changes in the nature of social and communal life: it has offered us new philosophies to replace the old ones. The process of secularisation, in other words, has been accompanied by corresponding doctrines and secular beliefs in the field of academic enquiry. Not all these philosophical changes pose a direct threat to the church. On the other hand we need to realise that many post-Enlightenment doctrines are at loggerheads with traditional Christian doctrine. There are many areas that we could examine – ranging from aesthetics to psychological theory – but I would like to concentrate on just two enquiries that I believe have become effective voices for enemy propaganda. These are science and theology itself. I believe that both scientific theorising and theology can be rooted in God, but when they submit entirely to reason, or the affections, they become transformed into weapons against the church.

I do not want in this chapter to pick a quarrel with science. On the contrary I want to support it and see it as complementary to the gospel. I think that such a claim is justified because, as the early Puritans recognised, science is not only the exercise of God-given freedom and creativity but it is also a means of grasping something of the wonder and mystery of God's created order.

Truth for a Christian is not divisible. A dualism that divides sacred from profane truth, or holy truth from scientific truth, is false. Truth is God himself, who is revealed in the universe as both person and action. Apprehending the truth may involve different approaches. We can, for example, approach God directly through the Holy Spirit. We can do this because he has already approached us directly in the historical person of Jesus of Nazareth. Reading the words of Holy Scripture also leads us to the Word, Jesus the Son of God, who through the Spirit shows us and unites us to the Father.

But our Holy God is also the creator God and he has endowed us with reason and human senses. Through these God-given attributes we can discover the truths of God's world, his creation, by discovery and quest. These truths are not synonymous with God himself, because God's world is not identical to his person (we are not heretics), but their existence is rooted in God, for he alone sustains and nurtures his created order.

Often we think of science as the disciplines of physics, chemistry, biology, botany and newer syntheses of the natural sciences (biochemistry, for example). Each of these disciplines has its own subject matter, theories appropriate to its subject, and a 'body of knowledge' accumulated over the years. What binds all these disciplines together, and makes them all science and not common sense or magic, is a common commitment to the scientific method. It is the method of science, the way in which it investigates reality, that makes it unique. And it is rigour that characterises this method. Of course many other disciplines employ rigour but not in quite the way of science.

In fact the logic of scientific enquiry is extremely complex and philosophers of science are divided over how in fact science actually works (Lakatos and Musgrave 1970). Strictly speaking, the philosopher Sir Karl Popper insisted, science must always be understood as a method which is the servant of truth; it is not concerned with truth *per se*, because that is the task of philosophy (Popper 1976: ch. 10). He preferred to see the procedures of science as leading to the validation of theories and hypotheses (ironically by trying to falsify them!).[1]

Given this difficulty, I want to say just a few things about the scientific method in order to find out what we are not going to quarrel with, for my fight is with what I want to call 'scientism' – and this has nothing to do with science at all, but an abuse of it by scientists and philosophers. Scientism arises, as we shall see, when philosophers – and sometimes theorists of society – insist that science encapsulates all reality and can be the only arbiter of truth.

SCIENTIFIC METHOD AND THE SCIENTIFIC STANCE

In everyday life we use our senses, but this is for practical reasons, not in order to understand and manipulate the world through theory. What science does is to look at the world through the eyes of a particular theory (or sets of theories). These theories are never absolute but always provisional. They are dependent on being sustained by hard evidence, evidence that is gathered by experimentation, hypothesis and observation. Theories are often not directly testable, but if they are sound one can deduce hypotheses or tests from them which are themselves testable through observation. If a hypothesis is successful it supports the general theory; if it is not, it calls into question the theory. Gradually repeated and rigorous tests derived from the general theory either support the theory or show that it is in need of modification.

Gravity, for example, cannot be tested directly, but its effects can. We could be rigorous and work out exactly how long it takes for an object to travel to the ground from a certain height. And we would not ask people to take our word for it; they could repeat the test themselves. If we were to drop an egg in space we would notice that it would float instead of drop. We would need to account for that fact. It could mean that gravity is not applicable in every part of the physical universe. In which case we would need to know why not. It might be that gravity is deficient as a theory. What will determine our answers will not be mere speculation (though science permits the wildest speculation) but further rigorous testing of hypotheses that will help us make up our minds.

Looking at the figure on the opposite page we can understand science as a treadmill or a continual process of hypothesis testing, observation, remodification of theories, and so on. A general theory may be able to generate many workable hypotheses and lead to many discoveries but still be ultimately unsatisfactory. In cosmology, for example, Ptolemy thought of the world as the centre of the universe (a geocentric model), but even though this was wrong he was still able to accurately chart the heavens and the almanack derived from his observations enabled medieval sailors to cross the oceans. When eventually it was realised that the earth was only one planet that was in orbit round the sun (a heliocentric universe) and Copernicus and Galileo restructured the whole of ancient cosmology and physics, the new universe that emerged was quite different to Ptolemy's system. In the seventeenth century Newton created a synthesis of the new cosmology and physics, but even though this synthesis was to lead to many great discoveries and remain scientific orthodoxy for well over two hundred years it too eventually had to give way to a superior theory (that is one with greater explanatory power), Einstein's theory of relativity.

Science, then, is a dynamic process that moves from fairly stable and settled work to periods of crisis and major change (Kuhn 1970). The scientist himself is a person whose approach to his method should be of the utmost rigour and criticism. He should be open-minded and prepared to accept

The Dynamic Process of Scientific Method

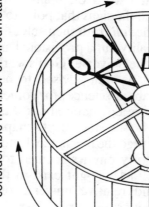

GENERAL THEORY
Theoretical propositions of relationships between facts thought to hold over a considerable number of circumstances

HYPOTHESES
Potentially testable hunches of factual relationships deduced from Theory believed to hold in specific circumstances

EMPIRICAL ENQUIRY
Discovery of new facts through observation to help test hypotheses

TESTING OF HYPOTHESES
Use of controlled experimentation and observation; must be capable of repeatability

confirmed hypotheses support the General Theory

Unconfirmed or partially confirmed hypotheses lead to modification or complete reformulation of General Theory

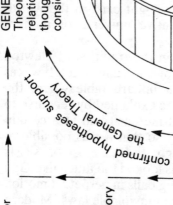

new evidence even if it contradicts cherished theories. (In fact scientists are often not like that at all, but that is the ideal.)

There is little place for complacency or dogmatic certainties in science. Scientific reality is extremely fragile and today's orthodoxies may be tomorrow's heresies. In this respect science is quite different from theology, because although theology should be rigorous and is always in need of reformulation its axioms are rooted in revealed truth (at least they are if we make any claim to a Christian orthodoxy).

On the other hand science and theology are similar in the sense that both theological and scientific formulations are not to be mistaken for the final word on reality: theological statements are the words and the signs that point to the Word who is truth; they are not the *full* truth themselves. Similarly science is not a mirror of reality but a provisional and always changing understanding of the universe (God's worlds).

Theologians today could be well advised to heed more closely what scientists say about science, for sometimes our modern theologians are more dogmatic about the universe than scientists themselves (see the next chapter). For example, one hundred years ago the mechanical and boxed-in universe of nineteenth-century physics seemed to offer no room or possibility that miracles might exist in the world. Today the open-ended and relative universe of modern physics holds no such certainties.

Nineteenth-century physicists in the tradition of Newton tended to see everything in terms of cause and effect. It was as if the universe was like a giant billiard table where the movement of all the balls could be explained by recourse to the billiard player who would strike each ball at a certain angle and with a certain velocity so that it was possible to predict where each ball would go. Indeed most physicists eliminated the billiard player (this looked too much like God the first cause) and saw the moving balls in perpetual motion according to their own invisible yet inviolable laws. Modern quantum theory in physics allows for random behaviour as well as cause and effect; that is to say, it has been observed at the level of subatomic particles that movement occurs that cannot be explained in terms of the cause and effect model so characteristic of earlier physics. The certainties of the Enlightenment philosophers, so influenced by Newtonian physics, that the universe had no room for surprises and unexplained mysteries are now shown to have been chimeras.

It is only as a result of criticism and modification of existing theories that science is able to progress. Work in the sociology of science has shown that in practice scientists will sometimes jealously guard their theories against falsification and may even doctor their data to give false results.[2] Even when their theories have been openly discredited they may hold on to them despite the evidence. This is to say nothing against science and its method, but only to point out that scientists are sinful human beings like you and me.

This sinfulness has led to the application of science to unethical ends. An obvious example would be the experiments in mass sterilisation performed by Nazi scientists upon Jewish women in concentration camps during the Second World War. This example demonstrates that science as a method is not automatically a force for good, but may be a powerful ally, or servant, of evil. In itself science is ethically neutral so far as its methodology is concerned: you can use it to blow up the world or to heal the sick. Once science is allowed to get away from ethical restraint then it is likely to cause havoc.

Science, then, will tend to reflect the ethical or unethical master whom it serves. Certain Hollywood horror movies still like to portray the scientist as the lonely seeker after truth locked away in his laboratory and hidden behind his bunsen burner and glass containers bubbling with garishly coloured liquids. In reality most scientists are dedicated professionals working for their paymasters who, these days, are likely to be governments, the military or industry.

THE MORALITY OF SCIENCE

Before we move on to seeing how science becomes scientism, we must reflect for a moment on the moral nature of scientific practice.

We cannot assume that all scientists are 'disinterested'; that is to say that men and women who practise science are only interested in knowledge for knowledge's sake (Merton 1968: 612). As Lewis points out concerning Faust, who is often thought of as the quintessential searcher after truth, 'It is not truth he wants from the devils, but gold and guns and girls' (Lewis 1978: 46). Some scientists, precisely because they are like you and me, may sell out to the highest bidder. Do we not find in our advanced societies that many of our greatest brains are engaged in building weapons of destruction (physical, chemical, and biological), or else are engaged in providing pointless toys to keep the general populace amused? Furthermore, science frequently responds to the market without looking too closely at the ethical issues involved in its products: consider how the demands of business take priority over the need to avoid the long-term problems of air and water pollution, or how abortion on demand can be practised without thinking of the personal and social consequences involved.

Science is the handmaiden of consumerism and the creator of mass media and micro-chip technology. She works for the United States Government but also for the Soviet Union. She will work for anyone if the price is right, because in reality her practitioners rarely work for themselves. Science may be value-free, but governments and industry are not. When scientists choose, or they are forced, to work for goals which lie outside science itself the results can be catastrophic. When, for example, the Allies were building the first atomic bomb at Los Alamos in New Mexico the rationale for this terrible weapon was the need to defeat the German High Command, who were themselves developing 'the bomb'. But in fact the so-called Alsos mission had discovered in 1944 that the Nazis were incapable of building the weapon and were at least ten years behind the Allies' own development. General Groves, the military and administrative head of the Los Alamos project, decided to go ahead, with government backing, even though the bomb was not needed and there were strong ethical arguments against it.

Many of the scientists were kept in the dark about the

situation, but it is significant that after the war many of the people associated with the Los Alamos project refused to be involved with the building of the hydrogen bomb (see Junck 1958).

Once in the hands of evil men science may even cease to be pure science. It becomes 'doctored' to fit the ideologies of government, racist theories, or business interests. Throughout the 1930s to the 1950s, for example, biology and agriculture were virtually destroyed in the Soviet Union by the theories of Lysenko. He did not believe in the genetic theories of Mendel, who had shown experimentally that individual characteristics of plants and biological organisms were passed on to subsequent generations. This was seen to be a tacit denial of the Soviet doctrine of 'dialectical materialism' that saw change being brought about by environmental manipulation. So what emerged in Russia with support from Stalin was not science but 'Soviet Science'. The *Sunday Times* on 9 January 1977 records the dissident scientist Vladimir Bukovsky as saying that Lysenkoism was still alive in Russia today!

And so we can see that scientists in Russia may support Soviet political ends and back a 'Soviet Science' that is not really science at all. Pseudo-science was a major feature of Nazi Germany. And we cannot say that scientists were forced, at all times, to follow it, for in many instances they championed it. Lenard and Stark, for example, were two Nobel prizewinners in physics. They joined the Nazi Party in the 1920s and insisted that the superiority of the Aryan race was a scientific fact. Conversely, they taught that Jews were on a lower point in the evolutionary scale to all other races.

Perhaps we could just pass this over as 'cranky' or merely unpleasant. The horror of the Holocaust does not allow us such a sanguine observation. I would like us to look at a document written by the Professor of Anatomy at Strasbourg University, Dr Hirt. It is addressed to Himmler during the war, and was used against Dr Hirt in his absence at the Nuremberg Trials. (He was never captured.) I intend to offer no comment on the content of the letter, but it is worth observing that much of its horror lies in the 'objective' and 'scientific' nature of its language. As George Steiner has put it: 'Language being used to run hell, getting the habits of hell into its syntax' (Steiner 1967: 122).

(Doc 085)
  Enclosure:
  Subject: Securing skulls of Jewish-Bolshevik Commissars for the purpose of scientific research at the Reich University of Strasbourg.
  There exist extensive collections of skulls of almost all races and peoples. Of the Jewish race, however, only so very few specimens of skulls are at the disposal of science that a study of them does not permit precise conclusions. The war in the East now presents us with the opportunity of obtaining tangible scientific evidence.
  The actual obtaining and collecting of these skulls without difficulty could be best accomplished by a directive issued to the Wehrmacht in the future to immediately turn over alive all Jewish-Bolshevik Commissars to the field police. The field police in turn is [sic.] to be issued special directives to continually inform a certain office of the number and place of detention of these captured Jews and to guard them well until the arrival of a special deputy. This special deputy . . . is to take a prescribed series of photographs and anthropological measurements, and is to ascertain, insofar as is possible, the origin, date of birth, and other personal data of the prisoners. Following the subsequently induced death of the Jew, whose head must not be damaged, he will separate the head from the torso and will forward it to its point of destination in a well-sealed tin container, especially made for the purpose.
  On the basis of the photos, the measurements and other data on the head, and finally the skull itself, comparative anatomical research on racial classification, pathological features of the skull formation, form and size of the brain, and many other things can begin . . .' (Mitschevlich and Mielke 1962: 223)

It would of course be outrageous to assert that this perverted and pseudo-science has much to do with real science at all. But science is what its masters and practitioners make it. Methodologically sound science may be harnessed to evil ends, or methodologically unsound science may promote evildoing. The simple point is this: science cannot be evaluated in its own terms alone (this is scientism); it needs to be judged by the canons of morality.

Perhaps we could assert that safe science is that science that seeks to discover knowledge for its own sake. Such an assertion, in my opinion, is unwise and naive. The interest in knowledge for knowledge's sake is born out of an itching curiosity. It can so easily cease to be a mere itch and take on the full stature of a human drive: the lust for knowledge. We are back with Eden and the desire to be gods. Is not this the motivation behind Mary Shelley's *Frankenstein*? Lust for knowledge is the drive behind the insistence that every curtain of mystery needs to be raised, whether it is discovering the secrets of the atom, creating life outside of the womb, or conducting experiments on unborn foetuses. The search for knowledge can lead to the most appalling ethical practices: 'we must know' can mean 'we must know whatever the price'.

To allow science to run itself, as if its own techniques could tell it what is right and what is wrong, is to slip into scientism. C. S. Lewis realised that if science is dominated by a philosophy that says that the quest for knowledge is without morality, is amoral, or is a mere question of technical know-how (as technocrats like to imagine), then what actually happens is that science is bent to the wills and lusts of men. 'What we call Man's power over Nature turns out to be a power exercised by some men over other men with Nature as its instrument' (Lewis 1978: 35).

FROM SCIENCE TO SCIENTISM

Science is a technical instrument and is not capable of knowing what is right and wrong. It is not intended to run itself by its own techniques. Something that is amoral like a machine or a bus is safe if it is in the hands of a careful and trustworthy driver. Strictly speaking, it is in order to say that science is rooted in philosophy in so far that it needs a philosophy (of science) to validate its procedures. Historically science was understood as natural philosophy and was seen to be part of the general rational and philosophical approach to reality.

This approach included a belief that ethics was itself a science; certainly it was the case that it was believed that there were objective moral realities in the universe.

But as science progressed in the era of the philosophical Enlightenment a hiatus occurred between traditional philosophical studies and the new empiricism. Like Prometheus unbound, science began to assert its own mastery. It was as if the technician was demanding to be treated as if he were an inventor. Or if you prefer, the Sorcerer's apprentice wanted to emulate his master.

Unlike the Mickey Mouse character in Walt Disney's *Fantasia*, science really does have a power of its own and a power that the philosophers have never been able to match. Philosophers can speculate about the universe and offer insights into 'eternal verities', but they cannot predict and hence manipulate the regular movements and fluxes of the created order. They cannot accurately plot the courses of the stars or measure exactly the speed of sound waves. The power to predict nature is only a step away from controlling nature. And to control nature is to have her under your power, to do your bidding, to submit to your will.

This very real power of science began to get away from the constraints of classical philosophy at the same moment that that philosophy came under attack by the Enlightenment philosophers. This classicism, since antiquity, and under the guiding influence of Christianity, had always believed in the moral nature of the universe. Science in breaking free of this moral world-view reversed the servant–master role just like the hired servant in Joseph Losey's film, *The Servant*, gradually gets the upper hand over his employer and eventually takes control.

Michael Aeschliman in an excellent essay on C. S. Lewis and scientism (1983) argues that science is safe and in its proper place when it is second to the wisdom and experience of classicism (the *philosophia perennis*). I remember the Thomist philosopher Jacques Maritain (1882–1973) saying some years ago that the moral universe is absolute because it has its origins in the life of God which is outside time. Like God himself it does not change with time or decay. But science by its very nature is always changing, always provisional, and deals with absolute truth in a relative way. Scientism comes about when the moral and the technical world are reversed.

Imagine it! Science which has no value in itself imposes its value of no value on values which really have value in themselves. Now, of course, this is not how it really happens, because it is philosophers and scientists who have brought this about. Perhaps at first science was seen as equal with traditional philosophy because of its phenomenal success. To back science was to back the winner. But gradually, as the servant gained the upper hand over its master, we saw a process of putting technical means before ethical ends. Empiricism took the place of rationality and fact of value; observation came before contemplation, and quantity before quality; and at last the material and phenomenal usurped the supreme authority of the spiritual.

It is a value judgment that says that scientific facts are superior to ethical or religious facts. But the rise of scientism during the Enlightenment cast doubts as to whether such things could be called facts at all. It is perfectly in order to say that qualities such as love, hope and beauty cannot be really apprehended by the methods of science. It may also be in order to say that such 'facts' are not like scientific facts, because they cannot be measured as quantities. Science deals with observable data that can be quantified and measured. It becomes ideology to say, however, that things that cannot be measured by the methods of science do not exist.

Scientism in its weaker form is a doctrine that claims science to be superior to all other methodologies and philosophies. In its stronger form, it demands exclusive rights to understanding reality. The latter and more pernicious doctrine begins with Hume and can be traced through Auguste Comte in the nineteenth century and the logical positivists of the Vienna Circle in the twentieth century. They would have all accepted Hume's empiricist position that,

'When we run over libraries, persuaded of these principles, what havoc must we make? If we take in our hand any volume; of divinity or school metaphysics, for instance; let us ask, Does it contain any abstract reasoning concerning quantity or number? No. Does it contain any experimental reasoning concerning matter of fact and existence? No. Commit it then to the flames: for it can contain nothing but sophistry and illusion' (quoted in Ayer 1959: 10).

The Harvard astronomer Gingerich has said that 'scientism is a . . . dogmatic philosophy that can develop from [scientific observation], saying that since this is the only way we can find out about nature, that is all there is' (quoted in Aeschliman 1983: 49).

And dogma is what scientific optimism becomes when it is converted into a belief in the absolute superiority of scientific thinking. None of this would matter too much if nobody took any notice of it, but throughout the nineteenth century scientism was a potent ideology that dominated Victorian thinking. When the French philosopher and founder of sociology Auguste Comte invented scientific positivism his ideas influenced nearly all the great thinkers of his day. Herbert Spencer, despite the fact that he liked to insist that his sociological theories were different from Comte's, was merely a tame imitator of him. Karl Marx eschewed positivism, and yet there are clear indications of it in his later 'scientific socialism', particularly in *Das Kapital* (1867). The Great British philosopher John Stuart Mill openly admitted his undying admiration for Comte (admiration that turned to disillusionment in his later life). Émile Durkheim the French sociologist never denied his great debt to Comte.

And Comte's position was to insist that it made no difference whether you wanted to investigate the natural or the social world, for all could be encapsulated by the methods of science. His scientism insisted on 'that necessary and permanent subordination of imagination to observation which constitutes the scientific spirit, as opposed to the theological or metaphysical spirit' (Andreski 1974: 139).

Comte thought that morality would eventually be reduced to science and that humanity could be investigated, in Chesterton's phrase, as 'common objects on the seashore' to be analysed as things with quantifiable properties. It would not be long before theologians started seeing the sacred scriptures in the same way and would begin to plunder their truths with the irreverence of iconoclasts let loose in a church.

Although scientism is essentially a philosophical doctrine there is also a tacit or functional scientism evident in the lay society. The proverbial man and woman in the street usually associates science with technology and engineering. It is the world of machines, inventions and consumer goods that brings science 'alive' for the ordinary person. Professor David Martin has argued that it is not scientific knowledge which impresses people, because such knowledge is neither directly accessible to ordinary persons nor is it comprehensible. It is the pace of scientific discovery and innovation that convinces them of the superiority of scientific reasoning (Martin 1973: 145–147).

Science is viewed as mysterious and miraculous. It is capable of great feats and wonders. We have an almost superstitious trust in it, for science is mystery in the modern world and magic come of age. (Is this not what the Grand Inquisitor offers the world instead of Christ and true religion? See Dostoevsky 1958: Bk 5, ch. 5).

This tacit scientism becomes evident in the way that the cult of numericity has taken over the Western world. The tyranny of numbers has been particularly oppressive in the social sciences, where many a true but totally trivial set of findings embedded in statistical tables takes on the aura of 'objectivity' and importance (see Cicourel 1964). Government surveys and bureaucratic procedures love to dress up their activities in the garbled wonder of numbers. Numerals and the power of cardinal numbers are greatly facilitated by banking, city finance and the rational properties of money. Micro-chip technology will ensure that numericity will wrap us in its jargon for a long time to come.

'DARWINISM' AND SCIENTISM

Scientism as a philosophical doctrine is what is described technically as 'reductionist': it always reduces all truth and reality to the methods of science itself. Some scientific disciplines attempt to reduce all other sciences to their own understanding of the world. This may be legitimate. There is a case to be made, for example, that sociology and economics could ultimately be reduced to the laws of biology. Other scientists have insisted that physics is the science that ultimately captures all reality. In practice, however, reductionism if often a disguise for scientism.

Nowhere is this better exemplified than by the enormous influence of Darwinism. The theory of evolution has a curious status within science. Sir Karl Popper believed that it was more of a 'metaphysical research programme' than a full-blown science. Unlike Newton's or Einstein's theories, he felt that it did not offer any possibility of being refuted. It was plausible; he accepted that there was overwhelming evidence for a belief in evolution, but felt nevertheless that it was very difficult to think up ways in which one could falsify the theory. (For Popper if a science cannot be falsified in principle it is essentially metaphysical.)

Given this curious status Darwinism would probably not have caused such controversy if it had remained merely a theorem in biology. C. S. Lewis and Karl Barth, for example, were just two notable Christians who refused to be bothered by it. For those Christians who believe in the theological truths of Genesis, believing them to be real yet mythological in expression, then the theory of evolution poses no problems at all. It makes no difference to them, for example, whether God created the world in six days or six million years. Neither does it really matter whether evolution exists as a mechanism of nature, for even if it does God is still creator-God and the fall can still be understood as both a spiritual and a historical reality.

For those Christians who are literalist in all matters scriptural then it remains true that Darwinism, even as a biological theory, poses insuperable problems (see Kitcher 1982).

But the problem with Darwinism both in the nineteenth century and today is that it has become much more than simply a biological theory: it has become an explanation to be applied to culture, societies and even spiritual life. C. S. Lewis correctly understood that Darwinism was the scientific legitimation of the doctrines of progress believed in by the philosophers of the Enlightenment. Kant and Hegel, for example, in their different ways taught that there was a natural teleology (or direction/purpose) in the universe. Capitalism was the materialistic affirmation of progress and in this respect so too was Marx's socialism. Darwinism added the final doxology to the progressive optimism of the Enlightenment.

But all this was illegitimate science and false enthusiasm. When Darwin's book *On the Origin of Species* first appeared in 1859 it contained almost no mention of the evolution of man, and absolutely no attack upon God as creator. His position was as follows. (1) Everywhere we look in the natural world we see a variety of forms and characteristics within species and between species. (2) It is clear that parents pass on their special characteristics to their offspring. Elephants pass on trunks, kangaroos marsupial pouches to females, possums the 'habit' of hanging upside down, etc. (3) If there is a sudden change in environment – ice ages, or a new group of predators, for example – not all groups will survive. Natural selection is a process of the 'survival of the fittest' (though this phrase is from the sociologist Herbert Spencer, not Darwin himself), not in the sense of the strongest individual but of the species whose individual characteristics best allow it to adapt to its environment.

Darwin's theory led in the latter half of the nineteenth century to a whole spate of neo-Darwinisms outside of biology. Spencer attempted to apply the theory to societies (with notable racist overtones!), Frazer adapted it to evolutionary stages in human development (as Comte had already done before Darwin's theory). The Fabian Society was a socialist movement that quite overtly believed in a scientific doctrine of progress. Both H. G. Wells and George Bernard Shaw thought that Darwin had provided objective grounds for a benign socialism. Even Karl Marx's (less benign) socialism took on a scientific hue by the time of *Das Kapital* (1867). Engels, his friend and co-author, saw Darwinism as the biological partner to scientific socialism; a view later held by Lenin.

Neo-Darwinism became embedded in the twentieth-century political realities of communism and fascism, and still lives on today in more respectable form (notably the sociobiology of Wilson, 1975).[3]

But it was religion that bore the brunt of the new Darwinism. Victorians began to think – and people still think today – that if the principle of natural selection is true then there is no need of a designer God. The idea that *homo sapiens* were themselves evolved from lower life forms suggests that man is not the centre of the universe. If evolution is true, when did human beings receive souls? If the Genesis account of the origin of creation is faulty perhaps the same could be said for other parts of the Bible? Could the created order be an accident, a whim of blind chance?

Some Christians became so convinced of the new evolution that it became the basis of new theological thinking. Process theology and the moral evolutionism of Teilhard de Chardin (1959) attempted to adapt traditional Christian theology to evolutionary insights. This in my opinion is really a form of scientism, for it is the task of theology to incorporate what scientific insight it can into its framework, not to adapt its framework to a scientific theory whose status is by no means clear.

We need as Christians to be reminded of one basic fact in all these matters. Science is a methodological tool for exploring the natural (and possibly social?) universe. It has nothing to say about God, and absolutely nothing to say about morality. It may be that science alters our spatial understanding so that we no longer think of heaven as 'up there' and hell as 'down there', but science has to remain silent about the reality of eternity or whether heaven and hell exist or not. Similarly, evolutionary theory may well present us with a mechanism for explaining the development of organic life on this planet, but it has nothing to say about God's existence or his nature, love and purposes. If it claims that it does then it is engaged in scientism.[4]

There are many other illegitimate uses of science that we

could examine, but I would like to end this chapter with a case study in scientism that has had disastrous effects on modernity: the attack upon moral theory.

SCIENTISM AND MORALS

The most potent brew of scientism in the last hundred and fifty years has been the doctrine known as positivism, and in particular the sophisticated version of Comte's theories known as logical positivism.

Comte, like Hume before him, believed that truth could be encapsulated by the methods of science itself. One of Comte's unfinished projects was an in-depth study of ethics. He intended to demonstrate that moral statements had no objective status and that morality itself could be explained by the laws of human behaviour. It was the sociologist Durkheim who took up Comte's project. He thought that values were social facts that could be accounted for and described by the methods of science. Typical of his thinking was to move from the social fact of human solidarity in the face of crime, for example, to seeing in this fact a principle of moral obligation. Even Hume could have told him that this was impossible, because you cannot make a statement of value (an 'ought' statement) from a statement of fact (an 'is' statement). The scientist Henri Poincaré once remarked to Durkheim that one could not derive the proposition 'Don't eat toadstools' from the scientific proposition 'A toadstool is a poisonous mushroom' (Lukes 1973: 500).

Durkheim's project foundered on uncertainty, and in Great Britain and North America it was probably utilitarianism[5] that remained the dominant moral theory in the latter part of the nineteenth century. (Though idealism remained strong in Continental Europe and flourished for a brief time in England also.)

In the twentieth century, however, both traditional ethics and utilitarianism have collapsed in most of our universities, and it is logical positivism that has primarily been responsible for this. But not directly: the attack upon ethics is almost a by-product of the undermining of traditional philosophy by the positivists. Logical positivism is extremely complex for those not versed in philosophy and logic, but at the risk of over-simplification we must try to grasp its central tenets. In our chapter on the coming of modernity (chapter four) we caught a brief glimpse of Wittgenstein writing his *Tractatus* in the trenches of the First World War. It was this philosophical work that became the bible of the new positivists.

Comte had been an empiricist, but Wittgenstein and the positivists of the twentieth century were logicians who developed a radical theory of language. Wittgenstein believed in what is known as a picture theory of truth: statements and propositions must correspond to observable realities. By this criterion, Wittgenstein asserted, it is obvious that philosophy fails to correspond to observable reality. Most statements, in short, are metaphysical. Only scientific statements can be said to measure up to the criterion of observable reality. So radical was this view that Wittgenstein also insisted that logic and mathematics were only true in a weak sense. That is to say they are true only according to their own rules, which are symbolic and not empirical. So for example the proposition that $2 + 2 = 4$ is true only because that is the way that numbers work. (For Wittgenstein this amounted to no more than tautological truth – rather like saying a 'brown cow is a cow that is brown'.)

What does all this boil down to? For Wittgenstein,

The totality of true propositions is the whole of natural science (or the whole corpus of the natural sciences) (*Tractatus* 4.11).

Furthermore,

The correct method in philosophy would really be the following: to say nothing except what can be said, i.e. propositions of natural science – i.e. something that has nothing to do with philosophy . . . (*Tractatus* 6.53).

Now I have no need to criticise Wittgenstein because he eventually demolished his own theories, but in fact the positivists misunderstood an essential aspect of Wittgenstein's thought. They were convinced that Wittgenstein had logically demonstrated that there were only two kinds of truths in the world: (1) the *a priori* truths of mathematics and logic, and (2) the statements of natural science. They proposed that all statements should be submitted to a 'verification principle': 'A formula which can be checked neither by observation of the world, nor by deduction from our definitions, has no meaning' (Gellner 1963: 79).

In short, for the logical positivists, traditional philosophy, theology, aesthetics and moral theory were not simply mistaken: they were meaningless. Wittgenstein's position was logically similar, but his conclusions were quite different. He did not think that metaphysics was possible, or that ethical and aesthetical truths could be demonstrated philosophically. But he did believe such truths existed. He was a mystic who was convinced that great truths could only be shown in the lives of men and by the actions of people. His students were told on more than one occasion that if they wanted to learn about morality they would be better served watching a western at the cinema than attending philosophy lectures! Wittgenstein's reticence and silence in the face of moral truths (which he felt was the correct moral stance) was misunderstood by the positivists to mean that there were no such truths. Many years later Rudolf Carnap (1891–1970), one of the leading members of the Vienna Circle, admitted that he and his colleagues had failed to appreciate that Wittgenstein's silence was ineffable mysticism. Like St John of the Cross he could say:

> '. . . I heard great things.
> What I heard I will not tell . . .'

My favourite story of Wittgenstein at this stage in his life (the 1920s) is what happened when he visited the Vienna Circle. The positivists were expecting witty philosophical aphorisms and logical truths. When he arrived Wittgenstein refused to play mentor and instead played the 'holy fool': he read to them the poetry of Rabindranath Tagore . . .

But by now the positivists were crusading for their scientism with all the fervour of holy prophets. Moritz Schlick (1882–1936), the leader of the Vienna Circle for many years, believed that ethics was a branch of science. He insisted that it could be reduced to psychology. Most positivists, however, refused to see ethics in this way. Ethical statements were not factual statements, they claimed, but meaningless ones.

A. J. Ayer was never one of the Vienna Circle, but his book *Language, Truth and Logic*, first published in 1936, popularised the doctrines of positivism for the English-speaking world (in much the same way as John Robinson popularised Bultmann's theology in *Honest To God* in 1963). Following Carnap, Ayer insisted that all traditional philosophy was to be abandoned, and that included ethical theories: 'we reject utilitarianism and subjectivism . . . as analyses of our existing ethical notions. Our contention is simply that, in our language, sentences which contain normative ethical symbols are not equivalent to sentences which express psychological propositions or indeed empirical propositions of any kind' (1963: 107).

What in fact Ayer, and some of the other positivists, offered us in the place of traditional morality was not a moral theory at all ('there can be no way of determining the validity of any ethical system') but a theory about ethics. In what came to be known as the 'third theory' or the 'emotive theory of ethics', Ayer insisted that when we *express* a moral idea we are doing just that: expressing or showing emotion. No wonder that G. K. Chesterton and C. S. Lewis saw this emotivism as an affront to common sense as well as to common morality!

How then are we to judge moral facts? By the principles of logical positivism we cannot, because there are no moral facts or objective values, only strong feelings which we show about things which matter to us.

Eventually logical positivism fell into disrepute. It did not deliver the logical goods it promised, and as science was now the sole arbiter of truth, there was not an awful lot positivism had to offer (as Wittgenstein had admitted of the new philosophy). Various philosophers, notably the Cambridge don A. E. Ewing, and Sir Karl Popper, had argued that the infamous verification principle was meaningless on its own grounds: it did not (1) make empirical statements about the world – it did not correspond to observable realities – and (2) it was not a logical or mathematical statement. Therefore it was metaphysical and according to its own understanding meaningless. Ironically it was Wittgenstein who had the last laugh, not only logically demolishing his *Tractatus*, but also in his introduction to Karl Popper's *Logik der Forschung* (1935)[6] pointing out that positivism had become a pseudo-philosophy so narrow in its interpretation of reality that it had become not the handmaiden of science but a source of dogmas: '. . . once this meaning-dogma has been elevated on the throne, it is forever beyond assault, "untouchable and final" ' (Kraft 1953: 37).

No doubt some readers may be wondering why we are looking at all this complicated philosophy if logical positivism is no longer a potent force in the world of ideas. Can we not dump it in the dustbin of history like so many other outdated theories of yesteryear? I would that we could, but in fact although it is true that positivism no longer has so many adherents its long-term effects in the field of moral philosophy are still with us.

Indeed it would not be untrue to say that since logical positivism demolished the utilitarian and idealist philosophies of the nineteenth century they have been unable to make a serious return in the twentieth century. Classicism is no longer believed by the majority of English-speaking philosophers. C. S. Lewis, who called classicism 'the Tao', was convinced that moral objectivity was essential for the moral health of any society. It was one thing for people to be immoral, he thought, but it was a more terrible thing if there were no common moral discourse or no agreed ethical ends (cf. Lewis 1978, Appendix). This is the situation that we now find in the modernity of the 1980s, and logical positivism has played a major part in destroying the moral and spiritual fabric of our traditional ethics.

In the English-speaking world the major philosophy to replace positivism has been conceptual or linguistic analysis. Unlike positivism, and no doubt under the influence of

Wittgenstein's later work in *Philosophical Investigations* (completed in 1945), linguistic analysts are not absolutists in their claim for superior logical languages. On the contrary, they shy clear of 'truth claims' of any kind, let alone scientific ones. However, two things can be noted. Firstly the sort of work that has resulted from this new approach to language may be called egalitarian or relativistic. There is now talk of 'language games' and illegitimate and legitimate moves. Elucidation of the puzzles of language and (in the title of J. L. Austin's most well-known book) *How to do Things with Words* (1962), became all the rage. (Except that 'rage' is not really a word to attach to the senior common-rooms of Oxford where the careful yet frankly inconsequential new philosophy developed.[7])

Perhaps the major attack upon this new philosophy is that it is trite and trivial. Rarely do such philosophers grapple with the traditional ethical and epistemological questions of the earlier philosophers (first-order questions as they are dismissively called). It was Karl Popper who argued that trivia, even if it is true, is not worthy of the name of philosophy, and he thought that much of the new analysis was dealing with pseudo-problems (see his conversation with Bryan Magee, 1973). One can imagine an earnest young student asking his tutor a question about beauty or goodness and being submitted to a barrage of questions concerning the meaning of the words he used and in the subsequent analysis of the meaning the question getting lost, and certainly never answered in its own terms.

The second thing to note is that the egalitarian practices of modern linguistic analysis are related to the fact that, following Wittgenstein and Ryle (1949), most philosophers are concerned with mapping out the different types of discourse (scientific, moral, religious, aesthetic, etc.) and making sure that one does not apply terms from one 'language' to another. Some philosophers, notably Winch (1958), have applied the relativism of languages to societies, arguing that there is not total or objective reality, but only a differentiated and cultural relativism, to be found.

But all this egalitarianism, where now ordinary language is

back in favour after the more mathematical or symbolic languages favoured by the positivists, is often a sham. Many philosophers may no longer insist on the superiority of science, but most of them still turn their backs upon moral philosophy as traditionally understood. Wittgenstein, for example, always remained hostile to metaphysics, though at least he was consistent in this: he maintained his ineffable approach to morals and religious issues. Other philosophers have felt unable to return to idealism, and Gellner has argued that when linguistic and conceptual analysts are forced to give an account of knowledge and the status of their own language as philosophers they are often driven back on positivistic explanations.

More tellingly, Gellner explains that without logical positivism the old philosophy could not have collapsed and the newer more relativistic though trivial philosophy could not have flourished: 'Positivism is like the paper in the children's game that can wrap the stone but can be cut by the scissors. Linguistic Philosophy is the scissors, that could not affect the stone though it can cut the paper. It is parasitic on the Positivism which it also destroys' (Gellner 1963: 86).

The void left by the demise of the traditional philosophy has never been filled in the advanced Western world. Continental Europe has flirted with existentialism,[8] but whatever else this 'mood' philosophy brings it does not reinstate traditional morality. Sartre thought that such morality was inauthentic and that men should face the void bravely, though with dread, and alone. Christian existentialists, such as Gabriel Marcel (1889–1973) and Nikolai Berdyaev (1874–1948) baptised their existentialism with the gospel, and that is quite a different matter.

It is not unimportant to note that Sartre eventually abandoned existentialism for Marxism. I have no doubt that one of the reasons why socialism remains so powerful among the intelligentsia of Europe is that it offers a way forward out of nothingness and inertia; it offers, in Wittgenstein's words, 'a form of life' which is better than no life at all.

But tragically Marxism, like positivism, is not built upon the traditional philosophies and is incapable of generating any moral theory: it denies moral axioms (axiological ethics) and inserts in their place the doctrine of class solidarity. So often students tell me that they have become socialists for moral reasons, and when I question them on these moral reasons they talk about justice and equality. But when I ask them to come and show me where Marx, Engels or Lenin talk about these things in any traditionally moral way they are unable to do so. For this reason I believe that it is impossible in principle for Marxist socialism to unite with the democratic and libertarian traditions of Western Europe and the United States of America.

But now we come to where all this has been leading. The long-term effect of scientism on the advanced industrial nations is that outside of Christian universities (notably Catholic ones) there is virtually no consensus of moral theory. On the contrary, what we find is a situation more akin to nihilism. At best there are residues of utilitarianism (which I believe are not Christian anyway) and intuitionism.

I do not think it is the case that we have arrived at this situation solely because of philosophy. As far as people in the street are concerned they never did know much about philosophy. The lack of moral consensus in our advanced societies is primarily due to reasons that I have already outlined in this book. Industrialism and urbanism combined with consumerism, hedonism and rampant individualism do not exactly make a recipe for morality. Add to this secularisation, privatisation, pluralism, and the all-pervading television eye and it is perhaps no surprise that there is so much immoral behaviour in our private and public lives.

But where the philosophy does come in and deals the final death blow is that when we turn to our intellectuals, our professional philosophers, our professors of ethics, they can do little except shrug their shoulders or ask us whether we are aware of the status of our questions or the inadequacy of their semantic components. Professor Alasdair MacIntyre, in perhaps the most significant book on moral theory in the last decade, believes that our civilisation is poised on the edge of nihilism (1981). Unless we return to something like the traditional morality, the *philosophia perennis*, then we have little chance of moral survival. He asks us to choose (as representatives of the two traditions) either Aristotle or Nietzsche.

We cannot blame scientism for our immorality. Sin, as Christianity has always taught, is from the heart. And we have learnt the habits of sin by also absorbing them into our culture, and from our culture into our hearts. But sin is our internal enemy. Our external Enemy, unless we have also taken him to our hearts, is the Evil One who resides in the world. Scientism has been one of his great successes, so subtle, so alluring, and sometimes so seemingly logical. Who has been able to gainsay it?

I really do not think that we realise the magnitude of our problem. Here we are in a world lost in sin and immorality, as it has always been, but we are also faced with the modern evils of materialism and the scientific means to unethical ends – not to mention the very real possibility that we are only a step away from eternity – and what do we find: we have no moral language any more!

My wife, who is a social worker, came home the other day in considerable distress. 'A terrible thing happened today,' she said. 'I had to deal with a case of teenage boys sexually molesting a three-year-old child.' 'How terrible,' I murmured. To be frank, I was thinking more of Susan's trauma than the effect on the small child. 'Yes, it was terrible,' she said. 'But the thing that upset me the most is that none of them thought that it was wrong!'

No doubt we could dismiss this as an atypical case that has no bearing on this whole issue, but it does. For ten years I taught moral philosophy to social workers who receive virtually no ethical training (preferring instead to do sociology and psychology). My abiding memory of those hundreds of students who each day in their profession would have to make choices that affect the lives of children, old people and the mentally ill (and who have to face so many other really difficult and complicated social problems) is the fog of moral confusion. It is not only social work clients who cannot tell right from wrong. The only absolute that many students held on to was that there were no moral absolutes.[9]

Many of them thought that abortion was entirely an issue of the woman's right to control her own body. They wanted to believe in justice but did not know how to express it except through the slogans of left-wing politics. There was a mish-mash belief in freedom, social justice, fair-play, hedonism, rights and duties, free-will, determinism, macrobiotic diet, mysticism, and objectivity. Of course they were not philosophers, but many of them were graduates who had never come across ethical theory, traditional beliefs in morality, or Christianity. I learnt to spot the Catholics and evangelicals who stood out like sore thumbs. Their intuitions and convictions were usually right, although they were often no better than their secular colleagues when it came to articulating a moral theory.

C. S. Lewis was concerned, long before Alasdair MacIntyre, that we were living in a world where we could no longer appeal to a common tradition. This is where we have arrived at in modernity. The processes of social change have taken us away from face-to-face reality, from personal and communal contact. These changes have been matched by changes in the intellectual map, so that we no longer know where we are, how to use a compass, or how to understand the contours on the map. The collapse of moral theory took place in the universities where many of us never go. Philosophy, like theology, is no longer of any interest to ordinary men and women. Like the science we so admire and trust, philosophy belongs to that other world of specialists and intellectuals.

When we turn to that world for help and guidance for our problems and confusions we find that they offer not solutions but a mirror of ourselves. Enemy propaganda works at all levels of society because evil works on our human condition, our frailties, conceits, cowardices, lusts – even our lust for knowledge – and self-interest. That is why scientism has been such a success and continues to succeed even among intellectuals. It has been one of the conceits of scientism that goodness is reducible to intelligence. Has not the progressive mind always seen ignorance as the enemy at the door? People who think like that do not realise that the Enemy is already within.

And it is the enemy within with which I shall be concerned in the next and last chapter on unholy propaganda. Secular philosophies are no longer merely residents in the secular world: they have made their home in the churches. At the moment, when we should be coming together to take our stand against the Devil in our fight to win the modern world for God, we are finding that we have to fight within the sacred walls of our sanctuaries. It is one thing to be impotent in the face of a pluralised and privatised world awash in televised amusement, but it is a far more serious matter to find ourselves up against our own brothers and sisters in the faith.

I do not believe that we should personally attack those with whom we disagree, but we must contend for the truth. Traditional morality bowed down to science and the result was scientism. The long-term effect of scientism, especially in its positivistic guise, has been to keep moral theory down and out. Theology has been giving way to secular methods and ideas, and the result has been modernism. It is this modernism, as we shall now see, which has been the Enemy's most successful frontal attack upon Christianity in modernity.

8   THE ENEMY WITHIN –
Modernism in the churches

WHAT IS MODERNISM?

Many of us know that much of modern theology seems to have difficulty with accepting the Bible as the 'inspired word of God', or in treating the resurrection as a historical fact, or in finding credible the doctrine of the incarnation. Belief in miracles is thought of by many today as being impermissible in the scientific age.

It is not always so easy to know how to characterise this theology. What we must not do is assume that it is all of a piece, for theology today is not only diverse, highly special-ised (just like science) and controversial, it is also without any consensus. Theology, like moral philosophy, finds it very difficult to agree on a common programme or common approaches. This is partly a function of the specialisation of modern scholarship. A feature of much scientific and socio-logical work is that even people in the same discipline find it difficult to talk to each other. Theologians too, I have found, live separate and insulated lives.

So often, for example, brilliant New Testament scholars have little grasp of what used to be called 'dogmatics'. And many dogmatic scholars, especially those in the Orthodox tradition, have little comprehension of the exegetical and hermeneutical work ('interpretive understanding') of the New Testament scholars.

The presuppositions of some scholars are so different from other scholars that real dialogue is very difficult indeed. I recall Fr Simeon Lash, an Orthodox priest and brother of Professor Nicholas Lash, once complaining that the work of traditional dogmatic formulation was impossible when such work was done in the hearing of New Testament scholars. The dogmatic theologians might say something about the doctrine of incarnation as exemplified in the Gospel of St John, and the New Testament scholars would tell them to 'hang on' because it was by no means clear, in their opinion, that the relevant passages in the gospel were truly authentic!

It can be very confusing in some university departments for theological students to attend a course in dogmatics where the lecturer assumes the truths of traditional and orthodox Christianity, and then to attend lectures on New and Old Testament studies where those truths are denied as not consonant with the 'authentic biblical witness'.[1]

It is because of this confusion that theology becomes difficult to define. A popular way to talk about those (often very different) sorts of theologians who cannot assent to credal formulas is to call them 'secular humanists'. The trouble with this phrase is that it is very misleading; many modern theologians are not humanists and do not see their theological positions as secularist – though they might accept the term 'non-traditionalist' with pride.

Another popular phrase, particularly in British evangelical circles, is the word 'liberal'. Liberal is an awkward word because it has strong political connotations in our secular societies. Furthermore, some 'liberals' are extremely conservative compared to the more radical modern theologians. Professor James Dunn, for example, is sometimes called a 'liberal evangelical', which is not a term he uses of himself. The tag 'liberal' has been attached to him because he believes that the New Testament is not always direct reportage but contains edited versions – in some cases – of differing New Testament sources (Dunn 1985). But most modern New Testament scholars would see Professor Dunn as 'fairly conservative'. Compared to the authors of *The Myth of God Incarnate* (Hick 1977), for example, he is extremely orthodox indeed.

The media love the word 'liberal' because they can oppose it to 'conservative'. I objected to using it on a television programme and was told 'please use it because any other term confuses people'. But in theological circles the word 'liberal' is the proper noun for a particular school of modern theology known as the 'liberal school of German theology' and following the programme of its founder Professor Albrecht Ritschl (1822–1889). It has very little in common with other so-called 'liberal' theologies.

I propose, therefore, that we use the term 'modernist' to encapsulate all those forms of theology that do not accord with the revealed truths of the gospel. (But it must be noted that this term is not exclusive to religion because there are modernist schools of literature and art.) Modernism, in religious terms, first became an issue in the Catholic church at the turn of the century. Modernist Catholic theologians such as G. Tyrrell,[2] were really against medievalism rather than for non-traditional theological doctrines. In the Anglican church, modernists were those who were seen to be opposed to traditionalism, and in America modernists were the antagonists to the movement known as fundamentalism.

I would like to use modernism in the way in which it has become normative in theological usage. And, for once, the *Oxford English Dictionary* can offer us a definition which fits this usage: 'A tendency or movement towards modifying traditional beliefs and doctrines in accordance with the findings of modern criticism and research.' This is a broad definition and may include the methods of science and modern historical techniques. It allows us to look at the influence of modern philosophy, both scientistic and subjectivist. It is essential that we include both for, as we shall see, one of the most interesting hallmarks of some modernist theology is not how scientific it is – little modern theology is truly scientific – but how subjective it is. Modernism is the philosophical and ideological face of modernity, and in this respect theological modernism is Christianity recast in the moulds of modern world-views.

THE EXTENT OF MODERNISM

I doubt very much if any church grouping is entirely free of modernism. Certainly it is the case that theologians who seek to preserve the sacred character of the scriptures and hold to the faith 'once delivered' from the apostles cannot themselves be entirely free from modern critical methods.[3]

Professor David Martin would argue that modernism permeates deep into church liturgical structures, even when churches deny modernism on a theological level. I am thinking in particular of those churches who sing 'sacred songs' to secular music, and adopt the 'star' system of the secular world in relation to their gospel singers and preachers. Clearly this is an extended usage of modernism, and perhaps fits more closely the process of worldliness (secularisation) than the philosophical dimensions of modernism.

On a theological level conservative evangelicals, Protestant 'fundamentalists' and the Eastern Orthodox denominations are the most adamantly opposed to modernism. This was once also true of Catholicism, but since Vatican 2, Protestant modernism and the evolutionary theories of the Jesuit Teilhard de Chardin have become more popular. The growth of so-called 'liberation' theologies particularly in Latin America have attempted to meld Marxism with traditional Catholic sacramentalism. No mainline Protestant denomination is unaffected by forms of modernism. This is true of Lutheranism, the world Anglican Communion, Methodism, Presbyterianism, and Baptists. When recently a former principal of a Baptist college in Britain could declare his disbelief in the fact of the incarnation, it became clear that there are very few places where modernism does not rear its head.

Modernism does not belong to a particular confession or a denomination: it cuts across denominational boundaries. It is possible, and it does happen, that in the pews of the Methodist chapel, the Baptist congregation and the Anglican parish people are sitting next to each other with opposing views of the gospel. Many priests and pastors do not believe in the virgin birth or the resurrection, and for some the Bible is a collection of outdated and outmoded myths that are no longer relevant to the modern world. (*Relevant* is a dangerous word in my opinion, being liked by too many modernists and traditional Christians alike. It is wiser to be concerned with truth rather than relevance.) It is a mistake to imagine that modernism is only a reality in the theological colleges and universities: it is dished up for Sunday sermons and in Sunday school classes. It is rampant in the educational system. The fashion for teaching religion as comparative religion, in the best liberal tradition, is itself one of the dreams come true of a whole school of nineteenth-century modernist thought.

In many British, European and American universities modernism in all its forms dominates the teaching and research agendas. There are many university departments in England where traditional dogmatics is given short shrift. Theology as it has traditionally been taught and practised since the early church fathers (and in this respect the Reformation fathers are in that tradition) is primarily kept alive in Great Britain in a few Catholic seminaries and evangelical Bible colleges, and perhaps supremely in some of the universities of Scotland.[4]

Even in churches and confessions that would not be seen dead touting modernist theology, hidden strains of it are often found. My colleague at the C. S. Lewis Centre, Tom Smail, has pointed out in an unpublished paper that we are often heirs of the Enlightenment without realising it. For example, in some charismatic circles – by no means the majority – the emphasis on experience is so primary that the Word of God (*Logos*) becomes less important than the direct word (*rhema*) from the Lord in the Holy Spirit. This extreme subjectivism, and the emphasis on individual experience over and above the revealed truths of scripture, is a major theme of modernism, stemming from the Enlightenment itself. Perhaps this is by no means obvious. Let us make it so by looking at the origins of modernism.

THE ORIGINS OF MODERNISM

Modernism was born in the heart of the philosophical Enlightenment of the eighteenth century. It is not necessary for us to trace the history of theology since that time as there are several excellent books which perform that historical task (see Heron 1980). But we can understand much of the development of the new theological methods and understandings if we see exactly what the Enlightenment did to critical enquiries.

In this we will have to be impressionistic and leave out some major figures (such as Hegel), but we cannot ignore the decisive effect of Kant's *Critique Of Pure Reason* (first published 1781). Prior to Kant most philosophers had accepted that the realm of ideas (the noumenal) could be studied in itself. The whole of medieval metaphysics, for example, rested on the premise that one could rationally describe and analyse reality beyond the senses. Kant argued, and argued decisively, that the phenomenal world was indeed open to investigation through the senses, but the world of ideas, of imagination, of pure reason, was not accessible to rational enquiry.

Such a view undercut traditional theology, which dealt with such issues as proofs for the existence of God, and an examination of what God was like in himself (the immanent God). To talk of 'things in themselves' as having being (an ontology), Kant declared, was impossible. This is not to say that Kant thought that such things did not exist – on the contrary, like Wittgenstein his problem was to know how to talk of them legitimately – but it is to say that he thought that traditional philosophy was no longer possible.

But Kant also made a distinction between pure reason and practical reasoning. He believed that pure reason, which tries to deal with the concepts of our mind, is empty of real content unless it is mediated through the senses (through our perceptions). It is experience that brings knowledge to life for us. Pure knowledge on its own was for Kant like a far distant island cut off from the mainland of our self-conscious and personal knowledge.

As autonomous individuals, Kant believed, we live out our lives engaging in practical reasoning which is related to action and moral behaviour. He did not believe that the world of pure reason is binding on any person. No moral system has truth in itself that should be followed simply because it is there. Nor can any external God or moral law command our

allegiance, for they are frozen in (conceptual) space away
from our direct knowledge and participation. On the contrary, demanded Kant, moral behaviour is entirely a matter of
following the 'moral imperatives' within.

Human beings for Kant are the supreme and sole moral
agents in determining correct behaviour. Man is a social
being, but all men and women are autonomous and are free to
choose either good or evil. In this autonomous world of moral
choice and self-understanding Kant made room for faith. God
could not be proved by 'pure reason' but he could be reasonably believed in as the basis for action and through the
medium of faith. Having cut the Gordian knot that bound
the noumenal world to the phenomenal world Kant saw no
option for Christians other than to discover God for ourselves
through our own choices, experiences and practical
reasoning.

Ultimately one always gets the suspicion when reading
Kant that for him the reality of God is dependent upon our
own reasoning: he exists in so far as he exists for me. It is
perhaps easier to understand what all this has to do with the
whole history of modernism if we see the contrast Kant made
between *autonomy* as the centre for practical reason and
conscience, and what he called *heteronomy*. Morality and
religion, as we have seen, belong to autonomy for Kant.
Authority for faith and action belong within us, are internal to
us. We are the final arbiters of truth. It is the exercise of *our*
reason which is crucial for determining religious sensibilities
and actions. Heteronomy, on the other hand, is any source
of knowledge that is external to us, whether it be the metaphysics of an Aristotle, the moral theories of the medieval
scholastics, or even the scriptures themselves. External
religion, in the form of dogmas, may very well command or
entice us to act in a certain way. It demands, as it were, that
we sacrifice our conscience and autonomy to it.

Kant was not impious in his attitude to scripture, but he
believed that ultimately it becomes active and imperative for
us only if it accords with our reason and conscience. Here is
the classic shift from the religion of tradition to the Christianity of modernism. Luther could speak for the universal church

when he said of anyone approaching scripture that one 'does not stand over the Bible and judge it, but below the Bible, and hears and obeys it'. Kant invites us to stand over the Bible and judge from the standpoint of our own autonomy as free-choosing and rationally free human beings. We are no longer to be authenticated by the word, but we will authenticate – through our reasoning and moral sensibilities – the words of scripture.

Extreme charismatics, and of course existentialists, choose autonomy over heteronomy and in so doing follow Kant's own course. Those fundamentalists who treat the scriptures as dictated word for word from God like automatic writing with no human interference or influence, look towards heteronomy, the external words of the Bible, with the same fervour that logical positivists treat the statements of empirical science. Not only can this lead to idolatry but it shows a view of scripture far removed from the fathers and Reformers. Calvin, for example, realised that the Holy Spirit wrote the Bible through the fallible and human minds of men. And like the early church fathers he realised (as too did John Wesley) that there had to be an engagement with scripture by the individual will through the Holy Spirit (the charismatic dimension is necessary for true understanding).

In short, the traditional view of scriptural knowledge was to deny the absolute distinction between heteronomy and autonomy, but it certainly would never submit the revelation of God through the scriptures to the authentication of human reasoning. (Karl Barth saw this as akin to blasphemy.) It is not coincidental that as modernism began to take shape and concrete form in the nineteenth century, reaction against it, particularly by those influenced by millenarianism, became increasingly attached to extreme literalism and doctrines of the inerrancy and infallibility of scripture (notably Scofield). These doctrines were tacitly believed by some of the early Reformers, but never as dogmas.

It would not be untrue to say that on the whole modernism tends to look at science as a source of external truths or dogmas, but at the scriptures in the light of Kant's personal predilection for autonomy. This certainly seems to hold for

Bultmann, for example, as we shall see. If modernism does not follow the dualistic path of a slavish adherence to the external truths of science (scientism is never stronger than when in the hands of non-scientific theologians) and a subjective or interpretative approach to scripture, it goes the whole hog and opts for pure autonomy.

It is quite extraordinary how one can look down the list of theologians and see how many of them side with Kant against heteronomy (when it comes to religion!). Geoffrey Lampe who, for example, was one of Britain's leading exponents of Christ as essentially a (Spirit) object of faith rather than a historical person who is indeed both Jesus of Nazareth and the Son of God, saw commitment in this way, 'One's commitment of faith can only therefore, be tested by reference to one's own experience and the experience of other people past and present' (Baelz *et al*. 1981).

SCHLEIERMACHER: 'THE FATHER OF MODERN THEOLOGY'

If Kant is the rational philosopher who set the scene for modernism, it is the romanticist[5] Friedrich Schleiermacher (1768–1834) who can claim to be the true 'father of modern theology'. On the one hand Schleiermacher accepted Kant's demolition of traditional philosophy, believing that religious metaphysics (the noumenal realm) was no longer possible. On the other hand Schleiermacher wished to resist sterile rationalism and present the gospel in a form acceptable to modern man. He followed Kant in opting for *autonomy* as the correct and only possible arena for theological reflection. But unlike Kant he rejected the rational approach of 'practical reasoning' and built the whole of his systematic theology upon the concept of religious consciousness and experience. This experientialism which incorporated feeling as well as self-conscious thought was the heart of Schleiermacher's attempt to find a way to express the truths of the gospel as neither traditional orthodoxy nor cold rationalism.

Schleiermacher's new dogmatics, which he first systematically expressed in *The Christian Faith* (1821–1822), is brilliant and original. So much so that he is undoubtedly the major theological figure of the nineteenth century, and a hundred years later Karl Barth, who fundamentally disagreed with his approach, recognised him as the modern giant with whom he had to contend. (Barth always maintained a love–hate relationship with Schleiermacher's theology.)

Despite its originality, however, Schleiermacher's theology is really a break with traditional dogmatics. I first read this great German theologian after studying the phenomenological philosophy of Edmund Husserl (1859–1938). What immediately struck me was how similar Husserl's attempt to describe the structures of what he called 'pure consciousness' is to Schleiermacher's belief that there was a pure realm of religious- or God-consciousness. Indeed the whole Continental fascination with consciousness and all the incredibly complex terminology of existentialism and phenomenology look almost like a secular version of Schleiermacher's work. If he were alive today he would recognise Husserl and Martin Heidegger (1889–1976) as his heirs.

Schleiermacher recast traditional Christian dogmatics in terms of religious awareness or 'affections'. The Bible has authority, but in shaping Christian consciousness, not in its own right as a source of divine truth (*heteronomy* in Kant's terminology). Schleiermacher's use of such phrases as 'absolute dependence' or 'God-consciousness' reflected his conviction that this consciousness itself is the true basis of theology.[6] Gospel truths as traditionally understood become in his theology the expressed awareness of God-consciousness. Jesus is the truest embodiment of God-consciousness.

One could attack Schleiermacher's whole theological approach by asking whether feeling-awareness-religious consciousness provides sufficient grounds for an adequate Christian theology. The fact that the doctrine of the Holy Trinity is relegated to the conclusion in his dogmatics suggests that it is not.[7] But far more crucially we have to ask these questions of Schleiermacher: Are his doctrines of God-consciousness, which look similar in many ways to traditional beliefs, actually tied to the revelation of scripture? Is the resurrection *necessarily* a historical event? Are miracles really miracles or are they expressions of faith-commitment? Is Jesus a reality because he is a datum of faith – of our consciousness of him – or is he a reality because he was the historical Jesus of Nazareth? I believe that the answers Schleiermacher would have to give to all these questions would be at best ambiguous and at worst would admit that the historical basis of Christianity – of the incarnation, the life of Jesus and the resurrection – were of secondary importance. In a sense, rather like Husserl's famous 'phenomenological reduction', Schleiermacher tended to 'bracket away' questions of historicity and dogmatic revelation as incidentals to the true reality of religious consciousness.

I have dwelt on Schleiermacher not only because he is the father of modern theology but because he led modern theology away from the dogmas of faith and adjusted those dogmas to his own criteria of authenticity. That is what modernism does: Christianity is adopted and adapted to a faith-commitment not in Jesus as Lord or the revelation of scripture but to a modern understanding of faith; such an understanding may be essentially scientific, subjectivist, existentialist, moralist, or political – anything, it would seem, but a faithfulness to the gospel itself.

This would not matter if we did not live in a fallen culture that needs to sit under the judgment of the gospel in order to be liberated from the control of the Evil One, but once that gospel becomes adulterated by secularist philosophies – however good in themselves they may be – it loses its transforming power and becomes harnessed to the energies of this world.

We can learn other things from Schleiermacher too. He was a passionate seeker after truth, a deeply moral man, and wanted desperately to make the gospel ring true for modern man. How often does this fine motivation repeat itself in the lives of modernist theologians! It holds true for Ritschl, Schweitzer, Bultmann and Tillich. None of them were evil men wishing to destroy the faith: all of them wanted a gospel for modern man, but all were convinced, for different reasons, that the old gospel would not do. Schleiermacher himself was deeply influenced by his pious upbringing, especially in the Moravian schools. His commitment to pietism and moralism remained throughout his life. Having turned his back upon the rationalism of Kant he tended to favour the experiential over the rational and the spontaneous over the systematic. In revolting against the Enlightenment he unwittingly capitulated to subjectivism. This is a general problem of pietism. (For example, the Calvinist theologian Edward Irving accused Methodism of becoming awash in sentimentality and refusing to submit to the objectivity of grace, which he understood as God himself.)

Romanticism can slip into irrationality in its very attempt to escape the tyranny of *heteronomy*. I do not think that we can accuse Schleiermacher of that, for he was the pioneer in early methods of biblical criticism and the discipline known as hermeneutics. But we do find throughout the nineteenth century that so many modernist thinkers, having cut themselves off from the objectivity of revelation, became unbearably moralistic. I am thinking in particular of Ritschl in Germany and Tolstoy in Russia.

But now we must put together the final touches that turn the old gospel into its modernist form. And here we are in familiar territory because we are back with scientism and optimism. Following the Enlightenment and the rise of the scientific world-view it was believed by many theologians that miracles were no longer credible. Once this was accepted it became a presupposition of a great deal of modern theology. It goes like this: 'There can be no miracles in the nature of things; therefore it follows that the "miracles" of the Bible are either false reporting or myths.' Needless to say most theologians opted for the second course.

Another way of looking at this, the Polanyi way (1973: ch. 10), is to note a switch in faith-commitments: away from the truths of God's revelation to understanding revelation in the light of science. Science is plausible and modern men and women like nothing better than to live in a comfortable 'plausibility structure'.[8] Once we have opted to live our lives in the light of what is plausible there is no room for surprises or heaven's disclosures; we will adjust our world-view because science is constantly changing, but we will allow nothing to cast doubt on the plausibility framework itself!

Once it was accepted that miracles belonged to an earlier age and that science alone held the key to the universe, what was more natural than applying science to the Bible itself? Here we can see how the objectivity of science and critical reasoning fits in with what I earlier called the classic shift from the religion of tradition to the religion of modernism (p. 196). For that shift moved from the authority of the Bible to the authority of reason and in particular the authority of indi-vidual *autonomy*. No longer does the church speak for us, and the Bible to us, but we speak of ourselves. There is no longer any holy ground which compels us to remove our shoes in godly fear. We are the gods and fear no one.

And so beginning with the pioneering work of Gotthold Lessing (1729–1781), the historical method was applied to the texts of scripture. I am not afraid of scholarship and believe with Professor Dunn that Christians have nothing to fear from it (Dunn 1985: 103), but I am convinced that once the Bible as sacred text becomes an object of investigation then it be-comes extremely difficult to hear the divine drama. At first the new historical methods or criticism were primarily con-cerned with dating the books of the Bible. It was not until much later in the century that there began the modern source criticism which investigates the texts and their origins. And with respect to Ritschl and the German liberal school of theology, despite the fact that under their influence we have gained enormous information about the Bible, we are no longer hearing the gospel.

THE INFLUENCE OF GERMAN LIBERAL THEOLOGY

Ritschl was very different from Schleiermacher in many ways. He had no time for God-consciousness and he does not really fit into that stream of phenomenological thought that we see trickling through much of German philosophy to the present day. He was greatly influenced by the general optimism of the nineteenth century – an optimism that characterises many of his followers such as Hermann (1846–1922) and Adolf von Harnack (1851–1930) – and an almost scientistic belief in progress. This was still the era of Comtean positivism and the worship of reason. Ritschl had no time for experientialism, or mysticism. He tended to see the gospel as a system of ethics. He stressed the message of Christ, and it was Jesus' proclamation of the kingdom which he emphasised rather than the person of Christ himself.

In a way, looking at Ritschl we are back with Kant and practical reason. Ritschl believed that the facts of the matter are a question of scientific and rational examination. But true religion and morality are those 'facts' that we value for ourselves. It is no wonder that Ritschl attempted to demolish the dogmatic basis of Christianity, for he saw the great truths of Nicea and Chalcedon concerning the Trinity and Christ's true nature as outmoded and divorced from the true Jesus of the New Testament.

Curious developments come out of the German liberal school. On the one hand we have the beginnings of modern scientific studies of the New Testament (studies that have shown that the synoptic gospels draw on common sources, for example). Alongside these scientific studies we also see a more interpretative exegesis (hermeneutics) that lays the emphasis on recreating the world-views of Hellenism and Aramaic Palestine. In addition we see the real beginning of the modern quest for the authentic Jesus. Jesus, the German school believed, needed to be rescued from the overlays of the early church theologians. It was believed that many of the scriptural texts were far later than originally thought and contained theological interpretations of Jesus interwoven into his historical life and teachings. The liberal school wanted to set the authentic Jesus free and allow him to speak for himself.

Frankly, I think that in some ways this was a sham, for Ritschl, for example, had already decided that Jesus was the historical embodiment of modern Enlightenment man with all the traits of a German nineteenth-century gentleman. Jesus was the hero of Carlyle, with the moral stature of a Tolstoy, and his kingdom rather resembled Comte's religion of humanity. He stood for decency, progress, valour and liberal values. As Professor Heron points out, Adolf von Harnack, that great populariser of German modernism, presented Jesus 'as a noble teacher and inspiring example of love and heroic self-sacrifice' (Heron 1980: 37).[9]

I think that we can legitimately level the accusation at Ritschl that his decision to interpret the gospel as that which has 'value for us' undercuts any pretence at scientific objectivity. There is, in short, a great deal more subjectivism in the German school than at first meets the eye. This becomes even clearer if we see how much its members were influenced by the dominant cultural ideas of the time. Frazer's *Golden Bough* was all the rage in the early twentieth century, leading to a fascination with comparative religion and the role of myth in human development. Popular at that time, partly following Frazer, was a belief that the ancient world was crawling with 'redemption myths' and the death and resurrection of God-kings. As a number of the school were already unitarian in their belief and not particularly attached to beliefs in the resurrection as a historical reality, redemption myths fitted the bill very nicely.

And for decades the belief in such myths dominated modernist scholarship. Bultmann, for example, accepted the resurrection myth as a matter of fact. Today, however, modernist theologians as well as traditionalists reject such myths on historical grounds. It is an axiom, it seems to me, that modernist theology is relativistic and changes its tune with each intellectual fashion. And, let us be quite clear, this is not because it is scientific. Science accumulates as it develops. If there is a major shift in theory it tends to incorporate the findings of the earlier studies into the new theoretical framework. But in much modern theology we get a different phenomenon: many of the earlier approaches are abandoned altogether.

Let us look at what happened with the liberal school. By the turn of the twentieth century the great rush to find the authentic Jesus was on. No more Christs of dogma and Chalcedon – simply the historical Jesus. The elements of this quest were partly scientific. After all, if you are claiming to find someone in history you are in the world of facts. But there was also a great deal of subjective interpretation coupled with more sophisticated methods of understanding stemming from Wilhelm Dilthey (1833–1911) and from Schleiermacher himself.

In 1910 Albert Schweitzer (1875–1965) published his *Quest of the Historical Jesus.* His remarkable study effectively put an end to the dominance of the liberal school, for he argued that what emerges from the New Testament is not a nineteenth-century liberal gentleman or a heroic man of destiny, but an obscure prophet from Galilee whose message was not essentially ethical but eschatological. Furthermore his eschatological longings were ended for him on the cross and his predictions were shown to be false by the course of history. All the noble Jesus-figures of the nineteenth-century theologians were not in substance the historical Jesus but creations of fancy. As Tyrrell the Catholic modernist put it, the re-creators of the authentic Jesus 'looked into the deep well of history, and saw there only the reflection of their own faces'.

I once attended a lecture in which we were told that Schweitzer's study put an end to the search for the historical Jesus, but this is untrue. It certainly aided the comeuppance of the liberal school, but it also did something else. Schweitzer, for example, rejected the historical Jesus in favour of the 'spirit of Jesus' and since that time a wedge has been driven between the Christ of faith and the historical Jesus of Nazareth. Some scholars today recognise Jesus as the Lord of faith who has no necessary link with the historical Jesus. (Professor Lampe recently held that position.) Other scholars accept that there is a real historical Jesus but one who is devoid of divinity, or even God-consciousness. (Don Cupitt in our time has resurrected the anthropological Jesus.) As far as I can understand his position, Professor Maurice Wiles finds virtually no evidence for a historical Jesus at all, but I cannot understand from his *The Remaking of Christian*

Doctrine (1974) what he believes about Jesus (though to be fair there is more substance in recent works).

In a less subjectivist and jargonised way than German theology the quest for this historical Jesus has continued in Anglo-Saxon universities. In Oxford, for example, and particularly among Anglican New Testament scholars, there has developed a rather careful and measured (and certainly reasoned) search for the empirical Jesus and his authentic teachings. This work has primarily concentrated on so-called source and form criticisms and has been mainly concerned to map out the different written sources and oral traditions represented in the canonical scriptures.

Some Scottish theologians trained in the dogmatic tradition believe that this is not theology at all but a sort of textual archaeology. They have argued that a great deal of the theology in Oxford, Cambridge and Harvard tends to reflect the linguistic philosophies that arose after the collapse of logical positivism. Their criticisms of this theology are similar to Sir Karl Popper's upon Oxford philosophy: that it is trite, trivial, parochial, and refuses to engage in the real problems of the modern world. (See A. Heron in Walker 1988.)

It is precisely because a wedge is driven between the human Jesus and the divine Jesus that historicity is able to be discarded in that whole stream of modernist theology influenced by existentialism. Before I look at Bultmann and the contemporary theological scene, we must face the most important reason for the demise of the liberal school and assess the importance of Karl Barth, who dominates the theology of the Western world from the 1920s to the 1950s.

What really destroyed the German liberal school was not Schweitzer, who ironically was trained in its methods, but the First World War. And in a way this is more curious than it looks. On the surface the answer is simply this: the horror of the war and the millions killed gave the lie to the optimism and faith in reason of the liberal theologians. After 1918 it was clear that liberal theology had no gospel to meet the needs of modern man. And yet in Great Britain, despite the fact that the war put a temporary halt to belief in progress in the realm of philosophy, science became the source of truth. And in Austria we had the logical positivists and the Vienna Circle.

And so it is not unreasonable to ask why did not modernist theology continue its inexorable way? I think that there are three answers to that question. Firstly, we now know from the perspective of the 1980s that the collapse of the liberal school and the rise of Barthian theology was in fact only an interruption, a pause, in the development of modernism. We have to understand that this pause was made possible because the effects of the war upon a defeated Germany were more demoralising and devastating than for the rest of Europe. Secondly, Barth's theology and logical positivism had this in common: they both rejected subjectivism and what Kant would have called *autonomy* and veered back towards *heteronomy*.[10] It is significant that when positivism collapsed by the end of the Second World War, and Barthianism a little later, there was a sudden rush of subjectivist and relativistic philosophies and theologies to take their place. Thirdly, Barth was a man of such intellectual stature that he forced modern theology to think again about its commitment to reason and autonomy.

I think that it is inappropriate to deal at length with Barth in this chapter because he is not, in my opinion, a modernist theologian. Many evangelicals have, however, treated him as if he was one. I would like to say something briefly about this and then, looking through Barth's eyes, see what he thought was wrong with modernism. His views are perhaps even more vital today than during his life-time.

KARL BARTH AND THE CHALLENGE TO MODERNISM

Barth's rejection by some evangelicals is understandable. His systematic dogmatics incorporates many of the insights and approaches not only of the Reformers but also of the Greek fathers. Barth is more at home in some ways with the Greek East than the Latin West (Torrance 1986). The fact that he also rejected much of the Aristotelianism and scholasticism of

Catholic theology has not endeared him to Roman Catholics (though Pope Pius XII called Barth 'the greatest theologian since St Thomas Aquinas'). Historically, however, this 'strange evangelical', as Professor Packer has called Barth, fell foul of certain evangelical opinion in Britain and Germany because he was not a thoroughgoing biblicist in the nineteenth-century evangelical tradition. He treated the scriptures as sacred, but in the sense that they revealed the revelation of God who is Jesus himself. For Barth the words of scripture were rather like ikons or pictures of the truth that pointed to their source who is God become man. In other words Barth rejected the idea that the words (ikons) of scripture were holy in themselves: they deserved to be treated with respect, but not to be worshipped or seen as the locus of truth. Truth for Barth resides solely in God's self-revelation. In short, Barth believed that the words of scripture reveal the Word, and it is Christ alone who is God's revelation and his person and actions should determine the content of true theology.

For this reason Barth was not particularly bothered by debates concerning dates and origins of texts, and he certainly would have been in sympathy with Lewis concerning the mythological dimension so important to the meaning (not the truth) of revelation. The fundamentalist movement in Great Britain and in America had little sympathy with this approach and many so-called conservative evangelicals still find it unacceptable.

What is so important about Barth is that he did not simply revolt against modernism – and what he usually called 'natural theology' – but he offered an alternative to it. So radical is this alternative that when it first appeared on the German scene it was felt by contemporaries that Barth had hurled the gospel at them like a stone. The only legitimate source of theology, declared Barth, is God's revelation. All theology that starts from below – from our natural reasoning and human experiences – is doomed to failure and is an affront to the gospel.

The entire content of theology should be determined by revelation and revelation alone, thundered Barth. To be a theologian is to explicate the content of revelation through faith and faithfulness to God's truth in Jesus. Barth was not against reason as a tool in the task of a truly systematic and faithful theology, but he denied its supremacy. This is what he thought of natural theology: 'By "natural theology" I mean every (positive *or* negative) *formulation of a system* which claims to be theological, i.e. to interpret divine revelation, whose *subject*, however, differs fundamentally from the revelation of Jesus Christ and whose *method* therefore differs equally from the exposition of Holy Scripture' (quoted in Avis 1986: 43–44).

For our purposes we have much to learn from Barth's neo-orthodoxy (as it is often called). He understood that once theology from above – that is, God's revelation to man – is abandoned then theologies from below, starting from man's historical, cultural, and existential position, will inevitably reject the content of revelation. Incarnation and resurrection cease to be primary data, or the objective data, and become merely elements in an understanding of God that is rooted in our own autonomous understanding. Furthermore, theologies from below reflect the myriad starting-points of our own concerns and needs: we project on to God our prejudices, hopes and subjective longings. What emerges is transitory, fragmentary and historically conditioned.

Barth's theological approach is so absolutist that it could be argued that he makes no concessions to human reasoning. Perhaps theology from below is possible, and towards the end of his life he seemed to be moving in that direction. There is certainly no reason why science, for example, cannot be incorporated into a world-view that has Christ at the centre. We see such adaptions of Barth in the work of Professor Tom Torrance (1984). There is no doubt, however, that Barth provides the corrective to the sort of theology, so dominant in Britain and America today, that seeks to follow the route of natural reasoning to God. Sooner or later such reason comes up against God himself and his self-revelation. No theology from below can cross that barrier (see Gunton 1983).

Personally I am convinced, on intellectual grounds, that

theologies from below just do not work. Have you noticed how existentialist theologies fall back upon themselves and become primarily existentialism? Or how Marxist Christianity ends up as Marxism? Try and mix revelation with human philosophies starting from the human end and you have a recipe not only for apostasy but failure.

Barth's theology can be rightly criticised on the grounds that it is too Christocentric. By which I mean that Barth tried to interpret the whole of scripture in terms of God's revelation in Christ. But I do not think this was a major cause for the collapse of Barthianism. In the first place Barth's insistence on the supremacy of revelation and the objective reality of God's incarnation was felt to be too restricting for many theologians. Barth had tried to turn back the tide of modernism. But he was like the boy with the finger in the dyke, and when eventually the swell of modernism broke through it burst the dam and flooded the world with a sea of theologies quite alien to orthodoxy.

To change our metaphor, many theologians felt hemmed in by Barth, as if he were containing them in a world under the sovereign judgment of a God who from above forbade them to think for themselves. Once Barth fell from grace (though he is still very much with us and will become more important in the future) it was as if the children had been let out of school. Under this new freedom, which really made its mark in the 1960s, the old nineteenth- and eighteenth-century modernisms were brought back with a vengeance. It was almost as if there had been no First World War and no Karl Barth.

BULTMANN DEMYTHOLOGISED

The fact that the theology of Rudolf Bultmann should become so dominant after Barth (though of course they were contemporaries for many years) reflects so much of the postwar period. Reacting against the 'dark myths' of Nazism and influenced by existentialism, Bultmann took up the old theological liberalism where Schweitzer had left off. Bult-mann (1952) did not find the New Testament immediate but remote. He saw no point in pursuing a historical Jesus. It was his *kerygma* (proclamation) that he thought was important. He wanted Jesus to speak to the modern world directly, and wanted human beings to respond to his message without recourse to the myths of old. Having shouldered aside Barth, who like some ancient Old Testament prophet seemed to have accidentally got in the way of twentieth-century modern-ism, Bultmannism really charged ahead in the 1950s and 1960s.

His demythologising programme for purging the New Testament of its mythological content in order to let the proclamation of Jesus reach the modern mind clear and uncluttered was enormously appealing. Like so much of modernism it seems to be scientific when it is in fact primarily subjective. That is because the subjectivism slips in as the only plausible way of dealing with religion in a scientific world. Consider Bultmann's most famous remark: 'It is impossible to use electric light and the wireless and to avail ourselves of modern medical and surgical discoveries, and at the same time to believe in the New Testament world of daemons and spirits' (1953: 5).

Robinson in *Honest To God* (1963) made the same sort of impact upon the English-speaking world when, following Bultmann, he insisted that we must do away with a God in the sky 'up there' and furthermore one who is an old benign being with a long white beard. How did so many people get taken in by this kind of theology? I mention this precisely because now in the 1980s Bultmann himself is no longer followed with any great enthusiasm. I think we have to see it like this. Bultmann appealed to science as evidence that miracles, demons, and the resurrection of bodies are no longer credible. This appeal is based on very little knowledge of science and there is no doubt that Bultmann's concept of science was influenced by nineteenth-century mechanical physics rather than modern science. Theological modernism, in fact, has its roots in Enlightenment philosophy and nineteenth-century science. There is nothing absolutely new about it, which is why I have

attempted to understand it in its historical context. Having,
however, pointed to the hard realities of science, Bultmann
appealed to our modern search for authenticity and in the best
tradition of Kantian *autonomy* sought to ground his theology
in existentialism. What threw so many scholars was the
elegance of Bultmann's demythologising approach. His hermeneutics seemed so scholarly, and his knowledge of myths
and their functions so sophisticated, that it was not clear on
the surface that much of this elaborate historical theorising
was more a question of personal interpretation than historical
analysis.

Bultmann used a distinction made popular by some of the
earlier liberal school between history (*Historie*) and those
events that can be said to be historical, turning events (*Geschichte*) in human development. This distinction is sharper
than it appears, for it follows (for Bultmann anyway) that
turning events such as the crucifixion are *Geschichte* because
of their impact upon history, but they may very well not
actually be historical (*Historie*) at all! Here you have the
classic problem with existentialism, which Sartre himself was
to recognise: it is ahistorical because it is entirely caught up
with self-authentication and subjective truth. If it is true
that Hegel and Marx bind us with the laws of history, as Søren
Kierkegaard (1813–1855) saw, it is equally true that
existentialism binds us to the transient 'now' of our existence.

Ultimately Bultmann's theology fails because it falls back
into existentialism. As Roberts points out (1977) Bultmann's
elegance and profundity turn out on examination to be basically about nothing at all except the reduction of all theology
to the one principle that man draws his 'self' into conformity
with his 'authentic self' that allows him to be. I apologise to
readers that I cannot put this more simply, but that is because
much of Bultmann's understanding of existentialism is taken
from Heidegger, whose 'profound nonsense' is impossible to
translate into simple English.

REFLECTIONS ON MODERNISM TODAY

As I said at the beginning of this chapter, I have left out Hegel in this impressionistic look at modernism. I have also not looked at process theology or the Catholic and Protestant liberation theologies. Instead I have tried to concentrate on the development from Kant, Schleiermacher, Ritschl and into twentieth-century modernism because I feel that most people want to be able to understand why the Bible is not believed as God's self-revelation. Or to put it another way, why it is that so many theologians do not seem able to accept the dogmas and beliefs of tradition. I have attempted to show that, following Kant, once the scriptures are dismissed as mere *heteronomy* the gospel disappears and becomes fragmented and diluted into modernist gospels that no longer are rooted in revelation but in reason or experience.

In the twenty years or so since Bultmann was popular in Britain, while in America Thomas Altizer was trying to convince us all that God was dead (his was such a radical emptying – *kenosis* – that he died on the cross!), we have been subjected to the swings and roundabouts of modernism in perpetual motion. Frankly the newest thing about modernism is the speed with which it travels. As Michael Goulder has put it: 'We are driving over the same course as our eighteenth-century forefathers, only at four times the speed' (Goulder and Hick 1983: 88).

Modernism is really sectarian rather than a broad church. There are still elements of the German liberal school alive in Oxford. Existentialism is still brooding in Europe and parts of Britain. Deism is doing well, and the pluralist theology of John Hick is doing very well, not only in California but in those sorts of Christian circles that favour inter-faith dialogue in the belief that at depth God is behind (or underneath) all religion (see D'Costa 1986).

Perhaps the rise of the media modernist is a relatively new phenomenon, but in fact the general public have not been introduced to new theology, merely to tired theologies. In Great Britain the media impact of modernism was particularly shocking to so many evangelicals because many of them were meeting it for the first time. (So privatised and pluralist is our society that dwelling in our churches and fellowships it is quite possible to imagine that we are still living in a world before the philosophical Enlightenment!) Conservative evangelicals, however, along with Anglo-Catholics and other traditionalists, rightly saw that the publication in 1977 of *The Myth of God Incarnate* heralded a more brazen attack upon the gospel. It was one thing to talk about the miracles of Jesus and New Testament demonising as mythical but quite another thing to suggest that we should learn to live with a Christianity which denies that God has entered into our humanity in order to redeem it from within. At a stroke such a contention removes the whole of Christian orthodoxy. Modernist theology since the Enlightenment has moved from trinitarianism to unitarianism and in one direction (Hick 1973) ends up with deism. In another direction we have so denuded the gospel of God's divinity and the action of the Holy Spirit that we are left with nothing but anthropology (Cupitt 1979).

Our attempts to strip the miraculous from the kingdom message of Jesus have left us with a denial of the historicity of the gospel story. There is no physical resurrection, no virgin birth, and no incarnation.

C. S. Lewis, reacting in particular against Bultmann, warned that the future of the Church of England would be short if it continued to go down the path of demythologising the scriptures (1975: 125). He recognised that myths are timeless truths that have been broken and differentiated by the process of imagination. But he recognised also that the great truths of the gospel are not myths in this sense. He saw that the incarnation has no mythic power unless it has a firm historical foundation. The incarnation is not a story to help us understand the fusion of the divine and human in human personality (as Professor Wiles would have it): it is a story of divine intervention and act, of drama. Yet it is not merely drama; it is the reality of God's love for us in that he came down from heaven and joined himself to our fallen humanity.

Professor Frances Young, who is now a very different theologian from the woman who contributed to the *Myth of God Incarnate*, followed a tradition in that infamous book which characterises much of modernist methodology. She sought to make the incarnation story plausible in terms of existing myths, Samaritan, Jewish, Hellenistic, etc. The trouble with this approach – trying to show historical antecedents to 'new' revelations – is that it always fails to ask the fundamental question of the revelations: Are they true? We do not want ultimately to know whether redeemer myths pre-existed Jesus. Ultimately we want to know whether or not he is the redeemer. I think it very likely, for example, that Christian belief in the Devil was influenced by Persian Zoroastrianism. So what? If this is true, and can be demonstrated historically, we still have to ask the fundamental question that I asked in chapter one, 'Is the Christian Devil a reality?'

Modernism cannot answer these questions, because no analytical method known to scholarship could possibly know how to decide the issue. The dualistic nature of much modernist thought comes out here. We notice its commitment to rational and empirical enquiry. This commitment states that if you cannot rationally demonstrate the correctness of your position by appealing to the facts or to *a priori* logical statements, you cannot make historical or theological judgments.

What you can do, and modernism does it *ad nauseam*, is to bypass truth claims altogether and operate in the interpretive or subjective mode. Having decided against Barth, and the whole of Christian orthodoxy, that revelation is not itself the objective datum of theology (usually on the grounds that such a position does not fulfil the criteria of modern rationality) we are left with a sea of subjectivism.

And so we have moved from the unity of theological belief to fragmentation. Without any overall picture to go by modernism builds analytic jig-saws, starting with scattered pieces and creating different pictorial forms. They are often elegant, and sometimes ugly, but they are always changing like a kaleidoscope.

Leslie Houlden has told us that 'we must accept our lot, bequeathed to us by the Enlightenment, and make the most of it' (Hick 1977: 125). The tragedy of modernism is that having accepted the Enlightenment it finds that it has very little left to make of anything. It is the truth that will set the captives free and we Christians have nothing to offer the modern world except the gospel. Modernism has made us timid in the face of its demands that we conform to the plausibilities and realities of the modern world-view. This timidity has kept us divided and afraid. Sometimes in reaction we have become anti-intellectual and belligerent, but we have rarely engaged in combat with modernism.

To talk of the 'enemy within' is often paranoid and much loved by people who believe in conspiracy theories. Modern theologians are not agents of Satan or paid-up members of atheistic societies. But I believe that the evidence is over-whelming that the Enemy has been at work: the gospel to modern man has been turned round to the gospel of modern men. We are never going to win for God the modern world – which longs to be free and delivered from alienation, separation and sin – with a modernist gospel.

I have tried in this book to alert us to the evils of modernity both in its social and in its philosophical aspects. Modernism in the churches is the evidence that we are scaling down our theologies to accommodate the modern world. But in the face of modernism and the merciless anti-Christian pressures of modernity, what can we do? The answer is that we have first to remember that we are a liberation army. Secondly we have to fight. I would like to end this book with some stratagems of combat.

Part Three

ENEMY ENGAGEMENT –
THE STRUGGLE FOR THE KINGDOM

9 KINGDOM MOVES

The New Testament exhorts us to resist the Devil (1 Pet 5:8), but does not give us detailed instructions on how to go about this. And this, it strikes me, is very wise. If our scriptures were a manual or an instruction book we would come unstuck every time we faced a situation that was not covered by the rules! I remember a girl in a social philosophy class once saying that she did not have a view on abortion because neither did the New Testament! On such grounds, I pointed out, it is difficult for us to have views on slavery, warfare or capital punishment. And if we wanted to specify problems in terms of the developments of modernity – the abuse of science, ecological mismanagement, atomic war, heart transplants, the effects of mass media – then it follows that the Bible will not have anything to say at all!

Clearly the scriptures provide the source for our theological doctrines, the general principles for our morality, and most importantly of all they provide us with spiritual nourishment through the Holy Spirit's guidance. Meditation and study of the Bible lead us into the truth which is Christ himself. As soldiers we take our orders directly from our captain, not from the stories about him. He in turn speaks to us through the scriptures themselves. We are exhorted to 'search the scriptures' (John 5:39). They are not a mirror in which we read the obvious or simply see ourselves; they are God's revelation of himself, and his revelation has to be grasped through spiritual and intellectual diligence.

There is, in short, a dialogue between God, us, and his self-revelation. If we take our instruction from the written words of scripture without relating them to their source, the living Word (Christ himself), we are in danger of slipping into a form of religious positivism (*heteronomy*). But because God is consistent, his being and his self-revelation in scripture are not contradictory. That is why whenever certain charismatic leaders insist that they have a word just for you (or us) which is not in agreement with scripture we should reject it. If on the other hand we give the Holy Spirit dominance over Christ (pneumatomonism) we slip into modernist *autonomy* (and lose the sovereignty of the Father; see Tom Smail 1987). Jesus reveals the Father to us through the Holy Spirit. The Holy Spirit guides us through the scriptures to Jesus, who shows us the Father.

If we are meditating on the scriptures and praying in the Spirit through the Son to the Father, then we are caught up into the triune life of God. This is the prerequisite to any offensive against the Evil One. Any move that we make off our own bat or from our own resources is bound to end in failure. We are only effective soldiers for Christ when we are serving in an army that is itself participating in God's own life. Now as soldiers, strictly speaking we are rebels who have laid down our arms and joined God's side. But to recall what we said in chapter two, we are not only followers of Christ, but we have been adopted by him into a new humanity.

It is sometimes difficult to believe that we are not only volunteers in God's army, but that we are also citizens of the kingdom to come. Only new creatures – members of a new humanity – can become citizens. The church militant is no less than God's citizen-army of the kingdom. Our strategy is to win other rebels to the great cause of Jesus Christ: that cause is the liberation of the world – the final completion of the victory over sin and the Devil won at Golgotha.

But how shall we fight and where? In this penultimate chapter I want to outline three practical areas for moving on to the offensive. They are not the only practical areas in which we can fight, but I believe they indicate the sort of offensive against modernity that we can make together. Briefly I shall look at a 'proper ecumenism', the need for a concerted attack on modernism, and the way towards a spiritual politics.

SPIRITUAL IMMOBILISATION

But first we have got to get moving. Before we come together, hit out at the Enemy and take the battle to the city (that is, away from the margins of our existence as privatised church-goers), we need to wake up and hear the call to arms. Until we hear the call – and we need to be awake to hear it – we are not going anywhere. If I have failed to help us all wake up, then obviously this book has been a waste of time.

My experience over the last few years is that many people are waking up and are being overcome by fear. They look around at the collapse of Christian civilisation, and the extent of modernism in the churches, and sink back into their comfortable television chairs, taking time off only to slink round to church on Sunday morning. Others feel so threatened by the world – and rightly so – that they seek comfort in their local church and settle for a decent pietism. And there is nobility in that course. A fervent, good-living and 'right-believing' Christian is an affront to the Devil. But to be on active service means by definition that we will be called to the Great Battle, which means joining up with our comrades. There is no such thing as an individualist war: the community needs us all against the Devil's dark collective.

To be immobilised by fear is to be like Peter, who turned from Jesus on the sea of Galilee and saw only the storm and the waves, whereupon the outward reality of his perilous position entered his heart and he was afraid. Fear consumes faith, and Peter sank. The early church fathers taught that cowardice arises from fear, not timidity. They taught also that fear destroys not only faith but all the virtues.

I am sure today that there are some non-Christian people who do not know what is right and what is wrong. Modern moral theories bring with them confusion, and confusion leads to inactivity or an inability to act morally. Christians who have internalised modern morality also experience this confusion. For many of us, however, the problem is not moral fog but fear: fear of the Devil, fear of our priests and pastors, fear of offending political authority, fear of our peer group.

Perhaps some of us fear our contemporaries more than the Devil himself!

Speaking for myself, I am convinced that cowardice has been a root cause of my luke-warm Christian discipleship. Looking back at the great mistakes in my life, they were nearly all caused by being afraid of standing for the truth or facing up to the truth. I do not know about you, but I do not like confrontation and naturally prefer appeasement. One day I heard on the radio Denholm Elliot, the distinguished actor, talking about cowardice. He argued that it lies behind most immorality. It is not so much that people do not know what to do, but that they cannot face the consequences of doing what they know to be right. Only love casts out fear and enables us to engage with the Enemy; every time we slip out of love's grasp fear enters our hearts as certainly as it did Peter's as he sank beneath the waves. 'Lord save me!' was the cry of desperation, not of faith, and love took his hand. That is the sort of captain that we have, that we combatants can rely on. We also know that he asks nothing of us that he has not already done himself. Jesus is not the sort of European commander who leads from the rear. He leads from the front, by example and deed.

But I think that there is a more pernicious reason for Christian inactivity, one that on the surface is moral enough, but at depth is the morality of the Pharisee. We all have a natural fear of pollution: we do not want to be contaminated by evil or apostasy. This righteous fear, however, can degenerate into false righteousness – a belief in our spiritual superiority. We who think that we are pure and clean cannot bring ourselves to rub shoulders with those whom we believe are unclean. Our spirituality is so precious and other-worldly that we will have no truck with those in the world, or even – dare I say it – with our brothers and sisters in other Christian denominations.

Let me be blunt about this. If we are not prepared to dirty our hands for God we are not much use to him. God's Son was prepared to 'contaminate' his uncreated divinity by joining himself to sinful humanity. In his earthly life Jesus drank with the 'winebibbers', consorted with prostitutes, and took a dying murderer with him to paradise. And we dare assert our righteousness – filthy as rags – over and above God! No wonder that Edward Irving in his great sermons at Hatton Garden in the 1820s used to insist that only people who believed in an unreal and romanticised Jesus (a docetic Christ) could remain aloof from fallen humanity. Jesus never condoned adultery and carnal sin, but it was spiritual sin that he saw as the root of religious failure. And it is spiritual sin, pride, triumphalism and exclusiveness, by which the Devil binds us Christians and keeps us immobile while he wreaks havoc through modernity.

The drive for purity in the Christian life not only keeps us divided from each other, but it also means that we are no longer alongside our captive brothers and sisters but against them. It is the Devil who convinces us that our enemies are really our human relations. God's answer to this lie is decisive: it is the cross.

Our self-righteousness, like any form of puritanism, has pragmatic consequences. During the Second World War, for example, a number of small Trotskyist groups refused to back Stalin against Hitler because they were convinced that he had betrayed the revolution. Despite the fact that it was obvious to the whole free and socialist world at that time that Hitler posed the greatest threat to world peace, they remained aloof from the struggle because they believed that they and they alone were the true vanguard of socialism! I once asked Metropolitan Anthony of the Russian Orthodox Church how he was able to reconcile his Christianity with his role in the French Resistance – a movement that included many communists. He replied that it was either a case of joining in the battle with dirty hands or staying clean on the sidelines.

If we translate this into Christian terms, how often do we find that there is a refusal to be involved in ecumenism or political activity because some of the people involved are not Christian? For example, in 1986 I talked to some Christian people who were convinced that the 'Green' movement was evil because it included socialists and pagans. There is no doubt that there are some socialists – the reds – who pretend to be green (there are socialist agitators everywhere, not least in my own church). It is also true that some of the ideologies of the Green movement belong to a non-Christian romanticism and deistic nature worship. So a natural reaction for some committed Christians is to have nothing to do with it. We see a similar reaction to CND and other peace movements.

But, I asked some of the Christian people concerned with the 'real' nature of the Green movement, what did they think about ecology? A number of them felt it represented a genuine Christian doctrine of stewardship. So why not, I suggested, form a Christian Green movement, and join in with the other Green movements when conscience permits, maintaining solidarity with them when possible, and keeping separate when it is not?

'Oh, we could not join in with them,' they said. 'Then don't be surprised', was my reaction, 'if you get nowhere.' Real politics means *realpolitik*. If we want to come out of the Christian ghettoes and make an assault on the city, which is controlled by the Enemy, we will have to fight alongside some of Satan's slaves. What a wonderful opportunity for mission! Fighting shoulder to shoulder with the captives against the common Enemy – the only Enemy external to ourselves that we have – is a chance to introduce them to our captain and 'turn' them to the greater cause.

The very same purity which keeps us out of real politics keeps us away from each other. Sometimes our deep fear of modernism leads to a refusal to come together in order to combat it! This is the work of our Enemy, for in coming together we not only gain strength through solidarity but we begin to move. I would now like to suggest a proper ecumenism for our time: to come together is to answer the call to arms.

CHRISTIAN MOBILISATION

Paradoxically the ecumenical movement is very divisive: it draws many to it and at the same time repels many others. There are those who are convinced that the World Council of

Churches is demonic. Catholics remain aloof from it, many evangelicals shun it, and the Orthodox are always threatening to withdraw from it.

There are similar reactions to the national councils in Great Britain and North America. The problem with so much institutional ecumenism is that it is the old trouble of the wheat and the tares. Some of us wonder if we will have to wait for the divine reaper to sift and separate.

Of course by having nothing to do with such bodies we also waive our right to influence them. The British Council of Churches, for example, would be a very different organisation if Catholics and evangelicals attended in full force!

Personally I think both the WCC and the BCC are too political. Socialist and centrist caucuses tend to hold sway at the expense of theological consensus. I find more disturbing the sort of professional ecumenical mentality that tends to see 'ecumenism' as 'where it's at'. There is often a dismissive attitude to those who feel less enthusiastic. And there are definitely groups of people who want togetherness at any cost and seem little bothered by differences of doctrine.

But having said all that, there are many great men and women of God who have given their time and talents to bring people closer together; and coming together for the common sake of the gospel is one of the hallmarks of the church. Jesus's great prayer to the Father that we may all be one remains a moral imperative for the militant church (John 17). This plea is not only for Christians, that they may see the glory of the Father; it is also for the world, that they may see the unity and believe. Unity, in short, is a question of mission and hope to a fallen and divided world.

Our indifference to unity is a sin. The real reason for our failure to come together is a refusal to repent. This, I believe, is the basic weakness of the bureaucratic approach to togetherness. No amount of theological commissions, whether they be Faith and Order reports in the WCC or the Roman Catholic-Anglican ARCIC talks, will ever promote unity. I am all for such theological discussions, and I am involved in them myself (they are preferable to perpetual politicking). But only direct encounter through repentance and common experience will bring us truly together, and turn us into an effective fighting force.

There is another difficulty with bureaucratic ecumenism: like government 'quangos' they have a habit of perpetuating their own existence. National and international councils are extra-denominational structures that pursue their own agendas – agendas that are quite often different from those of their member churches. Furthermore, such organisations have no real authority; they are not the sort of church council of the early centuries, where the churches were in communion and espoused a common faith. At the Council of Nicea (AD 325), for example, there was not a collection of different denominations, which is the present situation; each regional and national church belonged unreservedly to the universal church.

But the greatest danger of modern bureaucratic ecumenism, whether it be at the World Council level or bipartite talks, is that it glosses over the real issues. For example, when the Catholic and Anglican theologians discuss doctrine there is an assumption that they hold to that doctrine. The reality is different. Many bishops of the Church of England do not assent to their own thirty-nine articles. It is not uncommon for some bishops and theologians to deny fundamental Christian beliefs.

What is the point of having union between Anglicans and Methodists, or Baptists and Presbyterians, when the real divide is not between denominations but between orthodox Christians who accept the biblical revelation and the truths of the ancient creeds and those who do not? In this respect division cuts across denominational boundaries and operates within the individual confessions themselves.

What we should be aiming for if we are serious about mission and ecumenism is not a hotchpotch of denominations but the coming together of believing Christians. Bishop Lesslie Newbigin in a recent interview (Walker 1988) believes that we either define our confessions by the centre, that is Christ as Lord, or by the boundaries – the secondary elaborations of faith and practice (which may be rites, liturgical dress, cultural expression, etc.).

It follows that if we define the church by the centre there is not a great deal of excuse for our religious pluralism. It was Archbishop Temple who once said that we should do everything together except that which conscience forbids. When we look around at the contemporary Christian scene what we find is that people are quite happy and content with continuing in their own separate fashions. Even those denominations that give lip service to ecumenism show little evidence of giving up their autonomy and power.

In the next section I want to talk about standing against modernism. It is difficult to take a stand if we are not standing together. We do not have to tell the Devil about 'divide and rule': he invented it. Elsewhere (Walker 1986) I have likened the present situation in Christendom to a 'third schism'. The first divide was the visible split between East and West in 1054. The Western Reformation of the sixteenth century was the second schism. The third 'schism', I suggested, is an invisible divide between a believing church and a modernist church. Today the real issues of division are not methods of baptism, sacramentalism or pietism: the issues are a belief in and a commitment to a risen Lord and the trinitarian faith of the universal church.

And the tragedy is that our denominations are still fighting at the barricades of the last two schisms as if since then there had never been a philosophical Enlightenment or the rise of a post-Christian culture. No wonder the world laughs at our seriousness when it sees that we quarrel and fight among ourselves like any other human family. What sort of a new humanity is this! We are in the midst of the Great Battle, perhaps near the final moments, and we cannot even recognise our own comrades-in-arms. There is a solution to this problem: first find the right barricades and then the fighting ground itself will determine who are our comrades.

Catholics and Protestants disagree on certain interpretations of scripture, but they can agree on the common tradition that scripture is God's revelation. Eastern Orthodox and Baptists do not appear to have much in common, but both are committed to repentance and conversion. Episcopalians and Presbyterians are never going to agree on the 'correct' method of church government but they both recite the same creeds. Such differences as the Protestant division over Calvinism and Arminianism are real enough, but they pale into insignificance in the light of the common enemy of unbelief and heresy so rife in the churches.

When in the Church of England controversy broke out over the Bishop of Durham's remarks concerning the physical resurrection of Christ and the virgin birth, the most positive effect was to see the evangelical and Catholic wings of Anglicanism coming together in order to reassert the tradition of the church. Conversely, the most negative aspect of the recent decision of the General Synod to ordain women as priests is that it threatens schism on a 'secondary' elaboration of faith.[1] The long-term effect of this is that the evangelicals and Catholics will cease to stand together against modernism. We could even see a new 'Catholic' sect being established outside the present established church, leaving the evangelicals to fight it out alone inside that church while becoming increasingly entrenched in their defensive position.

I mention this example because our ecumenism, like our politics, also needs a sense of priority and *realpolitik*. We need to come together to save the faith of the historic church and then move on to deliver the captives. But we need to be realistic enough to acknowledge that we are always going to disagree on matters outside the central dogmas of the creeds.

To remind ourselves, the battle is not against one another: it is our fallen culture with its false ideologies and distorted social and economic structures that we fight. In fighting these we are fighting the Devil himself because they are under his control. We do not need to go looking for the Evil One. The Dark Power is everywhere where evil is to be found. As we are a liberation army, and as we seek to move among captive humanity like a 'secret society' (Lewis 1942: 61), a natural way to behave is to encourage the erection of barricades. During a revolution or in urban warfare a barricade is an instant method of resistance. The battlefield is the whole arena of modernity, but barricades are focal – and sometimes local – points for repelling the enemy. We need barricades to resist the forces of modernism in the churches, barricades to repel racism in the larger society (and churches), barricades to halt moral decline, barricades to prevent the plunder and pollution of our planet, barricades against false ideologies, barricades against the misuse of science, barricades against the plastic culture of the media. And of course we could go on. But what we do not need is Baptist, Methodist, Catholic, Lutheran, Orthodox barricades: we need simply Christian barricades.

Nowhere is this more obvious than in the field of evangelism. In practice evangelism means Catholic evangelism, Baptist evangelism, Pentecostal evangelism, etc. Evangelism goes hand in hand with denominational commitment. Billy Graham has always been a transdenominational evangelist, and in recent years has transcended even Protestant, Catholic, Orthodox boundaries while remaining faithful to his evangelical roots. If we want to resist heathenism and the false gods of affluence we need first of all to confront these evils with the gospel (erect the barricade) and then move on together in a combined offensive. We are entitled to have different views of effective and honest methods of evangelism, but we are not entitled to a muffled gospel. In this respect we are a preaching army chanting the saga of the Divine Drama as we engage in combat with the Enemy. Our propaganda is for the captives (the Devil knows the story and how it will end).

Sometimes we do not think through the consequences of our unilateral missions. We want to do something for God, so we zoom off against the Enemy on our own. In practice this often means that we end up competing against each other. In a recent as yet unpublished research paper[2] the C. S. Lewis Centre has charted the development of Protestant evangelism over the last few years, paying particular attention to new Christian movements. The overall pattern is to switch from missionaries to radio evangelism or to pull out of the Third World and home in on a nominal Catholic Europe. Catholicism is seen as fair game. Missionaries are also 'dropped' into Rumania on the grounds that the country is unchurched! (This situation works both ways as the Orthodox in Greece repress Protestants, seeing them as heretics and agents of modernism and Western culture.)

I believe that this sort of activity is understandable – sometimes it may even be laudable – but eventually it is regrettable: it often weakens the existing religious structure, leads to resentment and ends finally with Christian against Christian. This sort of example – stemming from 'free enterprise' evangelism – argues, I believe, for a far stronger grassroots ecumenism, where Christian brother and sister come together to find out if there is more in common between them than that which divides them.

Here such movements as Taizé are witnesses to a proper ecumenism, for unity can be found only in the lordship of Christ, who is head of the church and captain of the army. Improper ecumenism is a search for uniformity and organisational unity without the spiritual underground springs of repentance and reconciliation. A proper ecumenism needs to start with Christians accepting each other as fellow human beings – this begins with listening to each other – and then moving on to recognising each other as comrades of the new humanity.

C. S. Lewis believed that orthodox Christians everywhere can recognise each other 'and hold the main road' of Christendom (Lewis 1950: 13). It is that simple but effective vision that is needed in modernity. Is it not significant that most of us have no difficulty in recognising him as an exemplar of a 'mere Christian'?

I am sure that Lewis would expect us – orthodox Christians everywhere – to come together to fight the evils of modernity. Lewis believed that we do not need to change our denominational allegiance or renege on our churchmanship in order to do this (but we do need to meet). We cannot, therefore, afford to despise councils of churches, local ecumenical projects, interdenominational retreats and inter-church processes. Togetherness cannot happen in a vacuum. Neither let us reject our modernist brothers and sisters (though we must confront their theology with the gospel) out of a sense of our purity and righteousness. If we insist on meeting only with the righteous and the 'sound' we will end up meeting no one but ourselves!

Ultimately, however, a true and proper ecumenism needs to be more than a transitory phenomenon. Occasional meetings, glory conventions, council assemblies, and interdenominational evangelism may be good and proper in themselves, but they are not a real coming together unless there is struggle together (see Sheppard and Worlock 1988). It may very well be that committed Christian communities are the way forward in modernity. It is significant that, as different as they are, the Iona community in Scotland, Taizé in France and the Sojourners and Sword of the Spirit communities in North America are all ecumenical movements. Coming together and staying together, with all our unresolved differences, is the most challenging yet spiritual way of building up an effective fighting force.

THEOLOGICAL COMBAT

Coming together in community may mean a coming together on the basis of shared spiritual, ethical and political beliefs. Standing against modernism, however, presupposes a broad coalition of orthodox Christians who have a common commitment to the gospel. This will mean that although there will be wide disagreement on many theological issues, this will not be over fundamental dogmas – truths of revelation – but what the early church called theological opinion (*theologoumena*).

Two things were essentially wrong with the earlier great resistance movement of the 1920s and 1930s known as fundamentalism. Firstly, its base was far too narrow. It shunned Catholics and Orthodox, and also many believing Christians from some branches of Calvinism and Episcopalianism. Secondly, the fundamentalist movement foundered on philosophically doubtful premises concerning the 'inerrancy' and 'infallibility' of scripture. In some senses we all hold to the inspired nature of the Bible, but the theories of the American Presbyterian Charles Hodge (1797–1878), and indeed of the whole Princeton school of theology in the late nineteenth century, were too influenced by an oversimplistic and positivistic science on the one hand and a naive common-sense philosophy on the other.

The reason why these men and their successors were ultimately to lose against modernist thought was precisely because they relied too much on reason. Because we tend to think of fundamentalism as anti-intellectual and sectarian these days, we forget that in fact many of the writers of *The Fundamentals* (twelve volumes from 1910 to 1915) were in fact fine intellectuals. It is also worth recording in passing that many of these essays were broad and deep in character and demonstrated that fundamentalism was not yet an entrenched and bitter position.

The word fundamentalism was first coined in 1920, but long before that conservative scholars (notably from Princeton) had begun to attack the presuppositions of modernism. And all praise to the fundamentalists, for they identified many of the real enemies. When we think that they were opposed to what was then the new 'higher criticism', Darwinism, the growth of scientism, and the attack on miracles, it is clear that their instincts were correct. A considerable number of these scholars, however, were also committed to adventism and dispensationalism. Under the influence of Scofield – who saw his theology as science – and holiness revivalism there was a hard-line factionalism developing. It was this factionalism that was to lead to the disintegration of fundamentalism in the late 1920s and 1930s into a sectarian and warring movement.

Furthermore, in North America, where most of this was happening (though it was also happening in Britain under the influence of the Keswick Convention), the self-styled fundamentalists were increasingly alienating other conservative mainline Christians. Fundamentalism came to be identified with wild eschatologies which went every which way. This in itself somewhat gave the lie to a measured and reasoned defence of scripture. More significantly, by the late 1930s the impressive scholarship of the Princeton theologians became a thing of the past. In short the intellectual cutting edge disappeared from the fundamentalists. (See Marsden's great book on fundamentalism, 1980.)

The regrouping of many fundamentalists in the USA into

the broad coalition of the New Religious Right has not, at the present time of writing, produced intellectual thinkers anywhere near the stature of Charles Hodge, or his son Archibald Alexander Hodge (1823–1886), or, shall we say, Reuben Torrey and the Scottish theologian James Orr. These men, along with George Frederick Wright of Oberlin College (who thought that a limited though genuine evolution was possible), have yet to find their modern counterparts.

Looking at the 1930s to the 1950s in both the United States and Great Britain, we can see with the benefit of hindsight that the Catholic Thomists, the German Barthians, the Russian Orthodox in France, and later C. S. Lewis in England had much to contribute not only to a defence of the gospel but in terms of insightful attacks upon modernism itself.

It remains to be seen today whether the conservative evangelicals, Catholics, Reformed neo-orthodox, and Eastern Orthodox can learn from the mistakes of history and come together to save the historic faith. Many of the old problems will have to be looked at again. Conservative evangelicals, for example, are still influenced by the inerrancy/infallibility issues. These are not to be dismissed lightly, but they need to be seen for what they always were: secondary elaborations of faith based on a particular view of philosophy and reality. We could all do worse than ask each other whether we can believe the truths of the creeds! (see Bray 1984).

My major complaints against fundamentalism are not that it presented an inadequate defence of the historic faith (see Barr's seminal work on fundamentalism, 1981) but that it remained sectarian and failed to attack modernism with any intellectual rigour. But I cannot let fundamentalism pass without a genuine tribute. No one has a good word for fundamentalism these days, and even those groups who are still basically fundamentalist do not like to be so labelled! With all its weaknesses, however, and despite its increasingly sectarian stance, I believe that it did echo the truths of the Divine Drama.

In Eastern Orthodox churches the Drama is literally presented dramaturgically. The liturgy, the iconography, the church buildings, and even the priests' clothes are all related to the playing out, or telling-forth of the Drama. In fundamentalist churches, and still in many evangelical churches today, the Drama tends to be more narrative and epic. It is the preaching of the word that has kept the Drama alive.

Fundamentalists too have preserved the sacredness of scripture and with all their imperfections have maintained a belief in the Evil One, God's salvation through the incarnation and the cross, and a certain knowledge that Christ will return as the *eschaton*.

It is difficult to remain friends with fundamentalists if you are on the outside. Many Christians think that they are not worth talking to. No doubt most fundamentalists would reject my suggestion of a broad coalition, but equally many 'broad' Christians will have nothing to do with fundamentalists. Who, one wonders, are the Pharisees?[3]

Perhaps in the divine providence – for only God knows the full strategy of the Great Battle – fundamentalists have preserved the vestiges of the Drama in the midst of a perfidious generation.

BEYOND FUNDAMENTALISM

But now we come to the crux of the matter. We could make out a case and claim that something like fundamentalism, by its very primitiveness, keeps the gospel alive (however distorted it might be).

But it is not possible to go on for ever in modernity and never confront the ideologies of our day. The risk is of course tremendous. We have only to look at the whole of Protestant denominationalism over the last one hundred years to see that dialogue often means accepting the secular world's point of view. Modernism, by definition, absorbs and conforms to the philosophies of modernity.

I remember the great audacity – and not a little prophetic power – of a sermon given by one of the great ecumenical leaders of the modern world, Bishop Lesslie Newbigin. In London on the seventy-fifth anniversary of the Edinburgh

Conference of 1910 (sometimes thought of as the birthplace of the modern ecumenical movement), Bishop Lesslie was addressing Catholics and Protestants on the importance of Catholic participation in the ecumenical movement. After announcing his hopes he expressed his anxieties:

> To put it crudely, and at the risk of being wrong, I have a lurking fear that in the new-found fellowship with the rest of us, the Roman Catholic Church might be tempted to repeat the mistakes of the Protestants, that in being more open to the modern world it might, like the rest of us, become too much at home in the modern world . . .
>
> Will the consequence of the Second Vatican Council be that we are together able to bring about a truly missionary encounter at the deepest level between the gospel and the post-Enlightenment culture which we share with the rest of the so-called 'developed' world, or will it draw the Roman Catholic Church into the same timid surrender to the ideology of this culture which has so often been the response of the non-Roman Western churches?

(Perhaps the same question needs to be put to the Eastern Orthodox churches in the World Council of Churches!)

Bishop Newbigin accepts that as far as the Protestant world is concerned there can be no going back to a period of intellectual history before the Enlightenment: we have to confront it with the gospel now. In order to do this, those of us who have been exposed to modernism – and that means the majority of us involved in higher education or theological training – have to be prepared to engage with it.

The reasons for this are twofold. Firstly, it is a question of the successful spread of enemy propaganda: post-Enlightenment theology dominates our colleges, universities and schools. More seriously it has entered within the churches themselves. Modernism needs to be fought in the pews and the pulpits, not merely in the theological journals. Secondly, the rise of the media theologians, in Great Britain at least, has meant that modernism is now entering directly into secular homes.

If we are serious about getting into a fight we have to be

prepared for real combat. Fundamentalism failed because it never really fought the battle: it thumped the table and the Bible with great belligerence but ignored the actual content and methodologies of the new scholarship. Its resistance seemed to be the last-ditch stand of the fortress under siege. As these fortresses were dotted along the margins of the city they may have offered some refuge and succour but were incapable of launching a counter-offensive. That is what we need now.

Because we need to challenge the dominance of modernism in the Western world, we need to take the risk of being defeated by it. This is a terrible risk, but – under grace – it is a risk that needs to be taken. How many students have left an orthodox Christian home, say a Baptist or a Presbyterian one, and have lost their faith once they were exposed to critical studies? Precisely because it happens all the time Christians react by taking an anti-intellectual stance (doubt is evil, reason is evil, etc.). The net result of this intellectual evasion is that modernist theology continues virtually unchallenged. It is impossible to learn about hermeneutics, New Testament studies, existentialist and phenomenological thought, etc. without studying them in depth. Critical theology that is sanitised for conservative consumption still abounds in many Bible colleges.

We have been cursed for too long by the post-literary approach to scholarship. I mean the sort of committed Christian books – of the kind that clutter our shelves *ad nauseam* – which purport to tell us all about existentialism in two lines. Others give a potted and slanted view of church history in twenty pages. Religious publishing thrives on personal testimony and it is probable that tales of spectacular and charismatic faith form the staple diet of many Christians. We all love a good read (especially if it is entertaining), but we do not like so much to have to do any work.

There is nothing wrong with personal histories and testimonies; on the contrary they are uplifting and the retelling of the lives of the saints has a long and noble tradition in Christianity, but we cannot defeat modernism with paperback approaches to scholarship. This present book is no exception to that rule: this is a work of propaganda and invitation – nothing more.

This is the great challenge to orthodoxy: Are we prepared to engage in critical scholarship in order to learn and understand the modernism we are called to overthrow? We do not have to have a post-graduate qualification in theology to learn something about modernism. We find time for our television, our private hobbies, our fellowships, studying the scriptures, keeping up with technological and scientific changes in the world. Why, then, can we not start doing theology? In the eighteenth century ordinary Puritans and Methodists would read not only the Bible and Bunyan's ever-popular *Grace Abounding*, they would also wrestle with the works of Richard Hooker (1554–1600) and John Owen (1616–1683).

A great thing about Third World Christianity is the way in which Christians have not only rejected much of Western modernism, but they have also rejected Western conservatism. By that I mean they have been doing theology for themselves (see Wickeri 1984). For too long the Western churches have allowed theology to get away from spirituality and the worship of the church, and become almost solely an academic discipline practised by specialists in universities. The long-term goal of theological combat is to wrest theology back from the colleges (a point for which no doubt many of the theological advisers to the C. S. Lewis Centre are not going to thank me!).

We cannot all be academic theologians or intellectuals, but we can all work and fight harder. It is distressing to see that so few young Christians are interested in contending for the faith on the intellectual level. If we think of St Paul and the great tradition of Christian apologetics, the medieval scholastics, the Reformers, and the Puritan divines, they were all people who were engaged in theological combat. The early church during the patristic era had to attack the presuppositions of the pagan world. We are still in a pagan world, yet now the battle is being lost by default.

Ultimately the liberal/conservative divide is simplistic (Lash 1986: ch. 4). An orthodox Christianity is not liberal or conservative but radical: its roots lie not in sacred texts or religious feelings, but in God himself. Letting God be God is the starting-point of orthodoxy. Modernism, as we have seen (chapter eight), has its roots in a myriad places, excepting God. Nevertheless modernism contains a great deal of impressive, genuine, and thought-provoking scholarship. It is important to learn it well, for in so doing we will realise that we can no longer attack and defeat it from inadequate grounds. Even if we are overly conservative, any cursory New Testament studies will show us (if we are honest) that the sacred texts may be sacred but they are not dictated or word-for-word, blow-by-blow accounts of the events of the gospels. To deny the editing functions and diverse sources of the gospels is to fly in the face of truth.

The fundamentalist movement claimed that modern science disbelieved in miracles *a priori*. This is probably true still today for many modernist theologians. Equally, however, many non-modernist Christians decide to study modern theology with their own *a priori* assumptions and refuse honestly to face the evidence.

We can never approach evidence without any assumptions. I refuse, for example, to say that I will put aside my faith commitments to God and his revelation when I approach the Bible. Nevertheless I have learnt that I need to sift the evidence on its own grounds as well. I believe that the way forward is to take the attack to the modernists. This fundamentalism failed to do: it kept modernism out of its own churches but was unable to prevent it from spreading throughout the rest of Christendom. Fundamentalism failed not only because of its lack of intellectual rigour but also because of a lack of sobriety. It was overcome by the enticing lure of premillennial and adventist thought. This channelled its theological energies into fascinating but essentially diverting speculations. In the nineteenth century Edward Irving was considered by Samuel Coleridge to be the greatest thinker and reformer since Martin Luther. Irving's great trinitarian and incarnational studies, however, were caught up in adventist enthusiasm. His 'expanding mind' (to use Coleridge's own description of him) became enamoured with dreams of the last things and the 'signs of the times'. He went on to do some remarkable things in the rest of his short life, but he never did any more theology. The Bible is full of prophecy, and we should rightly await the return of the Lord, but enthusiasm for an imminent return can lead to a lack of interest in intellectual things; who needs refutation of modernism when Christ is returning any second?

We have moved a long way from the adventism of the 1830s, the early Pentecostal enthusiasms and the ingenious fundamentalist theories, but still the Lord holds his hand. Until the final trump the Great Battle continues unabated. We are not given permission to stop fighting because we think that we know when and how our Supreme Commander is about to make the final thrust! During the last one hundred years or so modernism has gained the upper hand. While many of us have enthused and prophetically insisted that modernism was a sign of the last times, modernists themselves have been gradually breaking down our resistance.

Recently Keith Ward and Gavin D'Costa, to name but two, have shown that modernism can be defeated on its own grounds (Ward 1985; D'Costa 1986). The alternative approach is to deny the legitimacy of the grounds altogether. If we want to take this path then we must consider, as Karl Barth did for much of his life, that a theology from below is just not possible. But all this is sheer fantasy unless we are prepared to meet together in conferences, fellowships, colleges, study groups and workshops; most importantly of all, we need to begin worshipping together. Let me end this section with two personal experiences of hope.

My first experience comes, perhaps surprisingly, from a theological commission. For four years, under the auspices of the British Council of Churches, men and women from the traditions of Catholicism, Eastern Orthodoxy and Protestantism have been grappling with the complexities of the doctrine of the Holy Trinity. Far from being dry, partisan and predictable, we have found through working and praying together that we have been caught up in the life of the triune God. There has not been unanimous agreement, but we have found that contrary to some expectations and past experiences we have been of remarkable accord.

The second experience has been one of sheer exhilaration at the way that eminent Christians from all denominations have come together to form the advisory board of the C. S. Lewis Centre. In a sense what has happened is that we have found ourselves on the swell of a great tide of resistance to the evils of modernity. We are resolved to swim together even though we disagree in many ways. It has been a joy, as we have been swept along, to find others bobbing in the waves. Linked together in this group, and in other groups too, we become comrades in adversity and no longer mere survivors. As the tide carries us relentlessly towards the enemy we do not expect to sweep away modernism in the first rush; but there is a surge of expectation that we will not leave it unmarked (see Walker 1988).

SPIRITUAL POLITICS

We have talked a great deal in this book about dualisms and divisions, but nowhere do we see a greater dualism than in orthodox Christianity's disjunction between its approach to theology and its attitude to the political and social order. For many people a conservative approach to theology goes hand in hand with conservative politics. Conversely, modernist theology often seems to cohere with liberal or socialist politics.

In the 1960s this was both symbolised and caricatured in the division in British universities between the apolitical and conservatively theological Inter-varsity Fellowship (IVF) and the radical politics but liberal theology of the Student Christian Movement (SCM). The IVF accused the SCM of not taking evangelism seriously and not holding to the gospel. Members of the SCM accused the IVF of retreating behind pietism and refusing to become involved with the great political issues of the day.

The IVF tended to see their commitment to Christ in terms of orthodoxy (*orthodoxia*), but the SCM saw their Christianity in terms of a discipleship that was related to actions more than beliefs (*orthopraxia*). Today in Britain, like the Campus

Crusade Movement in the USA, the IVF (now the UCCF) is doing very well; on the other hand the SCM has not exactly collapsed but it does seem to have lost its way.

Evangelical students have in fact returned to their more socially engaging roots of the nineteenth century (Bradley 1976). British evangelicalism can no longer be accused of hiding its head in the sand concerning political matters. 'Tear Fund', the wide Christian support for 'Band Aid', and the writings of Os Guinness (1983) and John Stott (1984) show an increased awareness of the social and political dimensions of modernity. The Greenbelt organisation in England and the Sojourners community in America demonstrate in their very different ways that being an evangelical does not necessarily mean that one is apolitical or right-wing. It remains a truism, however, that evangelicalism does not typically engage in radical or left-wing politics.

Although evangelical students have shifted from right to centre in their politics, hence covering much of the old ground of the SCM, the Student Christian Movement itself has failed to develop a radical and theological politics that connects with the roots of Christian orthodoxy. Furthermore, and I realise this is contentious, though I think it true that evangelical students have been 'politicised', their politics are not deeply connected to a Christian orthodoxy. In this respect they are closer to the SCM than meets the eye.

I have started with this example from British student Christian politics because I think that the same problems hold for the World Council of Churches, the American National Council and the British Council of Churches. Furthermore, it holds also for the New Religious Right. What I believe is disturbing about the apparent left-wingness of the WCC, for example, is not that it is left-wing but that its political stance is often couched in terms of justice and human rights, which are fine and noble Enlightenment concepts, but rarely obviously biblical ones. I do not mean to suggest that the gospel is not concerned with justice, but only to point out that justice in the gospels is never divorced from the kingdom. As Christians we are not called to make the world a better place: we are called to overcome it – to transfigure it with God's love. Conversely,

I fail to understand, theologically speaking, how the New Religious Right in North America relate their biblical conservativism to their right-wing republicanism.

I do not believe that we can say that the scriptures provide a model for the perfect political system. Nor do I think that we can say that being 'right' or being 'left' is in any way a biblical idea. Christianity confronts the world in every era and in every political situation. It is not our task to take absolutist stands on the temporal order, if by that we mean to identify the church with a particular political and economic system.

Dying feudalism tried to identify monarchy with a doctrine of the divine right of kings – a doctrine much favoured in Russia, but also prevalent in England in the seventeenth century. Kingship is personal and symbolises authority over the temporal order as being guided and legitimated by God. Kings can be seen as God's regents, or viceregents, as it were. To try and suggest, however, that the scriptures actually sanction kingship as the only legitimate form of political power is to fly in the face of the evidence. The New Testament does not offer us a political model that points to emperors. The fact that after Constantine there was an attempt to fit together the spiritual and temporal orders is more a question of tragedy than a matter for congratulation.

The Old Testament has to be used as the source for any attempt to ground a divine right of kingship. It is a very unsafe ground because the only clear political system that God seems to favour is the patriarchy of the Judges: a theocracy that has nothing to do with divine rights of humans at all. The eventual kingship of Israel is God's judgment, or second best, for his chosen people.

Democracy, C. S. Lewis believed, was a system worth following if you believed in the fall: it is a means of checks and balances to prevent absolute tyranny. Nowhere, however, does the Bible advocate democracy. Furthermore, to suggest that we can develop either capitalism or socialism from the New Testament is false. In the first place these economic and political systems of modernity have their roots in the Enlightenment and before that loop back to Greek antiquity rather than Palestine.

It is monstrous to suggest that capitalism, which is a system of self-interest and materialism, is somehow to be identified with New Testament Christianity. This is not to say that it is bad, or indefensible, but it is to say that the Bible does not order it. The parable of the talents (Matt 25:14–30), which is sometimes cited as praising free enterprise, is clearly a parable of the kingdom of heaven (v. 14), and concerns Christian stewardship; it has nothing to do with profit or investment.

Neither can we point to Acts 2:44 as evidence for socialism. And I do not mean by this that what is called 'socialism' in Eastern Europe, with its cruel and impersonal bureaucracies, is not 'real' socialism. Acts 2 tells of the direct and radical effects of the Holy Spirit upon Christian commitment. These effects are personal and communal. They are indeed the hallmarks of the kingdom and consequently are a serious clue to Christian politics, but socialism is quite another matter. Rosa Luxemburg (1871–1919), the famous woman socialist killed by right-wingers, wrote a booklet on Christianity and socialism before the Russian Revolution. She pointed out that Acts 2 advocated a sharing of goods in common, but not any kind of production system. There was not, in Marx's terminology, a taking over 'of the means of production'. A commune, a co-operative, and a policy of sharing are not the bases of an advanced socialist economic system. They may be models of communities, monasteries, simple co-operatives, perhaps even a William Morris or a Gandhi-style rural socialism. In no sense, however, can we use Acts 2 as the basis of Marxist doctrine.

TWO MISTAKEN CHRISTIAN APPROACHES TO POLITICS

It is a tragedy that we are so divided by our political allegiances, but I believe that we have to reject two approaches to politics and be prepared to accept two others.

The first approach to reject is to go hunting in the scriptures for the odd verse or line that happens to fit our personal political beliefs. In the advanced industrial societies we may be left or right, or liberal or conservative, for many reasons; these may relate to our personalities, where we happen to live, the strength of peer-group pressure, or our moral convictions. Naturally as Christians we like to believe that our politics belong to God and are sanctioned by scripture. The notion of scriptural sanction is, however, a two-edged sword. Slavery in the New World was defended by reference to Paul's injunction to servants in Ephesians 6:5 that they obey their masters (the Greek word *doulos* can be translated 'slave' or 'servant').

A feature that I have noticed in British Christian circles is the way that feminism, anti-racism, the need for social justice and many other issues are presented in essentially secular terms with a little bit of theological dressing sprinkled on the top that makes them look Christian. Often what happens is that single issue (constituent) politics – gay rights/liberation, feminism, racism, and peace – are presented without any worked out theological or spiritual position. This works fine if you happen to be committed to one or all of these constituencies. There rarely seems to be, however, any worked out orthopraxis from an orthodox Christian position. Quite often this is so because these political positions are essentially secular and in no sense relate to a Christian orthodoxy.

There are those who, seeing that much of Christian politics is really secular politics in disguise, opt to be apolitical. This can be either a complete indifference to politics or an ingrained conservativism that argues that 'rendering unto Caesar the things that are Caesar's' means an acquiescence in the political and social order. Such a position is a recipe for private pietism divorced from the realities of public life, and is the second approach to politics that I think we should reject.

It is the sort of politics, in short, that fits a privatised Christianity living on the margins of the city. It is not a biblical position, because it is the negative conservativism of Pontius Pilate: a refusal to get involved. Furthermore, it is a misuse of the Caesar text, because Jesus qualifies his statement by insisting that God must also have his due (Matt 22:21). The gospels clearly demonstrate a bias to the poor both in the sermon on the mount and in Christ's dealings with ordinary people. Rich people are not excluded from Christ's love, but they do come under his judgment. The rich young ruler is too attached to his wealth to receive salvation (Luke 18:18–25), but Zacchaeus in response to God's forgiveness gives away half his worldly goods (Luke 19:8).

As we have already seen (under 'Spiritual immobilisation') washing one's hands is often the outward show of the Pharisee. It is easy to condemn the zeal of radical politics while we refuse to dirty our hands. At first in Nazi Germany many German Christians looked the other way when they saw what was happening to the Jews. Later, however, a number of the leaders of the Lutheran church not only supported Hitler but in their support declared that Jesus was not a Jew! The extreme irony of this is that the people who were responsible for this heresy were the 'orthodox' Lutherans, not the more modernist leaders of the Confessional church.

Given that I have admitted that there are no easy answers in the field of politics, I would like to suggest two ways forward that I believe merit serious attention.

CONFRONTING THE POWERS

I argued in chapter one that we do not take the Devil seriously. Nor do we usually bother to wonder what it means to fight against 'principalities, against the powers, against the world rulers of this present darkness' (Eph 6:12). It is too glib to assume that the powers refer to the evils of political systems other than our own. As Dr Charles Elliot (1987: 139) has put it, 'No one economic system has a monopoly of alienation: no system is free of Powers that need to be redeemed.'

Nor can we say that evil is only personal evil. Systems become evil. Anything which dehumanises, turns people into objects, or exploits the vulnerable and weak is evil. To talk of powers is to talk of power. I am aware that much of the evil caused in the world is a direct result of individual and corporate sin. At the same time many good people are caught up in systems that they do not understand. It is very difficult for the affluent in Europe and the USA to realise what effect our economic machines have on the developing countries.

An acquaintance of mine who read Dr Elliot's *Praying the Kingdom* (1985) thought that his book was 'interesting but much too left-wing'. No doubt if she had had greater exposure to left-wing politics she would not have made such a misleading remark. It is precisely because Dr Elliot's background is in development that he sees the first-hand effects of the advanced industrial nations' upon the Third World. It is to his credit that he has avoided opting for a purely secular approach. Dr Elliot believes that we have to learn how to empathise with people who are the victims of the exploitative systems of the advanced nations: we need, he feels, to be able to enter into their pain and hopelessness. He thinks also that we must take responsibility for our own roles as consumers, producers and voters.

Firstly, however, we need to identify the powers of evil. If we are right-wing we tend to identify such problems as lawlessness, drugs, social disharmony, moral decline. Left-wingers tend to identify evil in terms of injustice and inequality, seeing the system of capitalism as the basic source of disorder. Right-wingers can also use system language when they want to, having no difficulty, for example, in seeing socialism as evil in itself. A Christian perspective, it seems to me, needs to transcend the left/right division in order to identify any power that harms, exploits, and crushes the weak. What we discover – if only we can peer beyond our secular horizons – is that modernity is characterised by a massive centralised power in the hands of the secular agencies. The public world – the city that we have left behind – is dominated by business, science, the military and government. This is the world, as we have seen (Captive Lives), where the church no longer has any authority. Is it so unrealistic to see it as the locus of evil powers?

Professor Walter Hollenweger once told me that he did not think that all the evil in the world could be explained by the evil of men: there is an objective Presence of evil in the world with which we must contend. This evil, if we take the Great Battle seriously, is the Enemy himself.

Just because the Evil One cannot be incarnated in the world as an actual person does not mean that he cannot be embodied in institutions and governmental 'power systems'. The Devil and his angels are not hordes of spiteful sprites swarming around the universe and occasionally dropping into earth to torment some poor soul. I do not mean that individuals are not tormented by objective evil that is external to them, but I do mean that the Devil's power as the prince of this world is also corporate and concrete power. If his power is purely cosmic – an anti-God 'up there' – then we have no need of him to explain evil in the world itself. I do not know in what ways the corporate evils of governments, bureaucracies, multinationals and scientific enterprises interrelate with, or are penetrated by, the cosmic forces of the Evil One. (See Elliot 1987: ch. 9.) I do know, however, that it is meaningless to talk of 'principalities and powers' unless we see them embodied in the evil institutions of the world.

From this perspective I do not think that it is totally incidental that the two great scientific economies of modernity – capitalism and socialism – dominate a world in which eight hundred million people still live in absolute poverty. These people are not the victims of blind forces of economics or the unintended consequences of affluence: they are the victims of neglect. Nevertheless, the systems themselves are capable of evil greater than the sum of the people who constitute them. Systems of defence, of international banking, of government bureaucracies are not made up of essentially demonic people but ordinary persons like you and me. Discovering the effects of systems we belong to or tacitly support takes effort and discernment.

For example, it is an unpalatable truth that many of the people living in great poverty also live in vital cultures that we unwittingly destroy. 'Those alternative systems may not be efficient in an accountant's sense. They may not even be very robust, in the sense that they can resist neither natural disasters nor inroads from modernisation; but maybe they preserve something essential to the human spirit – a something that capitalism systematically destroys' (Elliot 1987: 139).

You do not need to be left-wing to learn this truth about modernity: our missionaries throughout the Third World regale us with our unwitting folly. For example, a few years ago there was an incident when the nomadic Masai tribesmen of Kenya sent their young warriors into dry pasture that had been 'improved' by modern technology and water supplies; the young men destroyed the innovations. On the surface this seems no more than ungratefulness and vandalism. The background to this story reveals a different picture.

For hundreds, probably thousands, of years the Masai had wandered and roamed deep into the north of Kenya with their cattle. Gradually white settlers drove them into smaller areas in the south. In the 1960s, under Western influence, the Kenyan government gave the Masai tenure of the land. It began to deteriorate. The government appointed committees to run the group ranches. These committees were composed of younger men, not of the elders of the tribe, who were still accepted by the people as the true and rightful leaders. The elders, however, knew about ecology and the problems of over-grazing, so they realised that certain land needed to remain fallow. The water supplies were established by the government to improve grazing, but the Masai elders knew that deterioration would soon set in; so they sent in their warriors to preserve their way of life.[4]

If we are able to grasp what our modern economic systems can do to undermine the traditional ways of life of people in the Third World, is it so difficult to understand what high unemployment is doing to the communities of people in Dallas, Texas, or Liverpool, England? When I visited Merseyside this year I was shocked to see how the city was so shabby; the back streets were dominated by slogans and posters more in keeping with the cities of communist Eastern Europe. But to live in Liverpool, like living in the north-east of England, is to live in a dying community from which the rich south-east seems to be draining its energy and will to survive.

It is so much easier, and so much safer, to consign the Devil to our private world. We will fight him over trivial games such as *Dungeons and Dragons*, cast out demons every Sunday night at our charismatic meetings, and hold him responsible for our every tribulation. Suggest, however, that he is alive in the inner cities, Whitehall or the Pentagon, the South African government or South American dictatorships and you will be branded 'left-wing' (though if you mention Moscow people seem to be able to understand the concept of evil systems more easily). If we are to confront the powers we have to confront them where they are.

To take responsibility for own own (perhaps unwitting) role in an exploitative system is to begin the resistance. It may very well be that the demonic starts at home. The early church fathers understood the world to be the home of alienation and disorder. It is only the fallen world that can become the home of the fallen angels. Men and women are not demonic, nor are governments and institutions, but they are open to the possibility of demonisation. On the individual level, Dorothy Emmet (1979: ch. 7) has suggested, this amounts to insisting on being like a god – beyond good and evil. Paul saw some forms of demonisation as akin to idolatry (Rom 1:25). To worship power is always to run the risk of being possessed by that power. In a metaphorical sense we can be possessed by our material goods.

I am not suggesting here that we must try not to sin; that we can take for granted. Rather I am suggesting that we have to actively stand against evil in our private lives. We will not be very effective troops against the city if we are not liberated at home. The Devil is active everywhere. I am convinced, for example, that we will be more effective in our fight for racial justice if we have fought for it in our churches. Does it really matter what the Russian Orthodox Church says about South Africa when it has not yet dealt with the home issue of anti-Semitism? Voicing abstract views on other people's problems is an ineffectual and unspiritual way of dealing with the powers that confront us in our streets, our churches and our homes.

Having taken responsibility for our own actions and confronted the powers in (and against) our own lives, we can start coming together to take more concerted action. Maybe we will not be able to overthrow evil systems, but we can demonstrate the limits of their authority. This will never satisfy a fully politically motivated person: he wants to change the world, not make a gesture of resistance. It is this essenti-ally secular motivation that can seriously damage our central goal of fighting the Great Battle. We cannot turn our back upon politics, but neither must we assume that the gospel is to bring Utopia on earth through political means. Jesus rejected this identification unequivocally: 'My kingdom is not of this world; if my kingdom were of this world, then would my servants fight . . .' (John 18:36).

This is the great temptation of a Christianity that identifies with secular socialism. As the Orthodox theologian John Meyendorff (1978: 320) reminded the World Council of Churches, 'Christianity has suffered enough because it ident-ified itself with power, with the state, with money, with the establishment. Many of us rightly want to disengage it from these embarrassing allies. But in order to win its true freedom the Church must become itself again, and not simply change camps.'

To reject serious gestures of resistance to evil because they are ultimately not political or radical enough can also lead to cynicism, in which case we end up doing nothing. 'Why give aid to charities,' we sometimes say, 'when the long-term problems remain unsolved?' Any true spiritual and moral resistance with a political face is a genuine blow to the Enemy. God does not ask us to (re)build Christian civilisation, change the world through political means, or build Utopia, but he does ask us to take a stand on social and political issues. If we are really worried about the effects of television on our families, we can start by giving up television. (Our family has done without one for eight years and it's been a joy.) If we are worried about pollution of the atmosphere, we can give up our cars or buy lead-free petrol. Apartheid in South Africa disgusts many of us, so why do we still buy South African goods?

These individual examples of responsibility (the Lord prompts us, but lays down no rules) help us to move forward in God's power against the powers of this world. Jerry Falwell has received no praise from me so far in this book, but I think that in many ways his belief in the use of consumer power to hit the consumption of the city is good news. So far the religious right have targeted pornography and abortion. But Falwell has admitted that he learnt his techniques from the civil rights movement of the 1960s. Let us hope that we can begin to see both these issues as kingdom business and not insist that they are right/left concerns.

TOWARDS A TRINITARIAN POLITICS

A Christian 'third way' in politics, I believe, is to transcend the dualism of the Enlightenment children, the collectivist and the individualist man. Without the collective there can be no justice or welfare for the poor and elderly, the sick and the oppressed; and yet the needs of individuals and the basic dignity and freedom of humanity cannot be preserved in collectivist systems. It is appropriate, and right and proper, that as Christians our third way should be directed by the trinitarian nature of God.

God is not three persons in one because dogma and tradition say so. He is a trinitarian God because this reveals to us the nature of his being: God is personal and communal. We sometimes use the concept of *koinonia* to apply to the church as a fellowship or community, but some Orthodox, Catholic and Reformed theologians have understood this to be a primary attribute of God himself. The three persons of the Godhead are not simply modes or masks of God: they are God in unity dwelling in each other and for each other (*perichoresis*, or 'coinherence' as Lewis's friend, Charles Williams, called this mutual inter-penetrating love).

We have to refract the perfect love and tenderness of the Holy Trinity through the political prisms that we find in the secular world, but even these prisms should be ikons that point – however imperfectly – to their prototype. The German theologian Jürgen Moltmann has attempted a trinitarian politics (1981) that some would say comes out too left-wing. For my part I think he may well have projected his 'socialism' into the Godhead. We are used to God being made in our own images and expressing our wish-fulfilments. I think, however, that Moltmann has at least demanded that the kingdom must be seen as rooted in the trinitarian life of God. The kingdom, like grace, has become a reality which we tend to think of as something other than God himself – something he gives away. But the kingdom is not a list of divine rules, or even God's rule, that Christ tosses to us like a bone or largesse: it is his life in trinity which he offers to share with us.

A trinitarian politics would suggest that our political systems reflect a distorted vision of God. A Trinity that is understood as three 'persons' subsisting and interchanging in the being of God can easily become no more than modes of existence. If God's being is made to override his personhood we have a recipe for an impersonal collective. A true trinitarian model of God suggests that he is not three separate gods (tritheism), but that the persons of the Trinity, while united as one God, remain distinct, and there are functions that are proper and unique to the Father, the Son and the Holy Ghost. The Father and the Son, for example, are not to be understood as interchangeable units. It was this view that led in the third century AD to the heresy of patripassianism, which declared that it was the Father as well as the Son who was crucified at Golgotha.

We should resist the power of collectivism in society because collectivism, like an impersonal Trinity, treats individuals not as persons but as units, or atoms, that are interchangeable without distinctness and with no intrinsic worth.

We should reject the dominance of the individual in social life because it denies the common basis and unity of humanity. The unitarian God of the Enlightenment philosophers fitted individualism nicely. God is no longer in relation with himself: he is God alone. Individualism fails to understand that persons are not people living in isolation from each other. Persons are people in membership together – those who share a living relationship one with another. As individuals we are distinct from each other but share the same or a common nature (*physis*) just as God has one being (*ousia*). Clearly, however, the human race is divided. It is not in communion at the level of personal relationships. God's being, however, *is* communion and this demonstrates to us that he is love itself – outgoing and giving, yet residing in the mutual reciprocity of the three persons.

When we identify God solely as the sovereign Father we have a God that legitimates totalitarian and patriarchal systems. The concept of *monarchia* in the Trinity was an attempt by the early church to preserve the unifying principle of God in the person of the Father. This can so easily be distorted into the principle of dominance. (The old divine right of kings theories rested on a misunderstanding of earthly monarchy and heavenly *monarchia*.) At its worst the God who stands alone becomes no longer the loving heavenly Father, but the cosmic tyrant.

In terms of a spiritual politics a trinitarian view of society suggests that we need to try and reconcile the hopeless dualism of collectivism and individualism in the personal life of community. This may be pointing towards decentralised economies and a dismantling of massive bureaucratic systems, and is of course what Ernst Schumacher (1973) (and Mikhail Agursky, 1976) advocated.

Given that such a view seems Luddite and romantic, it probably will not politically transform the social order! But I do think that it points us towards the kingdom which permeates society like yeast in dough. This permeation can rightly be called metahistorical because the kingdom is no less than eternity penetrating into time itself. It is this kingdom life of which I now want to talk, for this is the true spiritual power that will overcome the evils of modernity like the presence of Aslan melted the snows of Narnia. Through our spiritual struggle for the modern world, we are revealing the nature of God's alternative kingdom. This kingdom is not only a reality that begins with the end of time. It began with the incarnation, when Jesus raised the first standard of resistance against the Evil One. Since the passion and Pentecost the kingdom has been thrown open to all citizens who have been adopted by the Spirit to become Christ's brothers and sisters, and comrades-in-arms.

When we enter into the spiritual heart of the Great Battle

we discover to our wonder, and for our fortitude, that we are not alone in the struggle. The 'cloud of witnesses' that surround us are not spectators but comrades. We think that we are battling it out alone when in fact the whole of heaven is behind our backs. To discover this truth is to discover how to live eschatologically. The great lion of Narnia calls out to his faithful followers an invitation that we must take up ourselves: 'Come further up! Come further in!' (Lewis 1980: 149).

10 KINGDOM COME

Throughout this book I have tried to focus our attention on modernity as the locus of our battle with the Devil. We fight, as I said in the foreword, on *terra firma*. But although our struggle involves intellectual and practical combat against the secular culture and ideologies of the age, we must never forget – even for a moment – that the nature of our struggle is spiritual. It is in the context of our fight against the principalities and powers and against 'spiritual wickedness in high places' that Paul urges us to put on the armour of a spiritual soldier.

The great apostle entreats us to fully clothe and arm ourselves not with any political or practical weapons but with truth, righteousness, the proclamation of peace, the spiritual power of God's word, his gift of faith. And then we are told to pray with all our heart and being in and to God the Holy Spirit himself. This prayer is for ourselves and for each other, and Ephesians 6:10–18 is full of the desperate need and urgency to cling to the Spirit.

Our spiritual equipment, our weapons, are available to us only after we have joined God's great resistance movement. Thousands of Christian books have been written on spiritual weaponry. I do not believe that we need to look for anything new or original to say (that's chronological snobbism for you), but I do think that we need to see that our struggle is grounded in hope. And in order to talk about this I would like to end *Enemy Territory* by inviting us to live eschatologically.

'FURTHER UP AND FURTHER IN'

Often we think of eschatology as the 'last things'. For some people this means the final judgment and the ultimate and mysterious 'restoration of all things'. For others it has become identified with living in the end-time and being able to discern the final signs of history as pointing to the *eschaton* – Jesus's return.

A belief in Christ's return is denied in many modernist circles. The idea that history and earthly existence will be snuffed out like a candle is one that many people find fantastic and repugnant. Certainly it goes against the grain of modern progressivist thought. Evolutionary beliefs still dominate in scientific modernity. We love to think of the universe unfolding and expanding, and civilisations improving and progressing. But as Lewis recognised, this is sheer fantasy (1975: 65–85). Darwinism as a biological theory offers no such picture at all, yet it has been one of the most potent myths of Enlightenment man.

History will end. What a difference it would make to our morality and politics if we really believed this! We would not be able to hide behind the argument that our unpleasant and perhaps monstrous actions will be justified by the effects they will have on future generations. 'The end justifies the means' looks pretty silly if the end – the future – is removed. How many five-year plans did Stalin legitimate on the grounds that future generations would benefit?

'The great getting up morning', as the American slaves used to say, is a certain hope or judgment for the whole world. And our final hope rests beyond human time, when the kingdom – with Christ – will be all in all. What I think is not very hopeful and useful in the Great Battle is to get carried away with the doctrines of the last things. A certain hope in Christ's return is one thing, but an over-fascination with it is enemy subterfuge. No doubt I am influenced here by my boyhood, when I was submitted to a barrage of premillennial and postmillennial theories. Nothing would excite our small congregations better than the latest interpretations of the scriptural prophecies.

And here lies the rub. There is nothing wrong with speculations, but they have a habit of creating undue excitement. When we should be fighting the enemy we are swooning with fear and anticipation of the parousia. When we should be blasting the heavy armaments of modernism we take time off for adventist investigations. We take up so much time reading the signs of the end-time that we forget the urgency of our struggle.

Sometimes our excitement leads us to believe that we alone have the true knowledge (gnosis) of metahistory and how it will crash into our finite world. Sometimes we think this knowledge means that we are a remnant especially chosen by God. Our own rapid church growth and come-alive liturgies seem to be evidence that the Lord is hurtling along at break-neck speed, carrying us along with him. Outbreaks of advent-ism leave us breathless and thrilled: there is the feeling of revival in the air and everywhere people are charging about, rattling their sabres, and threatening dire action against the Evil One.

But are we actually fighting? This is of course a question of discernment. Living in the Spirit and praying in the Spirit, as Paul suggests we soldiers should do, bring not only energy and enthusiasm: they breed the habit of sobriety. A mind baptised in the Spirit is not a mind buffeted by the passions of excit-ability and fanaticism. It is a mind that discriminates with spiritual judgment the genuine enthusiasm of the Spirit from psychological and even demonic forces (see McBain 1986).

There are rational grounds for believing that the end of time is near. Science has it within its power to destroy the world. Many Christians do not believe that God will allow such a thing to happen. I fail to see why not. What would be a more fitting comeuppance for a world gone mad than to blow itself up? God's intervention of judgment, when the angel shouts 'time', may very well be with a bang. There is no evidence in the scriptures that the universe will end with a whimper. God stays his hand for love of the captives – victims of the mad world and its ruler – and because he alone knows when time is up. And the Christ of glory will be the final moment of history. As the *eschaton* he closes time and becomes for us the door to eternity.

Whether in fact we are living in the end-time or not is, however, of secondary importance, for to live eschatologi-cally, as the early church certainly did (we have to give

Schweitzer that), is to live each day as if it were the last. Such a perspective changes the way we see the world. Even on the natural level, as we find with those who are dying, each moment is precious; all simple things become pregnant with meaning.

Once we can grasp the importance of living eschatologically we find that our spiritual lives change: we learn to rest in the Lord. Shall I be frank? I believe that Western Christianity is too obsessed with action and not enough with being. This is reflected in our approaches to theology: the great redemptive acts of Christ dominate the religious canvas. The Western world is masterful, energetic, powerful, dominating. And yet Jesus in becoming a baby in Bethlehem had already accomplished the great victory by joining himself to our humanity. His earthly life and passion were the fruits of his incarnational obedience to the Father. Jesus has saved us not because of what he did but by what he is.

We can look at this the other way round. The Lord, because of who he is, was able to win the great victory over death and sin on the cross. Similarly, as Christians of the new birth, it is only because of what we are, as living limbs of the risen humanity of Christ, that we can join in the uncompleted battle against the Devil. Jesus has in fact already defeated the Enemy at Calvary. We are not called to help Jesus win his victory for him. He has already accomplished that, but he calls us to our at-one-ment with him. 'If you want to join in my struggle,' he says, 'then you must be joined to me.' How do we best help our Lord to complete the victory already accomplished? Well of course we need faith and trust, but most of all we need to be united to the risen Christ and to rest in him. He is our head and we are mystically joined to him through the Spirit. This mystical body is the church and the door to the eternal kingdom. It is the door in our own hearts through which the kingdom shines with all the splendour and transfiguring radiance of God's glory.

That this does not seem to fit with our actual experience of God is due to the fact that we are too busy running around after him and not resting in him. If we are secure at the centre, spiritually alive in God, then we are living eschatologically:

from the Spirit outwards to the world. Dr Elliot's plea for an 'alternative consciousness' (1987: 119) in order to confront the powers of evil must be the 'consciousness' that is impregnated with the kingdom. The kingdom is always to be understood eschatologically, because it is eternity breaking into time.

I remember once reading a book about an Englishman in Greece. He was shocked and was piously offended when he visited a small Orthodox church where the priest was praying the litany of intercession and his wife was cleaning the church. While she was doing the housekeeping, he was lost in prayer. It struck me that this was a perfect model of our life in God. The man and the woman represent the inner life and its outward expression: the busy activity is facilitated – let loose – by prayer. Mary and Martha were in opposition to each other because in the story at Bethany (Luke 10:38–42) Martha did not understand that the outward (and necessary) show of work needs to be an expression of the inner life. It is by going inwards that we discover the secret springs of spiritual resistance where God nurtures our struggling and feeble efforts to live in the new humanity.

The old Adam needs to be conquered from within because our natural human lives are always in conflict with the new man and woman. If we cannot die to the old self then no matter how busy and warlike we may be our activity is not eschatological life.

To recapitulate, our relationship to God should be the in-relation of adopted sons and daughters. We are grafted on to the life of the risen Christ – the new humanity. Not only do we have no right to be there – we are not only sinners but sinful *creatures* – but we can only become fully integrated members of this new humanity by the activity of the Holy Spirit.

Living eschatologically, therefore, has a deeper, and ontological, meaning than simply living as if this were our last hour. (Such a view keeps us alert, like sentries at our posts, or commandos behind enemy lines.) The deeper meaning is to be manifested by living from the reality of the kingdom. This kingdom is not for the lazy (remember the foolish virgins) but for those who are prepared to take it by storm. By which I mean that although the kingdom cannot be won by us either by merit or faith – it is God's gift – we are encouraged to engage with it, to wrestle and to strive for it.

This inward struggle has nothing to do with the sort of outward fretting and excitable spirituality that is always looking for the new thing – the next shot of religious feeling or theological novelty. Inward struggle allows God to knit us ever closer to himself. A Christian army, unlike ordinary armies, does not march on its stomach: it marches on prayer. What we need in modernity, as never before, is a return to that spirituality and prayer of desperation and faith that causes us to cling only to God.

All the great saints of history – from the fathers to the great Puritan divines – were men and women of prayer. Not occasional or faddish prayer, but a 'rule' of prayer: a life lived regularly in the presence of God. That is living eschatologically.

Charismatic activity may be the outflowing of our inward spiritual life. *Glossolalia* – speaking in tongues – can be the desperate cry from the heart where our spirit groans to be united with Christ. Only if the Holy Spirit is also groaning within us can this be achieved. But outward phenomena may not be directly related to inward spiritual experience. Too easily charismatic chatter creates a barrier of noise and dislocation of mind so that we cannot hear the whisper of the Spirit in the temple of our heart.

To live in modernity is to live in a world of frenetic pace, noise, over-indulgence and novelty. All of these things militate against the spiritual life, and the rays of God's kingdom can be shut out by the shrillness and carnality of modern living. Worldliness characterises modernity. If ever there was a time to return to fasting in the churches it is now, and yet we find that both Catholics and Protestants have virtually abandoned regular fasting (though the charismatic renewal is beginning to recognise its importance). Fasting is always linked with prayer in the spiritual life. We fast to turn us from unfit and overweight combatants into spiritually honed comrades.

The Orthodox East has much to learn from the West

(though it finds it difficult to accept this). It certainly needs it (Zizioulas 1985: 26). Perhaps the West also needs to recapture the spirituality and prayer of the East. Prayer and meditation are activities that we need to be trained in. God takes us as raw recruits but expects us to become disciplined soldiers. The success in the 1970s of Metropolitan Anthony's books on prayer (1970) were primarily because they were written by a master practitioner of prayer. Living eschatologically, however, is not to attend seminars on prayer, or even to read good books about it: it is to pray.

But there is one more and even 'further in' way in which we can live eschatologically. An evangelical friend once asked me why Catholics and Orthodox dress up in such outrageous clothes, light candles, smother their churches in sweet cloying incense, and decorate their churches with gaudy pictures. So I pointed out that he had missed the vital ingredient: food. All this sensuousness is related to the simple fact that to go to the liturgy is to accept the invitation to a divine party. Every liturgy is a celebration with good food, fellowship and bright lights. The Eucharist is not only a remembrance of Christ's unique and once-for-all death; it is a participation in the life of the kingdom (Luke 14:15).

This seems to be a very materialistic way to go about it! But the kingdom is a banquet of feasting and rejoicing. The kingdom may not yet have come in its fullness and finality, but it is here nevertheless; and food is a fundamental fact of banqueting. Reacting against the idea that Christianity is just a moral idea or a set of beliefs spread by teaching, C. S. Lewis saw it this way: 'it's more like evolution – a biological or super-biological fact . . . That's why He uses material things like bread and wine to put the new life into us. We may think this rather crude and unspiritual. God doesn't: He *invented* eating. He likes matter. He invented it' (1942: 60).

In the Eastern churches the liturgy is not understood so much as going 'up' to feed on God, as God coming down to us. When the deacon intones the opening words 'blessed is the kingdom' it is believed that the kingdom is here: eternity breaking through into our spatial and time-bound reality.

This approach to worship and the kingdom may be strange

– and unacceptable – to some Protestants, but there is another dimension to it that is of direct interest to us all. The celebration of Holy Communion is not only a party to which we alone are invited: the whole of heaven comes along. I do not necessarily mean by that the great saints of the past, but the whole host of angels and the created order that have remained faithful to God and remain comrades-in-arms with him.

To live eschatologically is to discover that the militant church – the outpost of heaven – is in fact already surrounded by the church triumphant. To live in the kingdom is not yet to be physically transformed into our resurrected destiny, but it is to be united with the church of history and the *Christus Victor* of Calvary and the King to come. Kingdom life is not only abundant life, it is eternal life.

We may be an outpost of heaven, the advanced troops waiting for the final invasion when God will be all in all, but we already belong to a heavenly company. It is true that we are encompassed by the Evil One and his forces, but 'they that be with us are more than they that be with them' (2 Kings 6:16). I love the juxtaposition of ideas in the old spiritual that says,

> We are climbing Jacob's ladder,
> We are climbing Jacob's ladder,
> We are climbing Jacob's ladder,
> Soldiers of the cross.

Not only does the heavenly host come down, but we are called to 'move up a little higher': 'Come further up and further in.'

To live eschatologically is to share the power and the fellowship of the kingdom. Like the opened eyes of the young man who was overcome with fear at the might of the Syrians, we can have our eyes opened by faith and 'behold, the mountain . . . full of horses and chariots of fire'. No doubt great saints do not need to be reassured, but we who are trying to overcome our timidity and to struggle with the Evil One for the modern world need heavenly support 'lest our hearts fail us'.

I was once walking through the back streets of Teddington

when I came across a small group of Salvationists. Their flag was limp, and their message seemed to be falling on empty ears. Standing in a circle, these old warriors of Christ (they all seemed over sixty years of age) bowed their heads and prayed. I stopped and found that I was praying too. There was nobody within earshot and the whole scene was so incongruous it should have been laughable. And then quite unexpectedly, and without any visual images, I knew that I was standing on kingdom territory. A feeling of holiness so terrible and awesome came over me that I wanted to run and hide. The presence of God was so strong that I felt for a moment that those faithful old subalterns of Christ were in fact the crack troops of the kingdom.

Fanciful and wishful thinking? Perhaps, but something similar has happened to me once since then that was even more unexpected and full of hope.

It happened at the funeral of my brother who was mentally and physically handicapped and for over forty years was cared for in Tatchbury Mount in Hampshire. The funeral service was packed with David's friends, all severely handicapped. We struck up his favourite hymn, 'All things bright and beautiful', and the residents sang out in defiant triumph and victory. It was not merely touching: it was awesome being surrounded by 'angels unawares' breaking through the hostility of Enemy territory. I wondered then, and I wonder still, if they were not more whole than I, more holy, and more blessed; in Charles Williams' phrase 'my companions of the coinherence', my true comrades-in-arms.

THE MARKS OF THE KING

And this brings me to my final word, without which this propaganda is a lie. As we seek to live eschatologically in the kingdom, we begin to understand that there is something very strange about our captain and comrades: we fight, but in pain. Jesus still bears the marks of the cross – the outward sign of the 'wound of the heart' that God bears from all eternity. He stumbles upon those broken feet and reaches out to us to link arms with him in his suffering. Joined to him, we come to realise that we are joined also to his wounds. He will give us his peace and fill us with hope and 'good cheer', but he cannot keep us from his cross. If we wish to join with him we must take him as he is. To be joined to the new humanity and comradeship is to die to the old humanity. Not for nothing does the old Protestant hymn insist that 'the way of the cross leads home'.

It is only when we are joined to Jesus that we feel his vulnerability and the openness of his love. It is because he is open to hurt and rejection that he joined himself to our wretched condition in order that he could heal us from within.

Jesus the man not only joins hands with us, and links arms in solidarity, but also as God he links arms with the Father. Thus does he – and he alone – mediate between the holiness and judgment of God and our fallen(away) humanity. He alone declares the kingdom to us, and in the declaration he draws us into its life-giving power through the healing restoration of the Spirit.

But in his love and the pure fire of the Spirit he asks us to submit our belligerence and triumphalism to be burnt. He wants only that which is pure, new life. We are exhorted to stand up, but with tenderness. The way of victory is not to smash the Devil with hate and repugnance. Such a way is too open to his perversion: he does not care whom we hate, even if it is himself. Throughout the New Testament Jesus confronts the demonic world with great authority (*exousia*),[1] almost with respect. The fathers believed that Jesus treated the great rebel with justice, for he too was created by God.

The victory of the cross was a victory that stands military sense on its head: Jesus submitted to the powers. It is not Christ the *pantokrator* who looks down from the cross. Jesus as judge looks at us through the eyes of the *eschaton*: the rightful king of all the earth. But on the cross we meet redemptive suffering in the person of a servant.

In following this Lord we take to ourselves his stigmata: we are joined to him, and his wounds become ours. Together we offer the world not passive resistance but spiritual resistance. We are to contend vigorously for the truth, because only truth can set the captives free. In our moral resistance to evil and human alienation we will fight for the rights of others. But for ourselves we forgo all rights. Our captain forfeited his for the captives. He redeemed us and made us his companions by shunning his own glory that we might be free.

Our Lord asks us to remember that as volunteers in the great cause we are not fighting to win but to save. The further in and further up we go into the communion of the kingdom the more certain we become that the divine love has already conquered not by laying down his arms but by outstretching them and embracing us all.

Notes

PREFACE

1 Propaganda always runs the risk of degenerating into caricature, chattiness and raciness. Inevitably scholarship will be mixed with rhetoric. This is a caveat that needs to be inserted at the beginning of a book of this kind!

2 I do not mean to offend pacifists with my military-style language. Using language creatively always runs the risk of causing offence. I do not in any way endorse militarism or indeed the language of triumphalism.

FOREWORD: 'CHOOSE YOUR SIDE'

1 We have the 'happy are ye' of John 13:17 and the more devastating 'if ye suffer for righteousness' sake, happy are ye' of 1 Peter 3:14, but we are not offered happiness as an end in itself.

1 THE DIVINE DRAMA LOST

1 I have in fact counselled some Christians who are on the fringes of the charismatic movement that they would be better off if they took personal responsibility for their actions and stopped blaming all their failures on the Devil (or on demons). Everything they do that is good is attributed to their faith – helped by the Holy Spirit – but everything they do that is bad is entirely due to Satan. If they fall ill it is a demonic attack; likewise their unhappiness is caused by Satan – what has happened in their lives is that they have forgotten that they are simply human and subject to the same problems as people everywhere.

2 Following early texts, the Lord's Prayer included the line 'Deliver us from the Evil One.'

3 This is not a Lewis phrase, but I mean by it that for Lewis all true myths are eternal and 'memories' or 'echoes' of God himself. (Like some of Lewis's philosophical notions, such an idea clearly invokes Platonism.)

4 May I recommend that you try this for yourself using Arthur Moss's translation and ordering of the four gospels as one (Moss 1971)?

5 Though we often forget that propitiation is mentioned only twice in the New Testament (1 John 2:2 and Rom 3:25).

6 Luther also, on the whole, accepted the medieval view of the atonement, despite his emphasis on justification by faith. It is true, furthermore, that Luther's account of salvation is far more dramatic than the scholastic theologians' and that the Devil in his theology is more active than in the works of Thomas Aquinas.

Indeed Luther's *theologia crucis* is not only exciting – and original in many ways – but it also loops back to the earlier patristic era. Both Luther and Calvin – not a few evangelicals forget – saw themselves as the heirs of the fathers, not their enemies.

7 Though to be fair to post-Enlightenment Protestant theologians, subjective aspects of the atonement can be traced to Augustine.

2 RETELLING THE DIVINE DRAMA

1 Scholars are divided as to whether the Hellenisation of the early church resulted in a distortion of the New Testament witness. It certainly affected it in the same way that Latin altered the earlier Greek theology.

2 I do not mean to dismiss the Latin fathers, who are the dominant influence on the theologians of the Reformation. The version that I offer here is merely *a* version, not *the* version. It is the sort of version that one would expect from an Orthodox tradition. I accept that it is primitive (and mythological), but I believe that it is biblical and still a vital story for today's world.

3 We have become so used to God as the rational designer that it is worth recalling that St Maximus the Confessor (eighth century) saw God's creation as passionate and wild – a crazy love, *manichos eros*.

4 From the fourth-century poetry of St Ephraim the Syrian.

5 In the gospels the story of the 'vinegar' comes after the cry of 'Father forgive them . . .'

6 Matt 27:52–53; 1 Pet 3:19.

3 APPROACHING MODERNITY

1 And, of course, evil is not foreign to our own natures.

2 Romanticism or the Romantic movement in art and literature are not what I mean here, but rather the preference for feeling and imagination over reason. Blake, Coleridge and perhaps even Lewis himself could be said to be Romantics in the grand sense.

4 KNOWING THE ENEMY – THE COMING OF MODERNITY

1 See Thomas 1971. The brilliant demographic introduction to Thomas's book has supplied many of these facts about England in the 1700s.

2 'Dialectical materialism' is a phrase belonging to neither Marx nor Engels: it was invented by Soviet socialists. The phrase denotes the fact that socialism is a philosophy of materialism; or in a more Marxist vein we could say that there is a dialectic between the true philosophy of Marxism (superstructure) and the state-owned economy (infrastructure).

3 Leszek Kolakowski believes that the disappearance of taboos is, perhaps, the greatest danger of modernity (Kolakowski 1986: 12).

5 CAPTIVE LIVES – THE INSIDIOUSNESS OF MODERNITY (PART 1)

1 Though if the Lutheran church had stood up and proclaimed its direct opposition to Hitler from the beginning, things may well have been very different. The fact that the Dutch Reformed Church in South Africa has now withdrawn its theological legitimation of apartheid is itself an example of how words can make a difference.

2 I do not mean by this mortician beautification. This habit, it seems to me, is a 'dressing-up' of the body into something unreal and grotesque; as such it is a tacit denial of death.

6 CAPTIVE LIVES – THE INSIDIOUSNESS OF MODERNITY (PART 2)

1 This section is really impossible to write without employing hyperbole: the nature of the evidence concerning the media is primarily interpretative and impressionistic.

2 My sources for this statistical information were principally *BBC Data Publications (1985)* and the *International Television Almanac* for 1985; I am also particularly grateful to Dr David Docherty for some of this information.

3 This book was going to press during the final stages of the British general election. Radio reports demonstrated that people were so bored with the election coverage that video sales went up by twenty per cent!

   On a more serious level, was it coincidence that (1) the Labour party campaign really 'took off' immediately after the carefully crafted party election broadcast by the makers of the film *Chariots of Fire*? and (2) did not the double-act of the two Davids of the Alliance party fail to convince because it too closely resembled the comedy show *The Two Ronnies*?

7 SCIENTIFIC SORCERY – SCIENCE, SCIENTISM AND THE COLLAPSE OF MORAL PHILOSOPHY

1 This notion of falsification is what distinguishes Popper's philosophy of science so radically from the logical positivists (with whom he is often

mistakenly identified). For further clarification of Popper's position, see Bryan Magee's excellent small book on Popper (1973).

2   There is now strong evidence to show that Sir Cyril Burt's pioneering work on intelligence testing contains fictional data and falsified results: no small matter when we recall how influential this work has been on the education system of Great Britain since the 1944 Education Act.

3   I do not mean to suggest that sociobiology is racist, but I believe that it is closer to scientism than to science. See Michael Ruse's criticisms (1979) with their plea for a more sober sociobiology.

4   To say for example that evolution demonstrates that nature has a built-in mechanism for change and adaption is a far cry from saying that nature is random or blind.

5   As utilitarianism remains an emendation of pagan hedonism, despite the heroic efforts of Mill and Sidgwick to square it with idealism, I believe it to be opposed to the spirit of Christianity.

On the economic level the utility arguments of Bentham and Malthus have helped forward some of the most baneful curses of modernity.

6   The English translation, under the title *The Logic of Scientific Discovery*, appeared in 1959.

7   Of course this is a caricatured generalisation.

8   I regret not having the space to develop the influence of existentialism on the modern world. In English-speaking countries its influence is more noticeable in theology than in philosophy.

9   At least this is true on the negative side. On the positive side these sessions were the most stimulating lessons I have ever been involved in. The students themselves knew something was wrong without any directions or directives from me. My role was to clarify and to articulate problems, not to moralise.

8   THE ENEMY WITHIN – MODERNISM IN THE CHURCHES

1   Conversely, it is also the case that some dogmatic scholars are considerably more 'liberal' than some New Testament scholars.

2   Though in fact Tyrrell's work was condemned by the Vatican as heretical.

3   Works of propaganda, such as this one, invariably oversimplify. It is not modern methods themselves that are the enemy, but their usurpation of the tenets of the gospel.

4   There are still pockets of tradition in Britain's universities: King's College, London, and Durham and Birmingham are good examples. (In Edinburgh, since Professor Tom Torrance's departure, modernism seems to be alive and well!)

5   This is an oversimplified label. A more accurate description would be to say that 'Schleiermacher exhibited the traits of Romanticism, particularly in his earlier works.'

6   His notion of God-consciousness as being one of 'absolute dependence' even suggests a form of heteronomy (an accusation levelled
against him by Barth).

7   Heron (1980: ch. 1) sees this as no more than an appendix. Schleiermacher, on the other hand, saw it as the 'coping-stone' of his whole
system. His trinitarianism, however, is not the traditional doctrine of
the fathers and Reformers.

8   This concept, made popular by the sociologist Peter Berger, is derived
from the phenomenology of Husserl's student Alfred Schutz. For an
understanding of Berger's emendation of this position, see Berger and
Luckmann 1976.

9   If Scofield's Bible (the famous *Scofield Reference Bible*) is distorted by
dispensationalist and inerrantist doctrines, Harnack's commentaries
are riddled with liberal presuppositions. How many students have read
Harnack's gospel as the gospel?

10   Although the Barth who moved from dialectical theology to neo-
orthodoxy also argued for an autonomy of a kind.

9   KINGDOM MOVES

1   Though for many Catholics, Orthodox and Anglo-Catholics, women
priests are a denial of the fact that at the incarnation God chose to be
born a man; this for them, then, becomes a primary, not a secondary
matter. For my part the gender of priests is by no means a closed issue
on the basis of biblical and patristic evidence and should not therefore
be seen as on the same level as the central dogmas of the incarnation
and the resurrection.

2   Commissioned by Professor David Martin and researched by Graham
Baldwin, the paper 'New developments in sectarian evangelism' was
read at the Institute of Economic Culture, Boston University, in April
1987.

3   I first met Christ in a fundamentalist household, and so for my part I
feel a natural empathy for such movements. Like C. F. Andrews
remembering his Irvingite background, I can look back in love, not
anger (Andrews 1932: chs 1–4).

    It is a great joy for me when I am permitted to preach in a black
Pentecostalist church. No doubt in many ways it is what we would call
fundamentalist. What is obvious, however, is that the Divine Drama is
alive and literally dancing round the aisles! When I preach I do not
have to worry whether the congregation believe in Jesus as Lord, or
whether they have doubts about miracles or the reality of the Holy
Spirit. I always come away feeling that I have been the one ministered
to.

4   I am grateful to Simon Batchelor for this story.

10 KINGDOM COME

1 While it is true that in the gospels Jesus exercises power (*dunamis*) in his healing ministry, it is more usually the case that he exercises his authority over the demons than that he demonstrates his power against them. Authority is an altogether more Christian approach, it seems to me, than exercising (and exorcising) power; power-healing concepts so easily become abused and turn into 'biff-bam-zap' theology. (I am grateful to my colleague Tom Smail for first pointing this out to me.)

References and Bibliography

Aeschliman 1983	M. D. Aeschliman, *The Restitution of Man* C. S. Lewis and the Case Against Scientism (Michigan: Wm B. Eerdmans 1983)
Agursky 1976	M. Agursky, 'Contemporary socioeconomic systems and their future prospects' in A. Solzhenitsyn (ed.), *Under the Rubble* (London: Fontana 1976)
Ahern and Davie 1987	G. Ahern and G. Davie, *Inner-City God* (London: Hodder & Stoughton/C. S. Lewis Centre 1987)
Andreski 1974	S. Andreski, *The Essential Comte* (London: Croom Helm 1974)
Andrews 1932	C. F. Andrews, *What I Owe to Christ* (London: Hodder & Stoughton 1932)
Aulén 1965	G. Aulén, *Christus Victor* tr. A. G. Herbert (London: SPCK 1965)
Austin 1962	J. L. Austin, *How to Do Things with Words* (Oxford: Clarendon Press 1962)
Avis 1986	P. Avis, *The Methods of Modern Theology* The Dream of Reason (Basingstoke: Marshall Pickering 1986)
Ayer 1959	A. J. Ayer, *Logical Positivism* (New York: Free Press 1959)
Ayer 1963	A. J. Ayer, *Language, Truth and Logic* (London: Victor Gollancz 1963)
Baelz 1981	P. Baelz *et al*, *Is Christianity Credible?* (London: Epworth Press 1981)
Bailey 1976	E. Bailey, 'Religion of a Secular Society' (unpublished PhD thesis, Bristol University 1976)

Barr 1981	J. Barr, *Fundamentalism* (London: SCM Press 1981)
Bennett 1964	J. Bennett, *Rationality* An Essay Towards an Analysis (London: RKP 1964)
Berger 1969	P. Berger, *The Social Reality of Religion* (London: Faber & Faber 1969) (the original American title was *The Sacred Canopy*)
Berger 1979	P. Berger, *Facing up to Modernity* (London: Penguin Books 1979)
Berger and Luckmann 1976	P. Berger and T. Luckman, *The Social Construction of Reality* A Treatise in the Sociology of Knowledge (London: Penguin 1976)
Blauner 1964	R. Blauner, *Alienation and Freedom* (Chicago: University of Chicago Press 1964)
Bloom 1970	Metropolitan Anthony Bloom, *School for Prayer* (London: DLT 1970)
du Boulay 1984	S. du Boulay, *Cicely Saunders* (London: Hodder & Stoughton 1984)
Bower 1985	R. T. Bower, *The Changing Television Audience in America* (New York: Columbia University Press 1985)
Bradley 1976	I. Bradley, *The Call to Seriousness* The Evangelical Impact on the Victorians (London: Jonathan Cape 1976)
Bray 1984	G. Bray, *Creeds, Councils and Christ* (Leicester: IVP 1984)
British Council of Churches 1986	British Council of Churches, *Reflections* How twenty-six churches see their life and mission (London: BCC 1986)
British Council of Churches 1986	British Council of Churches, *Observations* on the church from Britain and abroad (London: BCC 1986)
Buber 1959	M. Buber, *I and Thou* tr. R. G. Smith (Edinburgh: T. & T. Clark 1959)

Bultmann 1952   R. Bultmann, *Theology of the New
                     Testament* vol. 1 (London: SCM
                     Press 1952)

Bultmann 1953   R. Bultmann, 'New Testament and
                     Mythology' in H. W. Bartsch (ed.),
                     Kerygma and Myth (London: SPCK
                     1953)

Carr 1981   W. Carr, *Angels and Principalities* The
                     Background, Meaning and
                     Development of the Pauline Phrase
                     hai archai kai hai exousiai
                     (Cambridge: CUP 1981)

de Chardin 1959   P. Teilhard de Chardin, *The
                     Phenomenon of Man* (London:
                     Collins 1959)

Cicourel 1964   A. Cicourel, *Method and
                     Measurement in Sociology* (New
                     York: Free Press 1964)

Cuff and Payne 1979 E. C. Cuff and G. C. F. Payne (eds),
                     Perspectives in Sociology
                     (London: George Allen & Unwin
                     1979)

Cupitt 1979   D. Cupitt, *The Debate About Christ*
                     (London: SCM Press 1979)

Davies 1982   T. Davies, *Merlyn the Magician and the
                     Pacific Coast Highway* (London:
                     New English Library 1982)

D'Costa 1986   G. D'Costa, *Christianity and Religious
                     Pluralism* (Oxford: Basil Blackwell
                     1986)

Dobbelaere 1981   K. Dobbelaere, 'Secularisation: A
                     Multi-Dimension Concept' *Current
                     Sociology* 29/2 (Summer 1981)

Dostoevsky 1958   F. Dostoevsky, *The Brothers
                     Karamazov* tr. D. Magarshack
                     (London: Penguin 1958)

Dostoevsky 1968   F. Dostoevsky, *Letters from the
                     Underworld* (London: J. M. Dent &
                     Sons 1968)

Dunn 1985   J. D. G. Dunn, *The Evidence for Jesus*
                     (London: SCM Press 1985)

Elliot 1985   C. Elliot, *Praying the Kingdom*
                     (London: DLT 1985)

Elliot 1987	C. Elliot, *Comfortable Compassion* Poverty, Power and the Church (London: Hodder & Stoughton 1987)
Emmet 1979	D. Emmet, *The Moral Prism* (London: Macmillan 1979)
Fisk 1986	M. J. Fisk, *Independence and the Elderly* (London: Croom Helm 1986)
Ford 1986	A. Ford, *Universe* God, Man and Science (London: Hodder & Stoughton 1986)
Galbraith 1979	J. K. Galbraith, *The Affluent Society* (Harmondsworth: Penguin Books 1979)
Gellner 1963	E. Gellner, *Words and Things* (London: Victor Gollancz 1963)
George 1982	W. George, *Darwin* (London: Fontana 1982) in the *Modern Masters* series
Gorer 1965	G. Gorer, *Death, Grief and Mourning in Contemporary Britain* (London: Cresset Press 1965)
Goulder and Hick 1983	M. D. Goulder and J. Hick, *Why Believe in God?* (London: SCM Press 1983)
Greer 1984	G. Greer, *Sex and Destiny* The Politics of Human Fertility (London: Secker & Warburg 1984)
Guinness 1973	O. Guinness, *The Dust of Death* (Downers Grove: IVP 1973)
Guinness 1983	O. Guinness, *The Gravedigger File* (London: Hodder & Stoughton 1983)
Gunton 1983	C. Gunton, *Yesterday and Today* A Study of Continuities in Christology (London: DLT 1983)
Gunton forthcoming	*Atonement as Metaphor*
Hammond 1983	F. and I. M. Hammond, *Pigs in the Parlor* (New York: Impact Books 1983)
Harrell 1985	D. E. Harrell Jr, *Oral Roberts* An American Life (Bloomington:

Indiana University Press 1985)

Heron 1980 — A. Heron, *A Century of Protestant Thought* (Guildford: Lutterworth Press 1980)

Hick 1973 — J. Hick, *God and the Universe of Faiths* Essays in the Philosophy of Religion (London: Macmillan 1973)

Hick 1977 — J. Hick (ed.), *The Myth of God Incarnate* (London: SCM Press 1977)

Hunter 1983 — J. D. Hunter, *American Evangelicalism* Conservative Religion and the Quandary of Modernity (New Brunswick: Rutgers University Press 1983)

Junck 1958 — R. Junck, *Brighter Than a Thousand Suns* (London: Victor Gollancz 1958)

Kamenka 1969 — E. Kamenka, *Marxism and Ethics* (London: Macmillan 1969)

Kelly 1968 — H. Kelly, *Towards the Death of Satan* (London: Geoffrey Chapman 1968)

Kelly 1977 — J. N. D. Kelly, *Early Christian Doctrines* (London: A. & C. Black ^{5}1977)

Kitcher 1982 — P. Kitcher, *Abusing Science* The Case Against Creationism (Massachusetts Institute of Technology 1982)

Koestler 1959 — A. Koestler, *The Sleepwalkers* A History of Man's Changing Vision of the Universe (London: Hutchinson 1959)

Kolakowski 1971 — L. Kolakowski, *Marxism and Beyond* (London: Paladin 1971)

Kolakowski 1986 — L. Kolakowski, 'Modernity on endless trial' in *Encounter* (March 1986)

Kraft 1953 — V. Kraft, *The Vienna Circle* (New York: Philosophical Library Inc. 1953)

Kuhn 1970 — T. S. Kuhn, *The Structure of Scientific Revolutions* (Chicago: University of Chicago Press ^{2}1970)

Kumar 1980 — S. Kumar (ed.), *The Schumacher Lectures* (London: Bloud & Briggs 1980)

Lakatos and Musgrave 1970 — I. Lakatos and R. Musgrave (eds), *Criticism and the Growth of Knowledge* (Cambridge: CUP 1970)

Lash 1986 — N. Lash, *Theology on the Way to Emmaus* (London: SCM Press 1986)

Lewis 1942 — C. S. Lewis, *Broadcast Talks* (London: Geoffrey Bles 1942)

Lewis 1950 — C. S. Lewis, *The Pilgrim's Regress* (London: Geoffrey Bles 1950)

Lewis 1955 — C. S. Lewis, *Surprised by Joy* (London: Geoffrey Bles 1955)

Lewis 1975 — C. S. Lewis, in W. Hooper (ed.), *Fern-Seed and Elephants* and Other Essays on Christianity (London: Fontana 1975)

Lewis 1978 — C. S. Lewis, *The Abolition of Man* (London: Fount 1978)

Lewis 1979 — C. S. Lewis, *The Screwtape Letters* (London: Fount 1979)

Lewis 1980 — C. S. Lewis, *The Last Battle* (London: Collins Lions 1980)

Lukes 1973 — S. Lukes, *Emile Durkheim* His Life and Work (London: Penguin Books 1973)

MacIntyre 1967 — A. MacIntyre, *A Short History of Ethics* (London: RKP 1967)

MacIntyre 1981 — A. MacIntyre, *After Virtue* A Study in Moral Theory (London: Duckworth 1981)

Magee 1971 — B. Magee, *Modern British Philosophy* (London: Secker & Warburg 1971)

Magee 1973 — B. Magee, *Popper* (London: Fontana 1973) in the *Past Masters* series

Malik 1982 — C. H. Malik, *A Christian Critique of the University* (Downers Grove: IVP 1982)

Marsden 1980 — G. M. Marsden, *Fundamentalism and American Culture* (Oxford: OUP 1980)

Martin 1973   D. Martin, 'Order and Rule: A Critique of Spontaneity' in *Tracts Against the Times* (London: Lutterworth 1973)

Martin 1978   D. Martin, *A General Theory of Secularisation* (Oxford: Basil Blackwell 1978)

Mascall 1977   E. L. Mascall, *Theology and the Gospel of Christ* (London: SPCK 1977)

Mascall 1980   E. L. Mascall, *Whatever Happened to the Human Mind?* (London: SPCK 1980)

McBain 1986   D. McBain, *Eyes That See* The Spiritual Gift of Discernment (Basingstoke: Marshall Pickering 1986)

McLuhan 1967   M. McLuhan, *The Medium is the Massage* (London: Penguin Books 1967)

Merton 1968   R. K. Merton, *Social Theory and Social Structure* (New York: Free Press 1968)

Meyendorff 1969   J. Meyendorff, *Christ in Eastern Christian Thought* (Washington: Corpus Books 1969)

Meyendorff 1978   J. Meyendorff, *The Orthodox Church in the Ecumenical Movement* (Geneva: WCC 1978)

Mitford 1963   J. Mitford, *The American Way of Death* (London: Hutchinson 1963)

Mitschevlich and   A. Mitschevlich and F. Mielke, *The*
Mielke 1962   *Death Doctors* (Elek Books 1962)

Moltmann 1981   J. Moltmann, *The Trinity and the Kingdom of God* tr. M. Kohl (London: SCM Press 1981)

Moss 1971   A. Moss, *The Four Gospels Arranged as One* (London: Citadel Press 1971)

Mumford 1934   L. Mumford, *Technics and Civilization* (New York: Harcourt, Brace and World 1934)

Neuhaus 1986   R. Neuhaus, *The Naked Public Square*

	(Michigan: Wm B. Eerdmans [2]1986)
Newbigin 1983	L. Newbigin, *The Other Side of 84* (London: BCC Publications 1983)
Nietzsche 1966	F. Nietzsche, *Beyond Good and Evil* Prelude to a Philosophy of a Future, tr. W. Kaufmann (New York: Vintage Books 1966)
Ong 1982	W. Ong, *Orality and Literacy* The Technologizing of the Word (London: Methuen 1982)
Polanyi 1973	M. Polanyi, *Personal Knowledge* Towards a Post-Critical Philosophy (London: RKP 1973)
Popper 1976	K. Popper, *Conjectures and Refutations* The Growth of Scientific Knowledge (London: RKP 1976)
Postman 1987	N. Postman, *Amusing Ourselves to Death* (London: Methuen 1987)
Roberts 1977	R. C. Roberts, *Rudolf Bultmann's Theology* A Critical Interpretation (London: SPCK 1977)
Robinson 1963	J. A. T. Robinson, *Honest to God* (London: SCM Press 1963)
Rogers 1964	R. A. P. Rogers, *A Short History of Ethics* (London: Macmillan 1964)
Ruse 1979	M. Ruse, *'Sociobiology': Sense or Nonsense* (Dordrecht: D. Reidel 1979)
Russell 1977	J. B. Russell, *The Devil* Perceptions of Evil from Antiquity to Primitive Christianity (Ithaca: Cornell University Press 1977)
Russell 1981	J. B. Russell, *Satan* The Early Christian Tradition (Ithaca: Cornell University Press 1981)
Ryle 1949	G. Ryle, *The Concept of Mind* (London: Hutchinson 1949)
Schumacher 1973	E. F. Schumacher, *Small is Beautiful* (London: Blond & Briggs 1973)
Schutz 1943	A. Schutz, 'The Problem of Rationality in the Social World' *Economia* 1943

Sheppard and Worlock 1988	D. Sheppard and D. Worlock, *Better Together* (London: Hodder & Stoughton 1988)
Smail 1987	T. Smail, *The Forgotten Father* (London: Hodder & Stoughton ²1987)
Sophrony 1964	Archbishop Sophrony, 'Principles of Orthodox Asceticism' in A. J. Philippou (ed.), *Orthodox Ethos* (Oxford: Holywell Press Ltd 1964)
Steiner 1967	G. Steiner, *Language and Silence* (London: Faber & Faber 1967)
Stott 1984	J. R. W. Stott, *Issues Facing Christians Today* (Basingstoke: Marshalls 1984)
Sudnow 1967	D. Sudnow, *Passing On* The Social Organisation of Dying (New York: Prentice-Hall 1967)
Suenens 1982	L-J. Suenens, *Renewal and the Powers of Darkness* (London: DLT 1982)
Templeton 1981	J. M. Templeton, *The Humble Approach* Scientists Discover God (London: Collins 1981)
Thomas 1971	K. Thomas, *Religion and the Decline of Magic* (London: Weidenfeld & Nicolson 1971)
Torrance 1980	T. F. Torrance, *Christian Theology and Scientific Culture* (Belfast: Christian Journals 1980)
Torrance 1982	T. F. Torrance, *Reality and Evangelical Theology* (Philadelphia: Westminster Press 1982)
Torrance 1984	T. F. Torrance, *Transformation and Convergence in the Frame of Knowledge* (Belfast: Christian Journals 1984)
Torrance 1986	T. F. Torrance, 'Karl Barth and the Latin Heresy' *Scottish Journal of Theology* 39 (1986)
Varghese 1984	R. A. Varghese, *The Intellectuals Speak Out About God* (Chicago: Regenery Gateway 1984)
Walker 1969	A. Walker, 'Science in Nazi Germany

and Nazi "Science": Their
Relationship to the Party
Weltanschauung' (unpublished MSc
thesis, Salford University 1969)

Walker 1986   A. Walker, 'The Third Schism: The
Great Divide in Christianity Today'
in T. Moss (ed.), *In Search of
Christianity* (London: Firethorn
Press 1986)

Walker 1988   A. Walker (ed.), *Different Gospels*
Christian Orthodoxy and
Post-Enlightenment Theologies
(London: Hodder & Stoughton/
C. S. Lewis Centre 1988)

Walker forthcoming   A. Walker, *Flesh of Sin* Atonement
and Christ's True Humanity
(London: Hodder & Stoughton)

Wallis 1986   J. Wallis, *The Call to Conversion*
(Tring: Lion Publishing 1986)

Walter 1979   J. A. Walter, *A Long Way from Home*
(Exeter: Paternoster Press 1979)

Ward 1985   K. Ward, *The Battle for the Soul* The
End of Morality in a Secular Society
(London: Hodder & Stoughton 1985)

Weber 1922   M. Weber, *Wirtschaft und Gesellschaft*
(Tubingen: J. C. B. Mohr 1922)

Wickeri 1984   Wickeri (ed.), *Chinese Theological
Review* 1984 (Foundation for
Theological Education in South
East Asia)

Wiles 1974   M. Wiles, *The Remaking of Christian
Doctrine* (London: SCM Press 1974)

Williamson, Parotta
   et al 1983   J. Williamson and K. Parotta *et al*,
Christianity Confronts Modernity A
Theological and Pastoral Inquiry by
Protestant Evangelicals and Roman
Catholics (Michigan: Servant Press
1983)

Wilson 1975   E. O. Wilson, *Sociobiology: The New
Synthesis* (Harvard University Press
1975)

Winch 1958   P. Winch, *The Idea of a Social Science*
(London: RKP 1958)

Wink 1984   W. Wink, *Naming the Powers* The Language of Power in the New Testament, vol. 1: The Powers (Philadelphia: Fortress Press 1984)

Wittgenstein 1976   L. Wittgenstein, *Philosophical Investigations* tr. G. E. Anscombe (Oxford: Basil Blackwell 1976)

Wolfe 1979   T. Wolfe, *The Right Stuff* (New York: Farrar, Strauss & Giroux 1979)

Zizioulas 1985   J. Zizioulas, *Being as Communion* (London: DLT 1985)

Index

Scripture References